MW00627953

Living Lilith:

Four Dimensions of the Cosmic Feminine

M. Kelley Hunter

The Wessex Astrologer

Published in 2009 by
The Wessex Astrologer Ltd
4A Woodside Road
Bournemouth
BH5 2AZ
England

www.wessexastrologer.com

ISBN 9781902405346

A catalogue record of this book is available at The British Library

Cover design by Dave at Creative Byte, Poole, Dorset

Printed and bound in the UK by Biddles Ltd, Kings Lynn, Norfolk.

Unless otherwise stated in the text, all astrological charts produced from IO Edition by Time Cycles Research

Calculations for Lilith positions calculated using Astrodienst

Acknowledgements

Sincere thanks to
Friends, colleagues, clients, class participants and others who have enriched my understanding of Lilith through conversations, insights, inspirations, art or through special interest in my work, some of whom have given various permissions: Verena Bachmann, Mark Beriault, Mary Blazine, Yasmin Boland, Lilian Broca, Erika Butler, Candice Covington, Elizabeth Cunningham, Mary Damian, Robert Diehl, Elsbeth Pryer Diehl, Faith, Lilli Farrell, Michael F., William Fregosi, Agnes de Garron, Demetra George, Ben Ginther, Spencer Grendahl, Jeanne Humphrey, Kenneth Johnson, Antonia Langsdorf, Lee Lehman, Luis Lesur, Tad Mann, Sheola Meigs, Patricia Monaghan, Grazia Murti, Katherine Neville, Vicki Noble, Juan Antonio Revilla, Louise Richardson, Jan Sandman, Barbara Schermer, Jan Collins Selman, Laya Shriaberg, Judith Simmer-Brown, Julie Simmons, Luvia Swanson, John Trevett, Linda Thurman, Paula Upton, Vicki Uzzell, Gail Van de Bogurt, Constance Wallace, among many others, whether they know it or not.

Special appreciation to
Margaret Cahill for excellent editing, cheerleading, patience and helping push the book through the black hole;
Paul F. Newman for his eagle eye and excellent artwork;
Lynn Bell for my two sojourns in her Paris apartment with her Lilith-rich library;
Dragon Dance players of *The Great Round* and directors Sam Kerson and Susan Bettmann;
Goddess Scholars Yahoo discussion group;
Dana Hunt for her playful artistic collaboration and Neptunian imagination;
Delphine Jay for her deep work on the Dark Moon;
AstroDataBank for their service and dedication to gathering accurate data;
Astrotheme website that allows criteria searches using Black Moon Lilith, an essential aid to my research. Merci beaucoup.

In memoriam appreciation to Vivian Bennerson for her mentoring, Medusa work and wicked chuckle, Grandmother Doris for her heart-sight, and to Jeannine Akimowa for starting the Lilith Yahoo discussion group.

This book is dedicated to my beloved daughter Sanja Jean DeCola and my angel in heaven Valley Hunter DeCola.

Contents

Chart Data

Chart data has been checked, when possible, with AstroDataBank which uses the Rodden rating system for accuracy. Otherwise, data source is given. Rodden ratings are as follows:

ADB=AstroDataBase, with Rodden Rating
AA = accurate data as recorded by the family or state
A = reliable data as quoted by the person, relative, friend, associate
B = data from biography   C = caution, no source
DD = dirty data, conflicting quotes

Andersen, Hans Christian
2 April, 1805, Odense, Denmark, 1:00am — ADB#AA

Anthony, Susan B.
15 February, 1820, Adams, MA, time unknown — www.susanbanthonyhouse.org/biography

Astor, Mary nee Lucille Langhanke
3 May, 1906, Quincy, IL, 8:10pm — ADB#A

Beatty, Warren
30 March, 1937, Richmond, VA, 5:30pm — ADB#AA

Bono, ne Paul Hewson
10 May, 1960, Dublin, Ireland, 2:00am — ADB#A

Boulanger, Marie-Juliette "Lili"
21 August, 1893, Paris, France, time unknown — www.naxos.com/composerinfo/Lili_Boulanger

Boye, Karin
26 October, 1900, Goteborg, Sweden, time unknown — http://www.karinboye.se/verk/index-en.shtml

Byron, George Gordon, Lord
22 January, 1788, London, England, 2:00pm — ADB#AA

Carey, Harry Jr
16 May, 1921, No. Saugus, CA, 5:00am — ADB#AA

Carroll, Lewis ne Charles Dodgson
27 January, 1832, Daresbury, England, 3:45am —ADB#B

Catherine II, "The Great"
2 May, 1729, Stetten, Germany, 2:30am — ADB#B

Cezanne, Paul
19 January, 1839, Aix-en-Provence, France, 1:00 pm—ADB#AA

Chisholm, Shirley
30 November, 1924, Brooklyn, NY, time unknown —
bioguide.congress.gov/scripts/biodisplay.pl?index
www.nytimes.com/2005/01/03/obituaries/03chisholm.html

Chopin, Frederik
1 March, 1810, Zelazowa Wola, Poland, 6:00pm ADB#DD
unverified time

Clapton, Eric
30 March, 1945, Ripley, England — ADB#DD conflicting
information on time

Coleridge, Mary Elizabeth
23 September, 1861, London, time unknown —
rpo.library.utoronto.ca/poet/70.html
(University of Toronto Department of English)

Corrine, Tee
3 November, 1943, St. Petersburg, FL, no time —
http://libweb.uoregon.edu/speccoll/mss/tee.html

Curie, Marie
7 November, 1867, Warsaw, Poland, 10:36am — ADB#AA

Dalai Lama, His Holiness, the 14th, Tenzin Gyatso
6 July, 1935, Taktser, Tibet, 4:38am? — ADB#A
Though ADB gives an A rating to a 4:38am birth time, they report various contradictions. For our purposes, not time-dependent, we use dawn as a common fallback position which is most likely close.

Depp, Johnny
9 June, 1963, Owensboro, KY, 8:44am — ADB#AA

Duncan, Isadora
26 May, 1877, San Francisco, CA, 2:20am — ADB#A

Embattled Garden
3 April, 1958, New York City, 8:00pm (?) —
www.gmu.edu/cfa/pressroom/view.php?id=268
www.gc.cuny.edu/press_information/current_releases/2008/march/surinach.htm

Enya nee Eithne Patricia Ni Bhraonain
17 May, 1961, Gweedore, Donegal, Ireland —
Numerous web sources suggest general agreement on birth date and place. Astrotheme gives 12:00pm.

Federer, Roger
8 August, 1981, Basel, Switzerland, 8:40am —
www.rogerfederer.com/en/rogers/profile/index.cfm

Fonteyn, Dame Margot
18 May, 1919, Reigate, England — ADB#DD time uncertain
4-5:00am given in *Margot Fonteyn: A Life* by Meredith Daneman

Fox, Michael J.
9 June, 1961, Edmonton, Canada, 12:51am — ADB#A

Friedan, Betty
4 February, 1921, Peoria, IL, 4:00am — ADB#AA

Garbo, Greta nee Gustafsson
18 September, 1905, Stockholm, Sweden, 7:30pm — ADB#AA

Gore, Al
31 March, 1948, Washington DC, 12:53pm — ADB#AA

Graham, Martha
11 May, 1894, Allegheny, PA, 6:00am — ADB#A

Grant, Joan
12 April, 1907, London, England, 8:00am — ADB#A

Hari, Mata nee Margaretha Zelle
7 August, 1876, Leeuwarden, The Netherlands, 1:00pm — ADB#AA

Harlow, Jean nee Harlean Carpenter
3 March, 1911, Kansas City, MO, 7:40pm — ADB#AA

Hoffa, Jimmy
14 February, 1913, Brazil, IN, 6:52am — ADB#AA

Hopkins, Anthony
31 December, 1937, 9:15am, Port Talbot, Wales — ADB#A

Jackman, Hugh
12 October, 1968, Sydney, Australia, unknown time —
www.hugh-jackman.com/hugh-information/biography
www.hugh-jackman.net/hugh-jackman-biography.aspx

Jagger, Elizabeth Scarlett
2 March, 1984, New York City, 1:37am — ADB#A

Jagger, Mick
26 July, 1943, Dartford, England, 2:30am — ADB#A

Jolié, Angelina nee Voigt
4 June, 1975, Los Angeles, 9:09am — ADB#A

Jung, Carl G.
26 July, 1875, Kesswil, Switzerland, 7:32pm — ADB#A

Kahlo, Frida
6 July, 1907, Coyoacan, Mexico, 8:30am — ADB#AA

Keeler, Christine
22 February, 1942, London, England, 11:15am — ADB#A

King, Reverend Dr. Martin Luther
15 January, 1929, Atlanta, GA, 12:00pm — ADB#A
King, Stephen
21 September, 1947, Portland, Maine, 1:30am — ADB#A
Lennon, John
9 October, 1940, Liverpool, England, 6:30pm — ADB#A
Liberace
16 May, 1919, West Allis, WI, 11:15pm — ADB#AA
Lilith, Asteroid 1181, Discovery Chart
11 February, 1927, Algiers, Algeria, time not confirmed — JPL Small-Body Database Browser
Lilith, the Opera
11 November, 2001, New York City, 1:30pm
New York Times article, November 9, 2001, section E, page 7
Lorraine, Lilith Mary Maud Dunn Wright
19 March, 1894, Corpus Christie, TX, time unknown — www.tshaonline.org/handbook/online/articles/WW/fwr19.html (Texas State Historical Association website)
MacDonald, George
10 December, 1824, Huntly, Scotland, time unknown — biography www.george-macdonald.com/life_outline.htm
Malcolm X ne Malcolm Little
19 May, 1925, Omaha, Nebraska, 12:02 pm — ADB#AA
Mandela, Nelson
18 July, 1918, Tanskrei, South Africa, time unknown — nobelprize.org/nobel_prizes/peace/laureates/1993/mandela-bio.html
Mankiller, Wilma
18 November, 1945, Tahlequah, Oklahoma, time unknown — autobiography, *Mankiller: A Chief and Her People* by Wilma Mankiller and Michael Wallis
Matsuda, Seiko nee Kamachi Noriko
10 March, 1962, Fukuoda, Japan, 5:30pm — ADB#A
Maxima, Princess of the Netherlands, nee Máxima Zorreguieta Cerruti
17 May, 1971, Buenos Aires, Argentina, 8:05pm — www.koninklijkhuis.nl/ (Dutch Royal House website)
www.netherlands.info/RoyalFamily.html#RoyalHouse
Mayawati, Kumari
15 January, 1956, Delhi, India, time unknown — http://uplegisassembly.gov.in (India legislative website)

McAuliffe, Asteroid 3352 Discovery Chart
6 February, 1981, Flagstaff, AZ, no time given —
JPL Small-Body Database Browser

McAuliffe, Christa
2 September, 1948, Boston, MA, 10:13pm — ADB#AA

McCartney, Paul
18 June, 1942, Liverpool, England, 2:00pm — ADB#A

McKillip, Patricia
29 February, 1948, Salem, Oregon, time unknown —
Locus, July 1996, "Springing Surprises" interview
Numerous web sources suggest general agreement on birth data

McLachlan, Sarah
28 January, 1968, Halifax, Nova Scotia, time unknown —
Numermous web sources suggest general agreement on birth data

Minh, Ho Chi
19 May, 1890, Hoang-Tru, Vietnam, 5:00am — ADB#C

Monroe, Marilyn nee Norma Jean Mortenson
1 June, 1926, Los Angeles, CA, 9:30am — ADB#AA

Morissette, Alanis
1 June, 1974, Ottawa, Canada, 9:39am — ADB#A

Mott, Lucretia
3 January, 1793, Nantucket, MA, time unknown —
www.americaslibrary.gov/jb/nation/jb_nation_mott_1.html
(U.S. Library of Congress website)
womenshistory.about.com/od/suffragepre1848/p/lucretia_ mott.htm

Nin, Anais
21 February, 1903, Neuilly sur Seine, France, 8:25am —
correspondence to author

Obama, Barack
4 August, 1961, Honolulu, HI, 7:24pm — ADB#AA
birth certificate posted on internet

Obama, Michelle
17 January, 1964, Chicago, IL, time unknown —
Numerous web sources suggest general agreement on birth data

Oldman, Gary
21 March, 1958, London, time unknown —
Numerous web sources suggest general agreement on birth data

Pankhurst, Christabel
22 September, 1880, Manchester, England, time unknown —
Emmeline Pankhurst: A Biography by Jane Purvis

Pankhurst, Emmeline Goulden
14 July, 1858, Manchester, England, 9:30pm — ADB#A
Family records indicate the birth may have been on July 15.

Pankhurst, Sylvia
5 May, 1882, Manchester, England, time unknown — *Emmeline Pankhurst: A Biography* by Jane Purvis

Pankhurst Walsh, Adela
19 June, 1885, Manchester, England, time unknown — *Emmeline Pankhurst: A Biography* by Jane Purvis

Picasso, Pablo
25 October, 1881, Malaga, Spain, 11:15pm — ADB#AA

Pitt, Brad
18 December, 1963, Shawnee, OK, 6:31am — ADB#A

Pompadour, Madame de, nee Jeanne Antoinette Poisson
29 December, 1721, Paris, France, 10:15am — ADB#C

Pope John-Paul II, ne Karol Jozef Wojtyla
18 May, 1920, Wadowice, Poland, 5:30pm — ADB#A

Presley, Elvis
8 January, 1935, Tupelo, Mississippi, 4:35am — ADB#AA

Rilke, Rainer Maria
3 December, 1875, Prague, Czech Republic. 11:50pm — ADB#A
Numerous web sources give 4 December as birth date. Rodden's Astro-Data II, p.359, Astrolog #34 quotes Marian Gluntz, data from mother of 'just before midnight', suggesting confusion across the midnight hour.

Roberts, Julia
28 October, 1967, Atlanta, GA, 12:16am — ADB#AA

Rossetti, Dante Gabriel
12 May, 1828, London, England, 4:30am — ADB#A

Sagan, Carl
9 November, 1934, New York, NY, 5:05pm — ADB#AA

Seberg, Jean
13 November, 1938, Marshalltown, IA, time unknown — www.imdb.com/name/nm0781029/bio

Seneca Falls Convention
19 July, 1848, 10:00am, Seneca Falls, New York — *Seneca County Courier* article August 4, 1848 issue cited

Sharon, Ariel
27 February, 1928, Kafr Malar, Israel, 7:49am — ADB#A

Shaw, George Bernard
26 July, 1856, Dublin, Ireland, 12:55am GMT — ADB#A

Shelley, Percy Bysshe
4 August, 1792, Horsham, England, 10:00pm — ADB#A

Sisters of Mercy
12 December, 1831, Dublin, Ireland, likely around dawn — given to author by Sister Cynthia, also on Sisters of Mercy website

Spencer, Lady Diana, Princess of Wales
1 July, 1961, Sandringham, England, 7:45am — ADB#A

Spielberg, Steven
18 December, 1946, Cincinnati, OH, 6:16pm — ADB#AA

Springfield, Dusty nee Mary O'Brien
16 April, 1939, London, England, time unknown — *Dancing with Demons: The Authorized Biography of Dusty Springfield* by Penny Valentine and Vicki Wickham

Stanton, Elizabeth Cady
12 November, 1815, Johnstown, NY, no time — www.britannica.com/EBchecked/topic/563303/Elizabeth-Cady-Stanton, www-distance.syr.edu/pvitaecs.html (Syracuse University cites The Women's Rights National Historical Society, *Elizabeth Cady Stanton: An extraordinary woman*, by Doris Wolf and Mary Ellen Snyder, 2000.

Steinem, Gloria
25 March, 1934, Toledo, Ohio, 10-10:30pm — ADB#AA

Sterling, George
1 December, 1869, Sag Harbor, NY, time unknown — Confirmed via webmaster at george-sterling.org

Swanson, Gloria
27 March, 1899, Chicago, IL, 12:20am — ADB#A

Van Gogh, Vincent
30 March,1853, Zundert, The Netherlands, 11:00am — ADB#AA

William, Prince of England
21 June, 1982, London, England, 9:03pm — ADB#AA

Women's Social and Political Union
10 October, 1903, Manchester, England, time unknown — *Emmeline Pankhurst: A Biography* by Jane Purvis

Woodman, Marion
15 August, 1928, London, ONT, Canada, 2:30pm — given in person to author

Woolf, Virginia
25 January, 1882, London, 12:15pm — ADB#A

List of Illustrations

1

Lilith Comes in Dreams and Myth

Originally I did not choose to work with Lilith; she chose me. Some years ago she came to me in a dream, a dream with a powerful charge, one of those Big Dreams. The dream was of

> *A female tiger. She is magnificent, powerful. We treat her with respect, awe, careful not to arouse her anger. She can hurt, but we are allowed to stroke her. Somehow she is surrounded by a round enclosure, trapped. A number of male cats come in and rape her. She is covered in blood after the second. After that, she is left encaged, her heart destroyed. Anyone who approaches her is stopped by a terrible, hateful, warning snarl. She is dangerous, destructive, defensive.*

The dream ended with a question: *Why such a royal upbringing to be led to this fate?*

I recognized Lilith from a recent reading of the occult fiction novel, *Lilith*, by George MacDonald, in which she takes the form of a large cat. MacDonald reinterprets a story of Lilith from Hebrew tradition that identifies her as the first wife of Adam, who deserted him and took up with the Shadow. The feeling impact of the dream led me to explore it through active imagination. Lilith began to speak as I wrote

> *I'm so ugly. They hate me. They cut me out of their lives because I am so whole, because I will not take a back seat, second place. I believe in wholeness and sharing. I undercut you when you're not being whole, when you cut yourself off, where you seek blood. I give — on my terms, elemental, the one woman before man. Am I the Creator — or the first emerged feminine? There is no difference. I am of that original Heaven. I would not leave it.*

Thus I started to know Lilith. This four-phase goddess of mysterious power continues to lead me through her winding labyrinth among the roots of the Tree of Life where she lives.

Lilith and the Huluppu Tree

I live in the Tree of Life,
with the serpent in the roots and the Thunderbird in its branches.
Why are you afraid of me, afraid of the tree?

Myths are the collective Big Dreams that convey essential truths of human experience. In their telling and re-telling, these eternal stories reflect the psycho-spiritual evolution of the human psyche. Myth is a feminine expression of history or "her-story," concerned with subjective meaning and cycles of life, rather than sequential dates and facts. Under her many names, Lilith shows her face in our very oldest mythology and in the most up-to-date artistic works. With her endless fascination and ambiguity, she taps into the essence of human experience.

Lilith first appears in our oldest literary texts, written on clay tablets. This cuneiform literature was deciphered only within the last century and a half, after being unearthed in excavations along the alluvial valleys of the Tigris and Euphrates Rivers. The great goddess Inanna is the star of one of the best-known stories from this land, inspired by the celestial movements of the planet Venus. This most radiant planet was carefully tracked by astronomer-astrologers of Sumeria and Babylonia, as well as the Mayans and other Native American peoples. Living half her life as Morning Star, the other half as Evening Star, Venus is a startlingly bright presence in the heavens, never too far above the horizon.

This myth, buried for thousands of years under sandy mounds in the deserts of Iraq, has spoken to the hearts of many in the years since its publication. It is a poignant story of a great goddess finding her power in a pantheon of increasingly powerful male gods. It holds meaning for the psychological growth of women and men. Diane Wolkstein worked with Samuel Noah Kramer, one of the pioneering translators of the Sumerian language, to create a lovely poetic and theatrical rendering in *Inanna, Queen of Heaven and Earth.* In *Descent to the Goddess*, Sylvia Perera gives a profound psychological analysis of this myth from a Jungian perspective. More works have joined these early classics on the Inanna book shelf. The myth chronicles the development of the Great Goddess divided from herself in the ascendancy of male gods. This division may be the source of the ambiguity of Lilith. Amidst a wild primordial storm, a tree, a *huluppu* tree, perhaps a willow tree, is uprooted and swept down river. The young goddess Inanna finds the tree tangled in some brush along the river bank and pulls it from the water. Inanna tends the tree, this centerpiece of her garden, the original garden of Eden. She plans to make the wood of the mature tree into her throne of queenship and her bed of marriage.

Creatures appear in the tree: a serpent winds among the roots, a wild bird nests her young in its branches and the "dark maid" Lilith takes up residence in the trunk. Wild and untamed, these primordial energies interfere with Inanna's plans. Perhaps they have come to teach Inanna what she needs to know to fulfill her destiny as goddess. Yet Inanna is not ready to embrace the full and potentially dangerous power of these creatures, of Lilith. She needs to establish herself on her own terms. Inanna calls in her brother, Gilgamesh, to get rid of the creatures. He kills the serpent and chases away the bird. Lilith refuses to be dominated, rather she chooses exile. With Lilith's exit, the making of Inanna's throne of queenship and bed of marriage can proceed.

The serpent, the bird and the tree itself, the World Tree, are aspects of Lilith's nature. They are found in world-wide myths as symbols of life-giving power associated with the goddess. The serpent represents the chthonic wisdom of earth, oracular powers, and the *kundalini*, the subtle life force that awakens consciousness as it courses up the tree of the spinal cord. Winding in the roots of the tree, the serpent also grounds the energy into the earth. Generally a more positive symbol in the East than the West, the serpent demonstrates rebirth through the shedding of its skin.

The *anzu* bird (or Zu) was said to be a gigantic lion-headed bird figure, gryphon-like, considered a manifestation of a god who stole the Tablet of Destinies from the sky god, Enlil. In *Lilith: The Edge of Forever*, Filomena Maria Pereira cites references to the anzu bird as "the personification of the thundercloud, imaged as an enormous vulture floating with outstretched wings in the sky." This evokes the Native American thunderbird, an equally powerful bird flashing lightning from its eyes and thunder in the beating of its wings, or the Eagle, king of the winged ones of the First Peoples of the North Americas. Wings archetypally denote spirit.

Lilith's bird is most often the screech owl that sees through the dark of night. The owl is also connected to Athena, Greek goddess of wisdom. A winged creature, the bird represents the world of spirit, though the owl is also associated with death. "The myths and legends about woman-animal hybrids reflect our fascination with the possibility of the animal nature of the female…still potent, raw, primal, fierce, instinctual, bodily, unrepressed," wrote goddess scholar Elanor Gadon.

Whatever kind of bird the fierce Sumerian Anzu may be, it is part of the tree with the chthonic serpent. Lilith, who is connected to both creatures, is a conduit from one to the other, from the instinctive wisdom at the roots to the spiritual enlightenment in the branches and back down. These creatures are part of Lilith's untamed, unconscious nature and have knowledge to give Inanna, who is not yet ready to accept it. Inanna is a young goddess in an increasingly god-oriented pantheon. In this part of the story she calls in her brother, Gilgamesh, to cut down the tree. The serpent is killed, the bird and its family fly off to the mountains, and Lilith departs for the wilderness, to consort with demons. Later, when she is ready for the knowledge of her inner self, Inanna descends to the Underworld and confronts Ereshkigal, an aspect of the dark goddess, psychologically representing the unconscious.

Lilith, through her various symbols and interpretations, is connected to nature and the subtle realms beyond and underlying the physical. This theme comes around again and again in association with Lilith and her various levels of expression.

Lilith as Seductress, Child Killer, Sacred Prostitute

You, you have summoned me with your desires
There are things you need to know about Love and Creation.
What can I know about Love, you ask?
I seduce, I destroy, I have no heart?
Those are lies. Lies they tell about me now. Lies they might tell about you later.

Lilith's name linguistically connects her to various creatures in Sumerian lore. There were the *lilitu, lilin*, and the *ardat lili*, restless female ghosts seeking sexual satisfaction. Greatly feared were the ghosts of childless women or of women who had died in child birth, who haunt the living, seeking babies. The *lil-la* demon can mate and produce human children.

The *lil-la-ke* dwelled in the primordial tree, a "tree of light" at the eastern horizon where sky meets the sea at the dawn of the world. Lilith seems to be merged with the lamashtu, a fetus and infant-killing demoness. Amulets were worn to ward off this crib death demon.

The Burney plaque from the third century BC shows a crowned goddess, winged with bird claws and flanked by owls. Long held to be an image of Lilith, she holds the rod and ring of power and may actually be a Lilith-Inanna figure. In the Biblical Garden of Eden, Lilith turns into the serpent that tempts Eve with the apple. The north side West Portal of the Virgin of Notre Dame Cathedral and Michelangelo's famous ceiling in Italy's Sistine Chapel both feature Lilith as a woman-headed serpent handing Eve the apple. Many more Christian art works from the fourteenth to fifteenth centuries show this woman-headed demon.

Carried into Hebrew mythology and Kabbalistic lore, mentioned in the *Zohar*, Lilith continued to be a widely-feared hag, baby-killer and seducer of men in their dreams. Lilith embodies the lure of the senses tending toward materialistic misuse of spiritual power. Among Lilith researchers, there are many references to the esoteric text, *The Alphabet of Ben Sira*, a midrash or interpretive text, in which Lilith is the first wife of Adam. In this alternate creation story, Yahweh shapes Adam and Lilith from earth using, it is said, impure sediment to make Lilith, whereas Adam is fashioned from pure dust. Clean mud and dirty mud?

Considering himself superior, Adam expects Lilith to be submissive to him. She takes exception to his macho attitude. Claiming equality, she will not be put beneath him, sexually or any other way. She utters the secret name of God — which only she knows — and flies away to lifelong exile near the Red Sea, where she consorts with evil spirits. Yahweh sends three angels to bring her back. Though threatened with the death of a hundred of her demonic children per day, she refuses to obey. Meanwhile Yahweh creates another partner for Adam, this time taking one of his ribs while he is asleep and carving it into Eve. She is part of Adam, created from him, not whole in her own right as was Lilith. "Perhaps this was really the impure birth?" Lilith might suggest.

I long for a mate, thirsty like water.
Come to me, I want you, I need your seed
or I wither and die, no fruit in my branches.

BUT...
I will not submit to you and be put beneath you like a serving maid.
I am his who dares to pay my price.
I ask too much, you say? Yet I give all. Why do you hold back?
I warn you. If you send me away, you will fall asleep,
And your rib will be taken out for your mate.
You banish me, but you will be cast out from the garden and struggle to be reborn.
I will return to remind you of what you really want.
How you feel broken with a mate who is but a part of you, like a crutch.

In the way of myth, there are variations on this story. Such esoteric texts invite many levels of interpretation. A literal interpretation constrains the meaning and may create problems if we apply it to social and personal issues. Several thousand years ago, Judeo-Christian religions, and others world-wide, began to elevate the masculine aspect of divinity. Earthy sensuality, often associated with the Great Goddess, was de-spiritualized, becoming unclean, unholy.

In the Sumerian and Babylonian lands of the Middle East, goddesses such as Inanna and Ishtar had been celebrated as the embodiment of love and honored in sacred sexual rituals. In various cultures, it was the goddess, often through the agency of a High Priestess, who endowed the king with rulership. Lilith was also known as the handmaiden of Inanna, calling men in from the fields for the sacred rites. As priestesses of sacred sexuality, such women served the goddess of love. The religious transition to masculine gods judged such sexual love rites as blasphemous, yet they did not disappear completely. The sacred marriage rite, the "conjunctio" of heaven and earth as well as of female and male, comes down to us even in the Old Testament, as the beautifully sensual "Song of Songs, which is Solomon's," slipped in between Ecclesiastes and Isaiah. "Let him kiss me with the kisses of his mouth: for thy love is better than wine," invites the dark-skinned beauty in the King James version of the "Song of Songs." Lilith has been associated with the Queen of Sheba who travels to meet Solomon, wisest of kings. In one story, she lifts her skirts to cross a floor of glass and her hairy legs and claw feet expose her bestial nature. Their love story is one of seduction and wisdom.

In his classic work, *The Hebrew Goddess*, Raphael Patai compares Lilith with the Matronit (or Shekhinah), a Kabbalistic female divinity, and notes the enduring significance of both, extending from fourth millennium BC Sumer through into 18 or 19th century Hasidic Jewish beliefs. Her dual nature as a she-demon on one hand and a goddess or consort of God on the other, reflects "ambivalence of religio-sexual experience." Any step we take in life can take us closer or further from God. Lilith challenges our intentions, questions our moral beliefs and the direction of our desires, testing the soul all the way, toward freedom or bondage.

Lilith speaks to women and men from their innermost desires and fears, tempting us beyond safe boundaries, enticing us to dive into the void, to ride the undercurrents that pull us into or out of our egoistic personalities into unfamiliar seas. The experience of Lilith is highly personal. She seems to know just what places to touch that will bring you to your edges. Is she an evil seductress or a strict daimon of the soul? Neither description will do, as she escapes all such binding definitions. Often she leaves us speechless. I dare to write about Lilith only because she insists upon it.

Periodically, as Lilith calls in no uncertain terms, I find myself again pulled into her potent cauldron and challenged by her sword of Truth. Lilith came in another dream, in serpent form, a dream that honors the healing power re-emerging from the depths of Earth herself for our shared awakening.

> *I am walking down a narrow path between apple trees. A large poisonous snake crosses my path. I retreat. It disappears and I walk on. I pass into a stone chamber. On the doorway there is a smaller snake of the same kind curled in a spiral on the door frame. In the chamber there are many snakes — on the floor, on a table, on a chair. I am afraid. (I start to wake up and go into lucid dreaming). I open my throat and let my voice sound strongly in various tones. I light a torch. I feel more comfortable with the snakes, though still afraid. I consider letting a boa climb up my arm. Will it strangle me?*
>
> *A new scene. I have requested a dab of snake venom to be put on my wrist pulse. I will die in 12 hours or 12 days. I continue on with my life. I go on a journey with a friend and visit my childhood neighborhood. I decide I do not want to die. A small yellow and black snake is on a table. It shows me a pattern, like an infinity sign. If I move around in this pattern, I will live. I do. The snake unfolds the center of her body.*

As the dark goddess will continue to unfold her meaning...

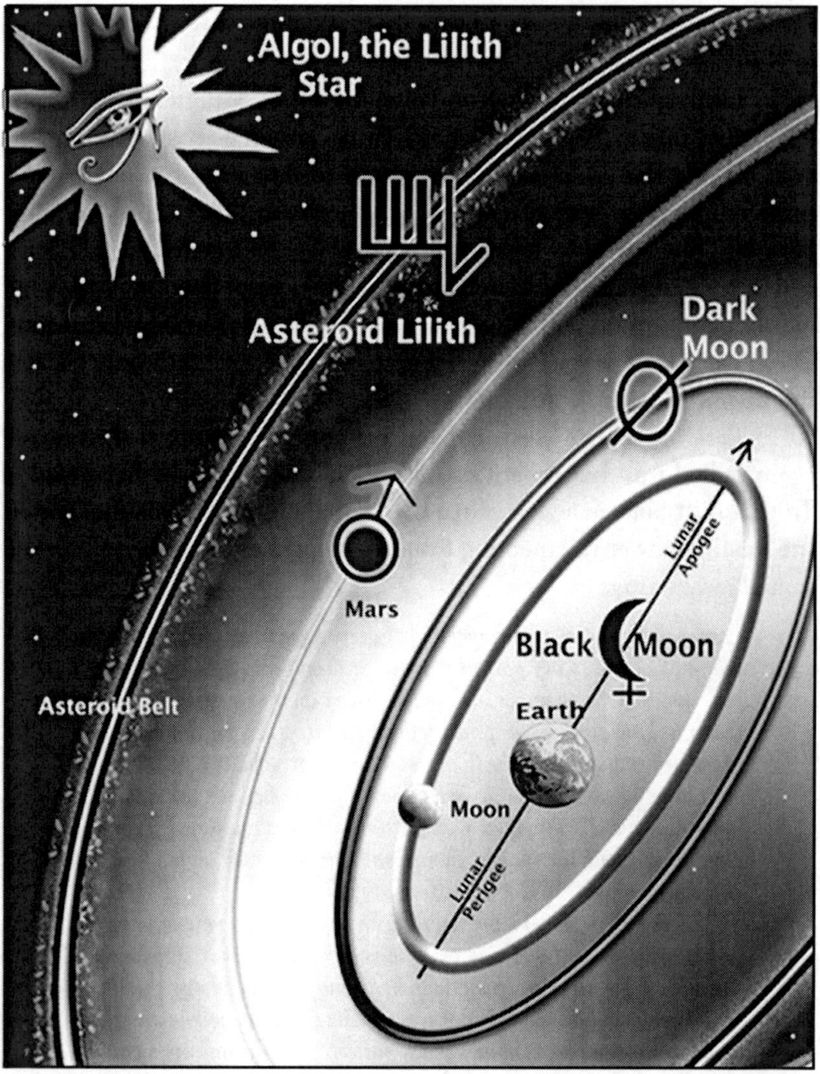
Algol, the Lilith
Star
Asteroid Lilith
Dark
Moon
Mars
Lunar
Apogee
Black
Moon
Earth
Asteroid Belt
Moon
Lunar
Perigee

2

The Four Liliths in Astrology

Several astronomical entities have been named Lilith, giving her special cosmological interest. It is as if Lilith appears at different celestial octaves. The **asteroid** Lilith is the most solid, a rock orbiting with thousands of other asteroids between Mars and Jupiter. The **Dark Moon** is a rumored, shadowy, yet unsubstantiated satellite of the Earth, which may or may not be real. The **Black Moon** is not a body at all; rather it is the second focus in the elliptical orbit of the Moon around Earth, an invisible but meaningful astronomical point of reference. The **star** Lilith is officially named Algol, the "demon" star, in the constellation Perseus. It was sometimes called Lilith by the Hebrews. Lilith, therefore, comes in many forms: a rocky asteroid, an elusive shadow moon, an orbital vortex in the Earth-Moon system, and a star. She gets around.

Because we can mathematically calculate the positions of these four Liliths, we have a way of tracking her in our lives. Resources for finding Asteroid, Dark Moon and the two Black Moons are found in the appendix. Algol is easy to find, at a fairly steady 26 degrees of Taurus. Weaving these positions into the cosmic patterns at birth or of any moment of time, we locate windows through which we peer into the eyes of Lilith. However, she doesn't make it easy to find her. The Black Moon is often referred to as the Dark Moon. There are few references that include all Liliths (see Appendix). Plus there can be a variation in measurement. The mathematics for both the hypothetical Dark Moon and the mean and true Black Moon positions are very complex, with technical choices to be made about the very base point for the calculations.

Here we will consider cosmic dimensions of Lilith and search for clues left by those who were born with an affinity for her intensity, power and allure. We learn most about Lilith from observing her mark in mundane moments. Some years ago I was writing one of my first articles about Lilith with the television on in the background. The television backdrop to Lilith included *The Accused*, the Jodie Foster movie about a woman who fights for justice after being raped; a news report on stalking; a rerun of *The Streets of San Francisco* about child stealing; *Hurricane*, a mythic Dorothy Lamour film showing the crossing of old and new cultures in old Hawaii; and *Stealing Home* (again with Jodie Foster). "Some MTV probably got in there," my daughter reminded me. All clues.

Though there are distinctions to be made about the effect of the various Liliths, there are underlying themes that connect them, like playing the same note in different octaves. The interpretations of each Lilith are not to be taken as isolated from the others. Pluck one string, the others will vibrate.

Asteroid Lilith

Men their rights nothing more, women their rights nothing less.
Susan B. Anthony

Asteroid #1181 is one of thousands of asteroids orbiting mainly between Mars and Jupiter. Like notes in a scale, the planets in our solar system are spaced harmonically in such a way that each one is about twice as far from the Sun as the last. Venus is twice as far as Mercury, Earth twice as far as Venus. According to this aesthetically pleasing arrangement, there should have been a planet between Mars and Jupiter. Perhaps there once was, one that somehow shattered and burst into thousands of space pebbles, strewn in a band as along the banks of a river, generally separating the rocky personal planets from the gas-giant social ones. The asteroid belt is quite a collection, coming in all sorts of shapes and textures, grouped in bands, some with renegade orbits. Ceres, the first discovered, in 1801, is the largest and roundest. It is now considered a dwarf planet. Named for an earth mother goddess of the grain, we could call Ceres the Mother of the Asteroids.

Asteroid Lilith was discovered on February 11, 1927 by Benjamin Jekhovsky, a Russian-Polish-French astronomer working in Algiers. Originally designated as 1927CQ, Lilith is in the main asteroid belt with an orbit of 4.36 years. The discovery degree of the asteroid itself was 8 Leo. The Sabian symbol reads: "Proletarian, burning with social passion, stirs up crowds." Many with a strong Lilith asteroid do just that.

The asteroid was named in honor of Marie-Juliette "Lili" Boulanger, a child prodigy musician born August 21, 1893 in Paris to a musical family. Her Asteroid Lilith was at 29+ degrees Libra sextile her Sun. Since she took her nickname in reference to the mythic Lilith, we can imagine she had a strong Lilith signature. Indeed she did. We'll take a fuller look at her chart and the Asteroid discovery chart later, after we have met all four Liliths.

The symbol for Asteroid Lilith was created by Tee A. Corinne (1943-2006), double Scorpio artist, when Al Morrison and Lee Lehman were preparing the first Asteroid Lilith ephemeris for publication in 1980. Lee tells the story

> *Tee was intrigued. I told her about the evolving convention at that point that whoever did the first ephemeris got to choose the glyph.*
> *I said whatever the glyph was, it had to be easily inscribable on a chart form by a person with limited artistic capability.*
> *Tee then drew the glyph.*
> *I asked her why, and she said, "Because Lilith did it with her left hand."*
> *Read her bio, and you'll understand that this was how Tee thought!*
> *I loved it -*
> *and I was certainly impish enough to just go ahead with it!*
> [communication to author, 16 June 2008]

[You can read her bio and see more work by this innovative artist and lesbian activist at http://libweb.uoregon.edu/speccoll/mss/tee.html.]

Tee Corinne's chart has Asteroid Lilith conjunct Uranus in Gemini, quincunx her Sun/Mercury. She also had two more planets in that quick-handed sign of the trickster. She was very handy! We can glean meaningful clues from these stories of asteroid history.

The symbol depicts a stylized hand, one of the most ancient symbols used by humans. It's easy enough to dip one's hand in some substance and leave a handprint on the wall of a house, a cave, or a rock canyon. The dexterity of the human hand is a key to our creativity and a mark of our intelligence. To match the Lilith symbol, it would have to be the impression of your left hand. If you were approaching someone, it would be your right palm up and out that would make the Asteroid Lilith symbol from the other's point of view. Such a hand signal warns, greets or blesses, depending on how you approach her. In the Sumerian myth, Lilith is sometimes called the "hand" of the goddess Inanna, bringing the men in from the fields for holy worship.

In ritual practices of the East, hand gestures called mudras refer to various expressions of the understanding of ultimate reality. In Tibetan tantra, *mudra* is called *chag-gya. Chag* is a word for "hand." In tantra it refers to immaculate emptiness and the experience of mind as transparent and spacious. *Gya* is a seal or imprint, used here to refer to the imprint of ultimate reality on all phenomena. This hand imprint, then, may sometimes express the power of an encounter with the sacred. Some experiences cannot be articulated in words; the immediacy of body language more fully demonstrates the impact of experience.

If considered as fragments of a one-time planetary body, the asteroids represent facets of a larger whole. The goddess asteroids can mythically be considered as reflections of various aspects of the Great Goddess. In this view, Lilith is one of the most ancient. Lilith is a fiercely independent goddess who refused to submit to the assumed authority of another or to compromise her autonomy. As the original, first wife of Adam, created from the same God Power and the same Earth, she demanded an equal relationship. The first man was not strong enough to agree, at least in that version of the story, at that time in history. That's over 5,000 years ago. We've come a long way, baby..? Lilith confronts us with issues of equality in relationship, and can reflect psychological issues of suppressed rage, resentment, sexual manipulation and self-exile.

Lilith can be seen to represent split off, demonized aspects of the feminine, the result of long-standing cultural projections that perceive powerful feminine roles and attributes as shameful, untrustworthy, and dangerous. Socially-imposed feminine role models often deny a woman's true instinct and vitality. Such cultural projections may define gender roles, but do not describe an individual. Both women and men struggle with the pressures of prescribed role models in their search for self-awareness and self-determination. A Lilith type of woman or man does not accept cultural stereotypes. They will at least stretch the fabric, if not tear away from it. Your Asteroid Lilith can feel like a shoe that cramps your toes. You can't walk without feeling that aggravation.

The Welsh *Mabinogion* records a story reminiscent of Lilith and Adam. We hear of Bloedeuwedd, a mythic sister of Lilith, her flesh fashioned from flowers. For some reason, not unimportant, mother-goddess Arianrhod disowns her sons and places a curse on the one named Lleu, that he will marry no woman born of the human race. Lleu is raised by his uncle Gwyddyon, a magician. Gwyddyon and his uncle Math fashion a lovely maiden from flowers, with skin as soft as rose petals, cheeks like apples. In her book, *On the Edge of Dream: The Women in Celtic Myth and Legend*, Jennifer Heath adds more details, that Blodeuwedd is created from flowers and plants with a purpose: oak for perfect speech, greatest intelligence, metamorphosis and transformation; meadowsweet for love and happiness; broom for stamina; and lily for unconditional love. Of course, lilies, as Lilith loves all kinds of lilies — lily-of-the-valley, water lily, tiger lily, day lily, peace lily, so many lilies — and the lotus. This exquisite flower, a primary goddess symbol in the East, grows out of dark, rank, decaying earth, and represents spiritual unfolding and the blossoming of the heart of wisdom. Lilith's path is similar.

To this blend of plants, the magicians add yeast, cow's milk, eggs, honey and their own urine and spit, then they sprinkle the body with water and sheep's blood to animate it. A rather messy mix, but not all that different from Yahweh taking Adam's rib. That must have been a rather messy operation as well. Thus the magicians create Blodeuwedd, a woman not of the race of men but rather made by them. They breathe life into her with magic spells and then they marry her to Lleu.

All is well until one fateful day when Lleu is away. A hunting party led by Lord Gronw Pebyr passes through and Blodeuwedd is obliged to offer hospitality. The two fall instantly in love. It takes a lot of time and work, but the lovers kill her husband. Gwyddyon finds Lleu in the shape of an eagle and restores him, turning Blodeuwedd into an owl, the bird often associated with Lilith.

Like Lilith and the rebellious Eve who ate the apple, Blodeuwedd awakens to herself and rebels against her creators. She follows her heart and asserts her will.

When birthing is claimed by males, the autonomous, powerful woman who expresses her sexuality is demonized, turned into an owl, a bird associated with wisdom, lunar mysteries and witches. Blodeuwedd is exiled, like Lilith, "ever banished to half-light, veiled by night ... a winged vapor... She had been truly alive only briefly and then not long enough to cultivate her soul."

One woman who has worked with Blodeuwedd as an aspect of her own female experience relates: "Blodeuwedd is a favorite virgin/maiden goddess to me and has often led me to love from the deepest part of me. I feel so whole, giving and impersonal when I feel her pulsate through me." In commenting on the creation of Blodeuwedd through human agency and magical intent, this woman comments

> *It seems that she was bred for free will and awakening and was an androgynous blend of male and female traits... I hear the positive magical intent of the magicians to alchemically create "The Yearning" in dynamic human form. It is not about vengeance and blood thirst, or even male and female. It is about love and free will. It is about yearning for what we already have.*
>
> [Louise Richardson, 12 June 2001, private communication.]

This interpretation moves beyond the socialized gender interpretation of the feminist perspective to an internal, subjective meaning of the myth. What really matters is that Blodeuwedd woke up to herself. The more self-awareness a woman or man possesses, the less s/he is possessed by the unconscious dimension of the archetype. A healthy expression of the Lilith energy is a sense of personal power and authenticity that disregards or challenges societal judgment and demonstrates capacities that stretch the status quo of gender definitions. The feminist movement in general is inspired by Lilith. In a later section we will look at charts of some of the leading women suffragettes. She specifically gave her name to a Jewish feminist magazine.

Considering that 1181 is in the main asteroid belt, Costa Rican astrologer Juan Antonio Revilla suggests that Lilith may work within the system for change, even with the marginalized outcasts of society, as contrasted to the maverick asteroids and centaurs that have less conventional orbits and live more obviously outside of convention. In *Asteroid Goddesses*, Demetra George and Douglas Bloch talk of Lilith as an intermediate "warrior" asteroid, transforming the lower octave energy of Mars to the higher octave of Pluto. With a potential of dangerously repressed anger, Lilith requires channels of expression, conflict resolution, mediation and negotiation, therapy or marriage counseling, before charged situations explode into abuse. The rage inherent in Asteroid Lilith is echoed, even amplified by the Lilith Star, Algol. Perhaps the asteroid offers a concentrated outlet for the star, which exists on a more remote, collective octave.

Dark Moon Lilith

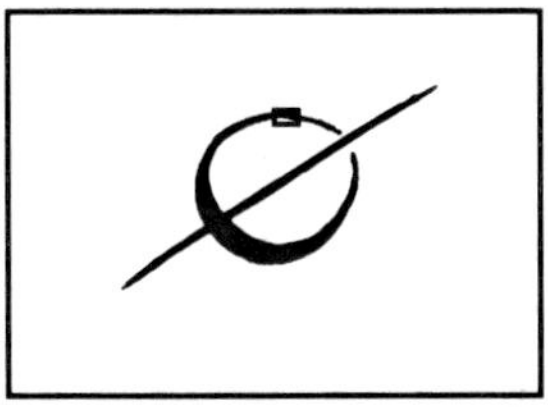

Two other Liliths are related to the Moon. Some say there is a second moon circling Earth — a mysterious, dark moon, seen only rarely when the sky is dark and it is either in opposition to or crossing the Sun's face. It has a dusky presence that absorbs light rather than reflecting it. One quarter the size of our familiar Moon, it is three times as far away, say astronomers who sighted it, or think they did. One-eightieth the mass of Earth, its orbital period is said to be 119 days, spending 10 days in a sign. Observations by astronomers were recorded as long ago as 1618, and through the next two centuries, including a sighting in 1898 officially documented by Dr. Georges Waldemath (or Waltemath), whose name is sometimes given to this object. This elusive moon came to broader attention through the work of astrologer Sepharial, who gave it the name Lilith. His 1918 book, *The Science of Foreknowledge* (recently republished), includes a chapter on "The New Satellite—Lilith," as well as a chapter on a possible third moon.

Why haven't we heard more about this second Moon? Perhaps it is the nature of Lilith. Its existence has not been completely verified. Though this controversial moon is dismissed by astronomers today, it is still of interest in occult circles in a symbolic way, along with a small bevy of other such shadowy dark moons said to absorb negative projections of human emotions. Juan Antonio Revilla suggests we call it a "ghost" moon. Perhaps it reflects the dark side of the Moon that always faces away from Earth. Perhaps its effect is somewhat like that of a full moon eclipse, when the Sun throws the Earth's shadow across the Moon. Perhaps it is a moon that used to be, or exists on an astral level. Perhaps it is the dark side of the Moon.

Finding correct Dark Moon tables is as elusive as Lilith herself. Questions about correct ephemerides, not to mention its very existence, make Dark Moon data suspicious. Web resources (see Bibliography) can be helpful. Because they seem to be the most accepted, and partly for ease, I use the Waldemath positions. Early books by Ivy Goldstein-Jacobson and Delphine Jay give ephemerides based on later positions given by Sepharial, but they are not considered totally reliable. (I understand that Delphine Jay is updating her books and tables.) I find Jay's psychologically sophisticated interpretations very revealing. She nailed me! I was startled by her astute analysis of my Dark Moon position that articulated so well unconscious motivations that I recognized as I read them, but had not previously risen to conscious awareness. Self-recognition in relation to this issue put some specific anxieties in a more restful space, but Lilith still trips me up in unexpected ways.

One of the original Dark Moon researchers, astrologer Ivy Goldstein-Jacobson associated Lilith with such words as sinister, frustration, temptation, self-undoing, betrayal, regret and denial. In *The Dark Moon Lilith in Astrology*, she describes the Dark Moon as an obscure enigma, difficult to understand, showing up when we are at our most vulnerable and likely to make unconscious, unwise choices. She points out the frailty of life and human nature, "her reason-for-being a mystery also, and difficult to distinguish in the darkness of life… She moves like a wraith…"

Delphine Jay agrees that it symbolizes denial, particularly of personal satisfaction in the area of life defined by its house position and aspects. Lilith pushes subjective issues into the impersonal realm, she writes in *Interpreting Lilith*. While the reflective Moon represents personal, subjective feelings, the Dark Moon represents a primal, objective and impersonal instinct that seeks identification beyond the physical and emotional realms. "This is the way it must be," she says clearly and definitively, like one of the Fates, harbingers of destiny. When her expression is self-centered, she can deny satisfaction and become quite negative. When the emotional content is channelled into higher centers, she adds power to creative, mental or aesthetic expression, even to spiritual practice. Lilith lures us into our more self-centered illusions for the purpose of purging negative desires and growing beyond our habitual patterns of unconscious conditioning. Jay views the Lilith dynamic as a physical and emotional maturing process stimulated by the impersonal levels of mind. Lilith requires the objective thinking approach or the higher mind to release the creative spirit imprisoned behind the narrow confines of social conditioning and the unconscious instinctive desires. The Dark Moon will expose mental and emotional immaturities that create blind spots in our approach to life. "Lilith is foreign to selfish desire. It is successful and inspiring only to mentally stimulating, creative or spiritual desire," writes Delphine Jay.

Lilith demands satisfaction of desire on some level. The desire body brings us into life, leads the way through life. Buddhists say it is the attachment to desire that gets us in trouble. Lilith agrees. Desire itself is inherent in biological existence. When we can't or don't follow our desires or do what we truly feel like doing, a cloudiness arises in our minds that affects our energy field until that desire is acknowledged in some way. Such condemned desires haunt us, creating a resistance that represses or redirects the natural flow away from its originally intended channels. Lilith nudges us to bring awareness to this process of sifting and sorting unconscious wants and inhibitions.

In *Lilith Insight, New Light on the Dark Moon*, Mae R. Wilson-Ludlam offers insightful interpretations of this "soulless" wilderness of Dark Moon, particularly as "a threat to making the right choices in life... the lure of forbidden fruit." The Dark Moon hints at places where we make regrettable mistakes in life. We make important, life-altering choices when sometimes we don't even know we are making them.

Dark Moon Lilith shows us where we tend to get caught in shadows, snared in regrets, compulsions, nebulous fears, trailing the dust of *sanskaras*, as the Hindus call soul impressions from the past that impact the choices we make in this life and may haunt us into future lives. The Anglo-Saxon *wyrd* refers to threads of destiny, the turnings and twistings of our lives based on the interdynamics between the (largely pre-conditioned) choices we make in response to what is going on around us, the larger Fate, and then the impact of our choices on that larger field. Each choice has a feedback loop with this larger field, leading to the next choice. There is an inevitability, like the tragic flaw that gets you in the end. This concept of wyrd seems to be connected to the outer planets, to the Nodes and also to the Liliths. There is no doubt that Lilith is "weird."

Some people with esoteric insight suggest the existence of a dark veil around Earth, like foggy gray smog, carrying emotional wounds and thought forms in the planet's energy field that we are all affected by in some particularly personal way. Unclear pieces of our own unconscious are activated by this darkened field of energy, catching us up in such emotional black holes as guilt, blame, shame, judgment, etc., binding us, like the hair of Lilith, into negative patterns. Through personal work we can heal these dark pockets, and help clear the Earth's vibrational field.

"The lower world is a secret duality: it is a black sphere outside with a shining white moon inside," reveals Jungian psychologist Marie-Louise Von Franz in *Alchemy*. Non-reflective, Dark Moon Lilith holds in her darkness — or her light. The Moon and Dark Moon are like the bright Sumerian Goddess Inanna and her dark sister, Ereshkigal, exiled in the underworld. After the tree is cut down, after ascension to queenship and after her honeymoon, Inanna opens her ears to the great below. She descends to her sister's realm, the underworld of the unconscious where the banished Ereshkigal cries in anguish and rage. The Dark Goddess takes one look at her luminous, beautiful sister who has gathered all the light and fixes her with the eye of death, freezing the growth of consciousness in the paralysis of repressed pain. Giving expression to the pain in some form releases us from our (often self-imposed) imprisonment in negative emotions. Lilith shows us the way, but she does not come out gently from behind her veil of darkness.

One woman met Lilith the child-stealer when her young son died on a new moon eclipse; the eclipse was conjunct her Dark Moon and

Saturn conjunct Asteroid Lilith, both in the 4th house. She can look back on that day and see each choice that led to the tragedy and the resultant disruption of home and family. For a long period of time she had to face and give voice to the guilt, emptiness and release within that was so deeply stirred by this death. In one version of Lilith's story, it is said that she takes children out of this dark lower world in order to return them to the Lord. Remember that Lilith's bird is the screech owl, the death owl. The veil between life and death is thin.

Black Moon Lilith

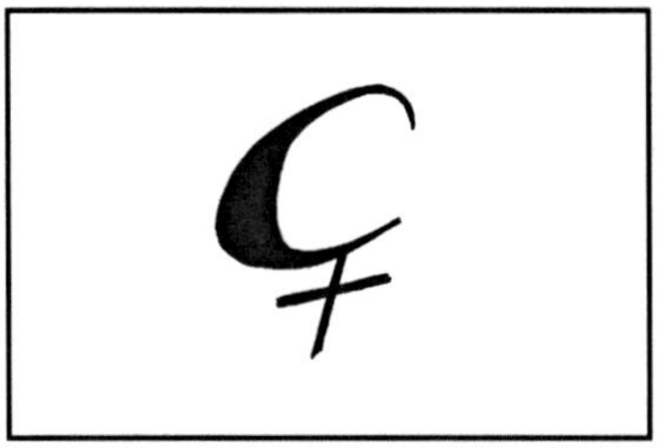

The Black Moon is not a physical body. The orbit of the Moon around the Earth is elliptical, as are all orbits. When Johannes Kepler figured this out mathematically, it was a shock to the prevailing religious mindset of the times. How could God make something that was not a perfect circle? Lilith was amused.

The ellipse is actually more interesting cosmologically. Rather than one "dead" center like a perfect circle, an ellipse has two orbital foci. The Earth is one focus of the Moon's orbit; the other is an abstract point called the Black Moon. This point is close to the apogee of the Moon's orbit (the place where it is the farthest from Earth, closest to the Sun), but is not always precisely the same. There are at least four ways of measuring this point. It wiggles and jiggles like a belly dancer in the complex gravitational dance between Earth, Moon and other solar systemic influences. An integral part of the Earth-Moon relationship, Black Moon symbolizes a central factor that is subtle yet potent, unseen but felt. Named for Lilith, this Black Moon also taps into the imagery of this ancient dark goddess, coming around again.

I first heard of the Black Moon at a lecture in Montreal. Mark Beriault described the energy of Lilith as a sword, deadly penetrating, sharply cutting through the veils of illusion, challenging our perception of reality. She will close all doors but the one true passage. She will not open it but pushes you right to the threshold and dares you to go through, offering no security as to the outcome. At the lecture, there was a woman dressed in a witch's black pointed hat in attendance. She must have known something about Lilith! This is how Lilith works. She is right there and gives you hints. She can be subtle in how she reveals herself, but you have to know how to listen and look. She offers no models to follow, she simply is.

The Black Moon takes 8 years and 10 months to circle the zodiac, close to a half-cycle of the Moon's Nodes, which are also non-physical and based on the relationship between Earth and Moon. Also like the Nodes of the Moon, Black Moon has a mean and true position. The mean position is based on its mean average motion. The true position is just that, tracking the frequent retrogradation of this point. The distance between them can be up to 30 degrees, sometimes located in two different signs. In *Black Moon Lilith*, I proposed a "Black Moon corridor," spanning the degrees from one to the other. Some charts would have a narrow band of Lilith influence, perhaps suggesting a more intensified experience, especially if in the same degree (an exact conjunction is fairly unusual, in my experience). Other charts would show a wide Lilith territory, often with two signs of expression. In this case, transiting planets would take longer to transit the two points. I also suggested that the Black Moon indicates an alchemical process, with the True Black Moon as the centerpoint of the transformational flame and the Mean position describing its overall status. The two relevant Sabian symbols can tell the story.

As a second center of reference, the Black Moon aligns with the Earth, suggesting invisible, subtle dimensions that underlie our conscious motivations, threading through both subconscious and superconscious layers. The subconscious contains personal, subjective material, stored memories and impressions that have shaped our personality structures and have been pushed down beyond conscious recall. The superconscious taps deeper sources of archetypal and spiritual energy. This may be what Jung called the transpersonal unconscious, "which is not only the basis of the conscious mind, but also the subjective or inner aspect of nature," wrote archetypal psychologist James Hillman in *Anima*. The dark light of the Black Moon reaches these deeper layers and seeks to reconnect our experience to the original source. As the inner aspect of nature, this experience is intimately linked to our bodies as part of Nature and our souls in resonance with *anima mundi*, the soul of the world.

The center of gravity between the Earth and moon is inside the Earth. As part of the Earth-Moon system, the Black Moon is an energetic vortex intimately bound to the center of the Earth. Black Moon and Earth are the two centers, or the double center, around which the Moon orbits. Lilith is a twin to the core energy of the Earth, its deep heart of molten matter, our hot mama – or perhaps an electrically charged crystalline grid. Science has not yet journeyed to the center of the Earth, no matter how many B movies have gone there.

The creative vitality of the Sun gives life to the Earth and fuels this central core, whatever it is made of. Representing the Moon's closest reach toward the Sun, Black Moon taps into a light-giving instinct for living life in cosmic harmony. Earth is a living energy stream, as our new technologies are revealing. Earth responds to inner impulses from its core, charged by the solar wind that enters through its poles, and it responds to cosmic influences reverberating in its magnetic field and sifting down through its atmospheres. We can imagine that the Black Moon moves in the invisible, aetheric dance of this energy and subtly informs the relationship between spirit and matter. This Lilith is the dark "sister" of the Earth. Not a physical body, Black Moon is a reference point that opens awareness into subtle dimensions essential to sustain spiritual vitality in our lives.

Black Moon shares some of the Dark Moon agenda to experientially confront us with our ego-bound self-centeredness.

Interpretations of the Black Moon and Dark Moon can be mutually informative. To make it confusing, as Lilith would, the Black Moon is often referred to as the Dark Moon. The Dark Moon as a dark energy cloud around the Earth has a different feel than the image of a second focus of Earth and Moon or an aetheric dynamic connector between Sun and Earth's core. Perhaps the Dark Moon insistence on non-subjectivity, taking us beyond our natal lunar patterns into heightened objective awareness, prepares us for the spiritualizing levels of the Black Moon. In the territory of the Black Moon, we question ourselves, our desires and feelings of power and powerlessness. Often experienced in a negative way, the Black Moon asks us to go beyond such judgments and extract the insight she offers for the growth of the soul.

In her valuable work on the Black Moon, *Lilith, Der Schwarze Mond*, Joelle de Gravelaine articulates aspects of what I perceive to be more clearly connected to Black Moon experience as it describes our relationship to the absolute, necessitating sacrifice and showing how we let go. The Black Moon insists that we set our ego-based selfhood aside to let the greater Whole flow through. It is an active receptivity when we are willing to "let Thy Will be done," to put our desires at the foot of the Great Spirit. The Black Moon faces us with a stark, still void, inherently uncomfortable, even terrifying. D.H. Lawrence exquisitely follows Lilith into that dark void, "ceasing to know…once dipped in dark oblivion, the soul has peace, inward and lovely peace."

A woman sensitive who works with powerful goddess energies reports of her explorations with Lilith, particular the Black Moon, after several years of intensive spiritual work. A grounded double Taurus, her Black Moon is conjunct Venus in Gemini, tuning into multiple wavelengths of the feminine energy.

> *I can now affirm, on a deep meditational level, that the molten core of the earth is the earth's core essence and the same vibration as Black Moon Lilith. It is definitely a fluidic gentle pulse for me now. As I bring that energy into my body, there is a very deep restructuring that is evolving in both my Haric and auric dimensions, especially my root chakra.*
>
> [Laya Shriaberg, personal communication]

Black Moon is an energy vortex involved with the Earth's celestial movement, perhaps a pathway for the incarnating soul. It can affect the hara, the power center of the body, as well as the subtle aura. Lilith lives in the Tree of Life, offering direct experience of wisdom if we can flow with her beyond our fears from the past, beyond our fear of the unknown. In part, it is a direction of mind which can trap us in the past, or turn us towards the true desire of the soul. As we bring these areas to light, through what we could call Lilith work, tapping into all her cosmic forms, we lighten and harmonize the anima mundi, the soul of the world, freeing the wisdom trapped from expression by the illusions of fear and darkness. In *Unremembered Country*, Susan Griffin beautifully articulates the essence of this core energy: "As I go into the Earth, she pierces my heart... she unveils me... she reveals stories to me... revelations, and I am transformed."

Black Moon Lilith lures us into self-centered illusions and demonstrates the undesirability of such a stance, so that we seek a deeper desire within our hearts, following the yearnings of our souls. She insists that we feel through, let go and surrender to something essential and transparent in us that is the bedrock of the soul.

The Lilith Star, Algol

...the Gorgon's head, a ghastly sight,
Deformed and dreadful, and a sign of woe.
Homer's *Iliad*

Algol, "the Demon," is the second brightest star in the constellation Perseus, located at the beginning of a curve of stars once called Caput Gorgonis or Caput Medusae, referring to the head of the Gorgon Medusa, the monster lady with snakes for hair.

Perseus holds Medusa's severed head that he cut off with a crystal sword. Algol marks the paralyzing eye of Medusa, with the look that turns one to stone. In any language it has a bad reputation, as stars go. Richard Hinckley Allen reports that the Chinese called it "Tseih She," meaning "piled-up corpses." Hebrews called it Satan's Head, he added, but also Lilith. This opens another doorway into mythic connections to Lilith, making an association with Medusa, another fearsome female image. Interestingly, there is a medical term derived from this star; "algolology" refers to the study of pain. It also gives its name to "alcohol," a substance that can make people "lose their heads."

A noteworthy star astronomically, Algol was the first eclipsing binary star to be identified, paving the way for a new scientific category of stars. Algol consists of two main stars that eclipse each other, causing variation in its apparent magnitude. Algol A is three times as big as our Sun and about twice as hot. It is more luminous than Algol B. Mutual gravitation between the two stars causes a bridge of gas to reach out from A to B. The light of Algol remains steady for about two and a half days (almost 69 hours) and then decreases rapidly to darken noticeably for a few short hours. It is easy to imagine Algol as the baleful eye of Medusa, winking or blinking and turning viewers to stone. *Sky and Telescope* magazine offers a user-friendly web page which forecasts the minima of Algol [www.skyandtelescope.com/observing/objects/variablestars/Minima_of_Algol.html.] Historical observation does not seem to refer directly to the star's variability, but does speak of an apparent redness, in spite of its classification among the white stars. See if you can see that red blink, and wink back — with respect!

The year 2000 zodiacal alignment point for Algol is 26 Taurus 10 using the modern measurement that refers to the equatorial poles. In *Brady's Book of Fixed Stars*, the author explains Ptolemy's original system based on the poles of the ecliptic, in which the year 2000 position for Algol is 25 Taurus 30. Bernadette Brady also gives this star's culminating point as 18 degrees Taurus, pinpointing yet another degree carrying its strong influence.

Generally a fixed star spends about 72 years in one degree. From the year 1900 to 2000, Algol moved from 24 Taurus 46 to 26 Taurus 10. At a rate of about 2.4 years per minute, we can expect Algol to move into the 27+ degree range around the year 2056. In any case, the star's sphere of influence can safely be stretched a degree either side, or more, depending on how strictly one uses the orbs of influence.

In *The Fixed Stars and Constellations in Astrology*, Vivian Robson called Algol "the most evil star in the heavens," a rather extreme statement. What is deemed "most evil" may be an important key to opening hidden, deeper levels of consciousness, as the study of powerful dark goddesses indicates. Feminist ears perk up when powerful women are demonized. In *Brady's Book of Fixed Stars*, modern star interpreter Bernadette Brady helps us re-vision the meaning of Algol, as the face of the feminine most feared for her raw passion and power. "She is female kundalini energy... the power of the feminine or the potential power of Mother Nature, not to be called evil for being strong." Algol carries the collective rage for the suppression and repression of this power. Brady cites Capulus, the right hand of Perseus which wields the sword, as the equivalent star for male rage.

Kalli Halvorsen of HerStar calls Algol the star of female passion and intensity. As the Eye of Medusa, Algol gives witness to the violation and abuse of feminine power and sexuality, she suggests, which gives rise to a profound rage. This rage can be self-protective, yet it often needs some kind of expression so that it does not turn in on itself from paralysis of repressed emotions, a cancerous emotional situation. In *Epheta*, Vivian Bennerson, "Mother B," a wise woman who worked with Medusa as I work with Lilith, wrote, "Let us become angry enough to care about ourselves… let self-love develop as it ought once we admit and realize that this power is within our grasp."

In her *Fixed Star Workbook*, Diana K. Rosenberg reports on Algol transits connected to catastrophes and violence, yet also finds a spiritual side — serious, patient, talkative, yet not bigoted. In the arts, it can show ghastliness and beauty at the same time; in politics, brutality along with high-mindedness. She gives the example of Picasso's "Guernica," a passionate anti-war response to fascist atrocities in the Spanish Civil War. Picasso had Jupiter conjunct Algol.

In *Starlight Elixirs and Cosmic Vibrational Healing*, researchers Michael Smulkis and Fred Rubenfeld report on the special qualities of Algol as a star essence. It tunes into internal harmonies that open a deeper awareness of life purpose, aligning DNA codes, reincarnational streams, and attunement with humanity's participation in the anima mundi, world soul. It can help us see how choices we have made impacted our development, for better or worse, so we can proceed more clearly with our destiny. "Awareness of how you have chosen to create resistant patterns to certain universal laws may come forth." Perhaps Algol is a point of focus for our collective consciousness where we can offer energetic contributions to support politicians to make decisions for the higher good, or not. In this regard, what can we learn from Ho Chi Minh, Pope John-Paul II, Ariel Sharon and Al Gore? All their charts are charged with Algol (see later section).

Medusa

I sat before my glass one day,
And conjured up a vision bare...
The vision of a woman, wild
With more than womanly despair....
"I am she!"
Mary Elizabeth Coleridge *The Other Side of the Mirror*

In 1882 young Mary Elizabeth Coleridge gave poetic voice to a vision of herself as Medusa, bereft of voice and words to speak her anguish and despair, "made mad because its hope was gone." Her "speechless woe" carries the weight of ages of female grief, rage, repression and hopelessness in an era that strictly proscribed options for women's lives. Coleridge expresses this basic theme of the Lilith star. Inclusion of the asteroid named Medusa, Asteroid 149, may add interest and more connections to the themes of the Lilith star. [We visit this poetess again in the later Dark Moon section.]

Algol and its Medusa connection is part of a mythic drama that involves several constellations that cover a large section of the sky: Perseus, Andromeda, Cassiopeia, Cepheus, Cetus, Pegasus and Andromeda. Greek myths do not offer many positive female role models. This section of the sky could do with a carefully considered revisioning! For now we can only take a peak into this big story. Let us reflect, as Perseus was advised, on Medusa. Even a brief investigation can help amplify our understanding of Lilith and the dark feminine.

In the Greek myth, Medusa was a lovely young woman, who caught the eye of Poseidon. He ravished her one day while she was serving in the temple of Athena. This did not please Athena, a virgin goddess, and she punished Medusa by turning her — and her two sisters, it would seem, for there were three Gorgons — into monstrous part-bird creatures with hideous faces and hair of hissing, twisting serpents, the original

Twisted Sisters. There is the bird and snake again. It might appear cold and unfair of Athena, yet she is the goddess of justice. In *The Centaur*, John Updike offers an unexpected nuance. He imagined the girl coming in to make an offering to Athena and taking a moment to look into the shining disk on the altar and tuck a stray wisp of hair back into place. Such a piece of vanity may be smiled upon by Aphrodite but not Athena.

There are multiple versions of most myths, evoking various facets of interpretation. Each has a perspective to offer and a psychological process to convey. Though a myth can be taken on its own terms, it is good to remember that they are grounded in a cultural context. This myth, in particular, may come out of Africa, connected to the Amazon culture, enemies of the Greeks in the Trojan War. A feminist historical reading by Barbara G. Walker interprets the Gorgon face as a ritual mask used by priestesses of the Moon goddess Neith or Anath or Ath-enna in North Africa. These priestesses were called Gorgons. The mask may have been worn to evoke the goddess and to produce awe and fear of her power. "Be advised you who approach." I imagine Medusa as an African high priestess who wore her hair in dreadlocks.

The serpentine hair of Medusa can also suggest the streaming rays of the Sun. Indeed, Medusa has been associated with the Sun goddess. Snakes and serpents are creatures that carry ancient, chthonic power in many mythologies. They are used in ceremony, ritual and healing through the ages, even today in various religious denominations in east and west. Images of goddesses and priestesses hold snakes, have snakes circling their arms or bodies, or undulating through their hair. Snakes symbolize an evocative mixture of male and female sexuality and regeneration. Snakes shed their skins and renew themselves.

Anthropologist and art historian David Napier, author of *Masks, Transformation and Paradox*, has researched gorgon-like masks across the world, linking Medusa and the Balinese Barong masks, an artistic expression of wild beasts. Such bestial lion-like Gorgon faces are the symbolic image of intense sensory experience, Napier believed, of immediate experience that is outside rational interpretation or understanding. Such masks express powers that tap into the fearsome irrationality of nature, those that stop us in our tracks. Beyond the mind, this Gorgon knowledge is instinctive and kinesthetic, purely biological experience. In Sumerian myth, the monster Humbaba, with his labyrinthine visage, was a guardian of the threshold that led to the transformative journey. Such ferocious creatures and faces may be protector spirits, guarding the sanctity of a temple or a home, to ward off evil. Two stone helmets, with the earliest known images of the Gorgon, from the seventh to eighth centuries BC, have been uncovered in Tiryns, the kingdom Perseus came to rule at the end of the story — after he cut off the head of Medusa.

The Mirror and the Eye

> *Carefully stepping backwards, feeling each footfall with jaguar stealth, Perseus kept his eye on the shield strapped to his left arm. He held it to his side angled like a rear-view mirror. As he retreated further into the Gorgon's cave, irregular light rippled like waves across the polished surface of the shield, moving in slippery serpentine forms. Startled, he realized he was seeing Medusa. Her back was to him, filling the shield's surface with dark slithering shadows, surrounding a faint image of his own face, seen as if from a great distance, haloed in undulating clouds. He felt suddenly as if he were underwater and took in a deep breath to steady himself. In that breath he could taste her musky scent, like some ancient salty perfume, evoking strange memories. Focusing again on the mirror, he was now looking into a vast single Eye, seeing his future unwind like a long dark tunnel...*

The Eye of Medusa. Is it open or closed? Is she awake or asleep? This powerful, penetrating and paralyzing Eye sees right through you and perceives "with an objectivity like that of nature itself and our dreams, boring into the soul to find the naked truth, to see reality beneath all its myriad forms and the illusions and defenses it displays," as described by Sylvia Perera in her rich volume, *Descent to the Goddess*. The eye is the window to the soul. The mirror is another. Mirror, mirror on the wall, who's the fairest of them all? It certainly isn't Medusa.

In past cultures where the Sun was celebrated as feminine in its life-giving nature, the mirror and the eye, the well and the web, the spiral and other such symbols of wholeness were associated with the goddess. The mirror is a sacred object of Amaterasu, the Shinto Sun Goddess in Japan. As recounted in the book, *Turbulent Mirror*, an ancient Chinese legend tells of the chaos that ensued as the world of humans became increasingly separated from the world of mirrors. Perhaps it refers to the mirror of Nature, perhaps the sky. The use of bronze mirrors in China dates back to the late Shang dynasty, 13-11 centuries BC. The sophisticated astronomy and cosmology of the Chinese is chronicled on such celestial bronze mirrors.

Perseus used a mirror-like shield of brass or bronze to avoid a direct confrontation with Medusa. The mirror reflected the demon's image. We conquer our dark passions by reflection, otherwise we can be paralyzed by them — a big hint in working with Lilith placements! Perseus then wields the crystal sword of skillful means given by psychopomp Mercury/Hermes. His skill in using the sword depends on the clarity of the mirror image. To effectively coordinate both is tricky; the mirror image reverses, like a telescope. He sees himself in the mirror as well. Or, in another version, he positions the mirror so that Medusa looks into it and turns herself into stone.

The word mirror derives from the Latin *miror, mirare*, "to wonder at, to be astonished." The Latin word for mirror is *speculum*, which gives us such words as *speculate*, (which originally meant to divinate with a crystal ball or mirror) and *spectacle*, as well as *telescope*. Edward Edinger discusses this in his book, *The Eternal Drama*. The mirror of the universe reflects the depths of our souls, immensely spacious like the dark energy theorized by current astrophysics. Making up over 90% of the universe, dark energy presents incalculable potential in our collective process of consciousness evolution. Perhaps Lilith works in this dimension.

In the mystery of the Lilith star dwells the power of recognizing the essential beauty beyond the terrifying darkness of the unknown. The "awe-full" beauty of Medusa carries so much of our own untapped power that we dare not look her in the face. And if we do, we may be terrified of what we see. There is a Hindu word, *bhey*, that means a sense of awe bordering on fear, a fear of offending or dishonoring, particularly God. To see deeply into the dark side of life, its wilderness and chaos can be profoundly transformational and freeing if one can endure the intensity of this encounter that strips the ego bare, exposes the naked soul. Algol can bring us to this edge.

The variability of this binary eclipsing star may create a periodicity of strong desire or purpose that fuels our intent, followed by a lull, fallow moments when we may feel empty and lose heart. In this dangerous or blissful desireless moment, we face that void or emptiness of Medusa's Eye. Are we stopped by it, is a resistance formed? Can we handle both desire and desirelessness? Buddha reminds us that attachment to our desires creates bondage to the world. Can we see through our desires, sexual and otherwise, and let go? Can we let go of superficial desires to commit to the strongest, truest desires? Lilith does not compromise; she compels us to seek the path of most vibrant life force. Ultimately the Eye of Medusa faces us with the inevitability and paralysis of our own death. How do we see through death?

In front of the deep dark endless space of modern cosmology, we may feel insignificance, terror and despair. We are confronted with the immense question of free will, a choice to willingly participate consciously — or not. This is the existential dilemma Perseus encountered in front of the primordial Eye of Medusa. In his book, *A Sense of the Cosmos: The Encounter of Modern Science and Ancient Truth*, philosopher Jacob Needleman expresses the profound nature of this critical, sacred moment of reflection and self-questioning, "for there is nothing to guarantee that we will be able to remain long enough or deeply enough in front of the unknown." In such a moment of stillness, we are petrified in a state of internal transformation, of potential awakening. Needleman identifies the core question as an emotional one, facing us with the unknown and stripping away our illusions. He says the question to be answered is, "Do I fear the darkness more than I love the awakening?"

This is a question humanity as a whole faces in the throes of a paradigm shift such as we are experiencing now. We each have our personal moments of confronting fears of the unknown, the void, the fathomless gaze of Medusa.

The Severed Head

"Off with her head!" said the Red Queen.
Lewis Carroll, *Through the Looking Glass*

When Perseus cuts off Medusa's head, he masters her serpentine kundalini power and penetrating third eye of intuitive sight. Psychologically this is the process for a man to claim his own power in relation to the dark feminine. The intention behind cutting off her head is the key. Is the intention to cut off from the body, retreat into mental abstractions and mind-over-matter, or to free the natural instincts from the domination of negative thinking and programmed rationality? Do we go "out of our minds," or "lose our heads"? What do we release when we "cut to the quick," when we free our deepest instincts and our deepest desires? Desires are natural, built into our biology. Condemned or repressed desires create an underlying nervousness that redirects the natural flow. Such desires seek satisfaction at some level before they let us go. Lilith is in charge here. When we acknowledge these desires, we free the energy, whether we use it to satisfy the desire or redirect it.

Out from the severed neck of Medusa flies Pegasus, the Flying Horse. Perseus can now soar on the wings of imagination contained in the body of the dark goddess. The imagination is freed from the paralyzing fear of the ego when confronted by the dark eye of primordial vastness. The symbol of the decapitated head appears in alchemy, associated with prophecy, creativity and transformation. Drops of blood from one side of Medusa's head become a healing potion, from the other side a poison. The book, *Off with Her Head!: The Denial of Women's Identity in Myth, Religion, and Culture*, edited by Howard Eilberg-Schwartz and Wendy Doniger, offers a series of perspectives on gender issues related to women's heads, hair, veils and cosmetics, to show that, "From ancient myth to contemporary culture, the metaphor of beheading has been used to express the dehumanizing of women." We could see this as an Asteroid Lilith level of interpretation, valid on its own terms.

On the other hand, skulls and severed heads can have spiritual meaning, as seen in the iconography of Hindu goddesses. Often the dark blue Kali is poised holding a sword and a head. "One left hand holds a severed head, indicating the annihilation of ego-bound evil force, and the other carries a sword of physical extermination with which she cuts the thread of bondage," explains Ajit Mookerji in *Kali, The Feminine Force*. Kali has two other hands which make gestures to dispel fear and to offer spiritual strength. She wears a long necklace of shrunken heads or skulls.

Kali has a bright side named Lalita, a Lilith-like name. Dressed in blood-red, flower-bedecked, sensual and Self-willed, her true form is too bright for mortal eyes. She keeps track of our spiritual lives, aligning thoughts and senses with the Great Spirit. When our minds become undisciplined, she gives us a nudge with her goad. If we resist, she tosses a noose around our necks and reins us in.

Other facets of Kali are expressed by the Ten Mahavidyas, a decemvirate of powerful goddesses that arose to surround Shiva when he tried to leave Kali (even Shiva can be overcome by this goddess!)

Half of them wear garlands of severed heads. Some brandish swords and carry heads still dripping with blood. Chinnamasta is especially striking, seen cutting off her own head. Streams of blood pour into her own mouth and those of her devotees, nourishing them. While decapitating herself, she might be sitting on a copulating couple, or in the act of intercourse herself. The blood shoots forth amidst plant-like growth. On a mystical or meditation path, the practitioner seeks to go beyond ego-bound mental states. This is sometimes symbolized by offering the head as a sacrifice. The blood suggests the infusion of new life in transcendent states.

Decapitation is a preferred method around the world for killing sacrificial victims, animal or human. Mayan ritual ball games recreated cosmological beginnings as told in the Mayan equivalent of the Bible, the *Popol Vuh*. In this exotic story, filled with decapitations, the Ball Court was the sacred Place of Ballgame Sacrifice, a portal to the primordial time and space of the Otherworld. Ball games were the highest religious rituals of the early Americas — and still seem to be for many people today! Carved panels in the great ball Court of Chich'en Itza depict two teams facing each other across a ball engraved with a skull. The player next to the ball holds the severed head of a captive, whose corpse is kneeling on the other side. Seven serpentine streams of blood fountain out of his neck. One showers the victim, transforming into water lilies from the Otherworld, symbolizing the life-giving vitality of his sacrifice. Ix-Chel, the goddess of healing, holds a serpent and wears such a Lilith lily on her head. Blood was a central religious and cultural substance in the Mayan culture. Bloodletting was considered a means to release soul essence from their bodies, offered as drink to the gods in an act of communion. In *The Power of Myth*, Joseph Campbell reports that the captain of the winning team is sacrificed to the gods as the finest representative. What would happen to our wide world of sports if that honor were reinstated?

In Christian teachings, the blood of Jesus is considered a divine substance. The beheading of John the Baptist is seen as a necessary sacrifice to empower Jesus in his work. In *Signs in the Heavens*, the authors, Bento, Tresemer and Schiappacasse, connect events in the life of John the Baptist, including his death, with meaningful alignments of the Sun with the star Algol, the decapitation star. They also called attention to the two major comets of the 1990s: Hayakutake in 1996 and Hale-Bopp in 1997. The trails of these two comets moved perpendicular to each other, crossing at a point of intersection with the star Algol.

In his provocative discussion, "The Seduction of Black," James Hillman suggested that decapitation is the way to release the soul from its identification with the literal, reductive and depressingly empty — black — state of the soul. In the alchemical process, the stage of *nigredo* is black, a dark emptiness in which meaning is occluded and occulted. Black negates the current state of being, is "a harbinger of alteration, of invisible discovery and of dissolution of attachments to whatever has been taken as truth and reality, solid fact or dogmatic virtue."

"She comes in colors," sang the Rolling Stones. And goddesses do — blue, green, red, brown, white, yellow — but black is most powerful. Non-reflective, black absorbs all colors and is absorbed in itself, "the black of starless midnight, a state of translucence or transparency that is beyond dark and light... a radiant black, " wrote China Galland in *Longing for Darkness*. The Lilith star, Algol, shines out of the endless dark of the night sky, with both her seductive wink and unblinking stare.

3

Lilith in the Arts

The fascination of Lilith has endured through the ages, inspiring artists across the spectrum: Goethe, Victor Hugo, Dante Gabriel Rossetti, John Keats, Thornton Wilder, George Bernard Shaw, Robert Browning, Anais Nin, and Martha Graham have all explored themes of Lilith. A modern sculpture of Lilith by Kiki Shuth is seen climbing down a wall in the Metropolitan Museum of Art in New York.

Lilith is also the name of a Jewish feminist magazine that addresses issues of spirituality, politics and culture. The 1962 movie, *Lilith*, starring Jean Seberg, Warren Beatty and Peter Fonda, has become a cult classic. The opera *Lilith*, a year 2000 production by the New York Opera Company composed by Deborah Drattell, is one of the latest and boldest dramatic expressions.

In the 2006 "Circle Trilogy" *(Morrigan's Cross, Dance of the Gods, Valley of Silence)* by popular novelist Nora Roberts, Lilith is Queen of Vampires, training an army of demons to conquer the universe. A band of three men and three women time travel through a circle of stones to gather together and confront Lilith's army. A witch, a wizard, a warrior woman, a queen from ancient Ireland, a shapeshifter, and a thousand-year-old vampire once turned by Lilith, this circle of six trains as a unit to live up to their destiny, developing courage, physical and moral strength, honing tools of magic and of battle, shape-shifting abilities and, most important of all, love, to vanquish the evil vampire army. The vampire is an enduring archetypal image for the blood-sucking dark side that seductively turns us away from ourselves. Lilith as vampire queen ultimately caused each of these characters to move forward to advance on their spiritual path. This trilogy can be used as a fictional text on Dark Moon.

Lilith is a character on the T.V. shows *Cheers* and *Frazier*, and she even made an appearance in an episode of *Doctor Who*. She gave her name to the Lilith Fair music fest created by Sarah McLachlan, featuring all female singers giving voice to women's autonomy, creativity and power. Lasting for several years, this hugely successful traveling show was considered a risky venture by the music world when it began in 1997. Just so, to allow Lilith into our lives and to express that power is risky business. We risk judgment and ostracism for demonstrating such passion and creativity as is demonstrated by this powerful goddess. Women who live out their Lilith-like autonomy are still called bitch, as are some men who love her.

Lilith in the Victorian Era

Lilith was a popular and highly ambivalent image for artists in the 1800s and into the early 1900s as the Victorian era progressed, with its highly self-conscious distrust of, and fascination with, the feminine. Most often Lilith is portrayed as an evil demoness and femme fatale. Likely drawing from the earlier *Hebrew Zohar*, Johann Wolfgang von Goethe reintroduced the seductive Lilith in *Faust* (1808) as Adam's first wife to be wary of

> *Her beauty's one boast is her dangerous hair,*
> *When Lilith winds it tight around young men*
> *She doesn't soon let go of them again.*

In *Lamia* (1819), John Keats writes somewhat sympathetically of this Lilith-related, multi-hued and shape-shifting demon who takes a woman's form to seduce men and devour them. He describes her, in part, as "some penanced lady elf,"

> *...full of silvery moons, that, as she breathed,*
> *Dissolv'd, or brighter shone, or interwreathed*
> *Their lustres with the gloomier tapestries—*

This seductress was later painted by John William Waterhouse in *A Mermaid*, and *Lamia* (1909). She is shown by both poets and artists as shedding her snake skin. Artists John Collier (in 1887) and Kenyon Cox (in 1892) showed Lilith as a beautiful woman embracing a large snake.

Lady Lilith (1868), by Pre-Raphaelite painter Dante Gabriel Rossetti, shows her brushing her long golden hair. It was this painting that truly brought Lilith into the modern era and opened the way to feminist attention. The Delaware State Welcome Center greets visitors with a large poster of this painting, as the original oil is in the Wilmington Society of Fine Arts. Rossetti's watercolor version is in the Metropolitan Museum in New York. Lilith gets around. Rossetti later wrote *Lilith* or *Body's Beauty* to amplify the painting, in which he spoke of her dangerous beauty and hair that binds and strangles (as in *Faust)*. In his erotic ballad, *Eden Bower* (1869), Rossetti tells how Lilith makes a sexual deal with the serpent as she seeks revenge against Adam and Eve still living happily in Eden.

In the ear of the Snake said Lilith:
(Eden bower's in flower.)
'To thee I come when the rest is over;
A snake was I when thou wast my lover.'

As the ballad sings on, Lilith tells her own version of the fall and elicits sympathy along with revulsion. If his 4.30am birth time is correct, this Lilith-loving painter and poet was a double Taurus with the Lilith star Algol close to his Sun and Ascendant.

Robert Browning gives a radical re-visioning of Lilith in his poem, *Adam, Lilith and Eve* (1883), in which Lilith and Eve are friends. Lilith reveals her eternal love for Adam, while Eve confesses she never loved him at all.

George MacDonald's *Lilith* (1895), my first introduction, portrays her as willfully claiming the sole power of creation over the Lord, based on her ability to give birth. She wants Adam to worship and obey her, and when he will not, she deserts him and takes up with the Shadow, who makes her Queen of Hell. At night, she turns into a wild cat, a leopardess, perhaps in memory of the Sumerian lion-headed *lamashtu*, or the lions who guard the thrones of many goddesses. We are reminded of the jaguar power of Mayan shamans. The spots on the cat's body are the darkness and shadows that stream out from her eyes. In her passion for freedom, she considers surrender to a higher power a form of weakness and slavery, yet she is unable to see her own destructiveness and cruelty toward others. Addressing the Eve character, Mara, she proclaims her autonomous will and self-creation. Mara gently rebukes her in a reminder of divine will, "a light that lights up the darkness behind it: that light can change your will, can make it truly yours and... not the Shadow's." This exchange epitomizes an essential theme of *Lilith*, self will or divine will. Once Lilith sees her true self, she is horrified and blames God for making her the way she is. She continues to resist surrender and renewal in the will of God. She is left suspended in a state of purgatory, leading the reader to believe that she will eventually come through it and find herself. (MacDonald's Lilith signature is described later.)

On the other hand, in a 1907 play by Isolde Kurz, *Die Kinder der Lilith (The Children of Lilith)*, God blames the woes of mankind on Adam's betrayal of Lilith, the First Woman, who embodies the perfected glory of heaven on Earth. Lucifer invents Eve to lure Adam away from Lilith, who then turns into the fiery angel that banishes Adam and Eve from the garden with the flaming sword of truth.

With dancing, red-hot sparks about,
All of a sudden her wings spread out,
Dreadfully changed she seems to him,
Kin of the flaming Cherubim.

Back to Methuselah: In the Garden

Heading further into the twentieth century, Lilith continued to be a compelling archetype in the transformation of the collective consciousness. George Bernard Shaw's 1922 play *Back to Methuselah* includes one of my favorite dramatic sketches of Lilith. The serpent in Eden speaks to Eve in a "strange seductively musical whisper" of Lilith, mother of Adam and Eve. It was Lilith, reveals the serpent, who first embodied the feminine power of conception and rebirth. She was alone in the Garden. When she first saw a creature die, she realized that in order to survive she must find out how to renew herself. "She had a mighty will: she strove and strove and willed and willed for more moons than there are leaves on all the trees of the garden." And she reproduced herself into two, Eve and Adam. The serpent tells Eve Lilith's secret

You imagine what you desire; you will what you imagine; and at last you create what you will... In one word, to conceive.

It is this power to create something out of nothing through desire, will and her capacity to love that is the creative nature of Lilith. Her vitality is the life force that manifests out of the unmanifest, out of the invisible substance of the universe, the dark energy physicists are now searching for so intently. This power of conception belongs to the feminine alone, says the serpent. Man must give his desire and his will to the woman to share in the power of conception. Similarly in Buddhism, it is the insightful wisdom of the feminine that informs the skillful means of the male principle. "I dared everything," confides the serpent, "it was by meditating on Life that I gained the power to do miracles."

The Soul of Lilith: Power vs. Love

> *Where love rules, there is no will to power; and where power predominates, there love is lacking. The one is the shadow of the other.*
>
> Carl Jung

In *The Soul of Lilith*, Marie Corelli's novel from 1892 , El-Rami is a brilliant and charismatic practitioner of the esoteric arts. He revived a young girl named Lilith from death. Like a sleeping beauty, he keeps her in a secret room, tended by an old deaf woman from the Arabian desert. The reader is first impressed with Lilith's ethereal beauty, like "a creeping of some subtle fire through the veins which made the fair body seem the mere reflection of some greater fairness within." She holds a star-shaped ruby on her breast, shining as brightly as Antares, the red supergiant star that marks the heart of the Scorpion. In Vedic astrology Antares is associated with the ruby. As one of the four Royal Stars of Persia, it was the Watcher of the West, the god of the dead who beckoned souls to the afterlife. In classical astrology it is a star of extremes that promises success, but warns of willful ambition that leads to self-undoing. Lilith holds this star at her heart, a symbol of her death-in-life and life-in-death journey — and a silent warning to the man who considers himself master of her soul.

El-Rami commands her spirit to travel into other realms seeking knowledge of the universe, of any sign of a god, of death, of the sorrow and darkness he believes underly life. She can find none. She brings back reports of peoples on Mars and Sirius, of other worlds and distant stars, of eternal life, light and the omnipresence of Love, but he cannot believe her. "How is it that she never comprehends Death or Pain? Is her vision limited only to behold harmonious systems moving to a sound of joy?"

His mental hubris rejects God and faith as improvable and disdains love as worldly and coarse, but eventually he has to admit that he loves her, fiercely holding on to his control and possession. She urges, "Love me, not my shadow!" As she reveals her soul-self, an angelic presence so full of light, he is overpowered and collapses. Lilith is released to the light, and El-Rami finishes his days in sorrow of separation and devotion to the angelic memory and the immortal vision of the soul of Lilith

> *Beautiful, indestructible, terrible Lilith! She permeates the world, she pervades the atmosphere, she shapes and unshapes herself at pleasure… She is the essence of God.*

Martha Graham's Embattled Garden

> *Love, it has been said, does not obey the rules of love but yields to some more ancient and ruder law.*
>
> from program notes

Martha Graham, innovative pioneer of modern dance, choreographed numerous evocative and provocative ballets. Following her first Saturn return, she founded the Martha Graham Dance Company in 1926, and created a vast repertoire over several decades. In 1958, well into her

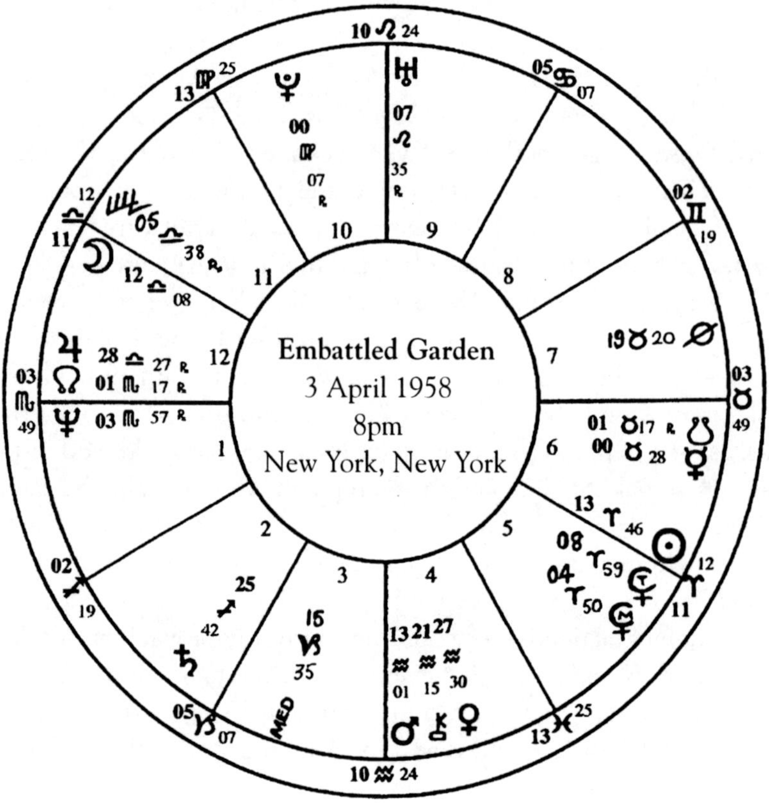

sixties, she created *Embattled Garden*, interpreting the story of Lilith as the first wife of Adam. The serpentine Stranger appears with Lilith to disrupt the harmony in Adam and Eve's garden with seductive, dark, comedic undertones, as innocence is lost and love found again. This dance premiered right on the Full Moon of April 3, 1958, with Black Moon conjunct the Aries Sun and Asteroid Lilith conjunct the Libra Moon. The Dark Waldemath Moon was in Taurus square a combination of Mars, Chiron and Venus in Aquarius. This work followed the long tradition of creative engagement with the Garden of Eden story, a foundational myth in the experience of male-female relationships.

Graham herself had a Taurus Sun widely conjunct Mercury in an Earth grand trine with mean Black Moon and Asteroid Lilith in Capricorn, and Ceres/Chiron/Dark Moon Lilith in Virgo. She had a wide

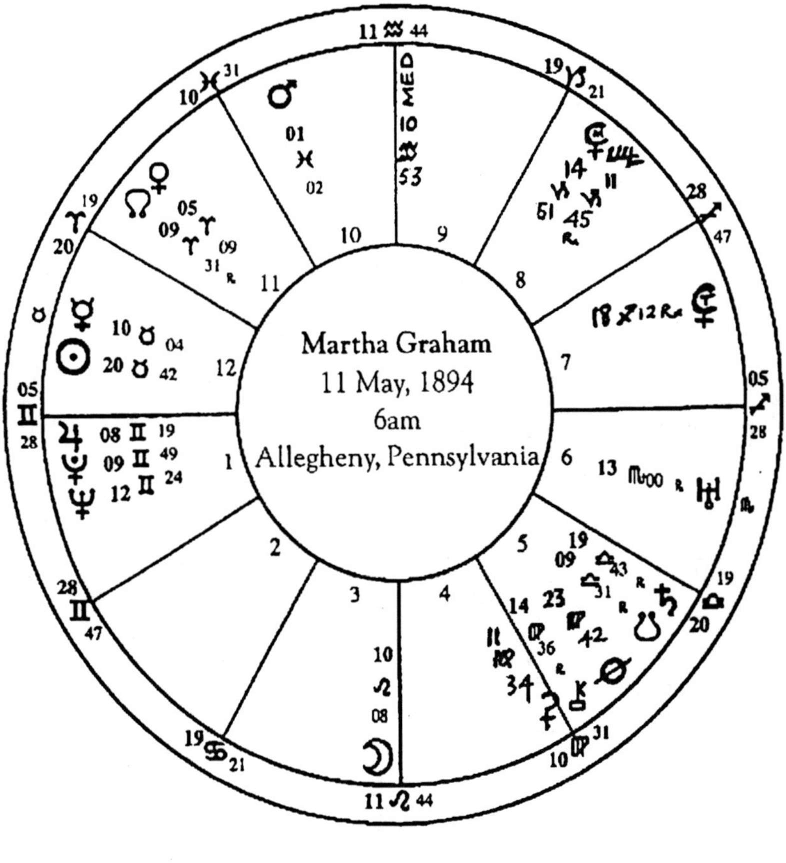

Black Moon corridor, with true Black Moon in Sagittarius twenty-six degrees away from the mean position. That oscillating Black Moon made a grand Fire trine with Moon in Leo and Venus/North Node in Aries. With trines in both Earth and Fire, she could well experience imagination in motion. "Movement never lies," was her motto. "It is the magic of what I call the outer space of the imagination." Her dancing and choreography were deeply erotic, and often challenging to American cultural mores of the early and mid-twentieth century. "Desire is a lovely thing, and that is where the dance comes from, from desire," she wrote in her autobiography *Blood Memory*.

The Lilith synastry between the choreographer and the dance piece is rich. The chart of the dance premiere shows that Aries Sun/Black Moon on Graham's Venus/North Node conjunction, and the Waldemath Dark

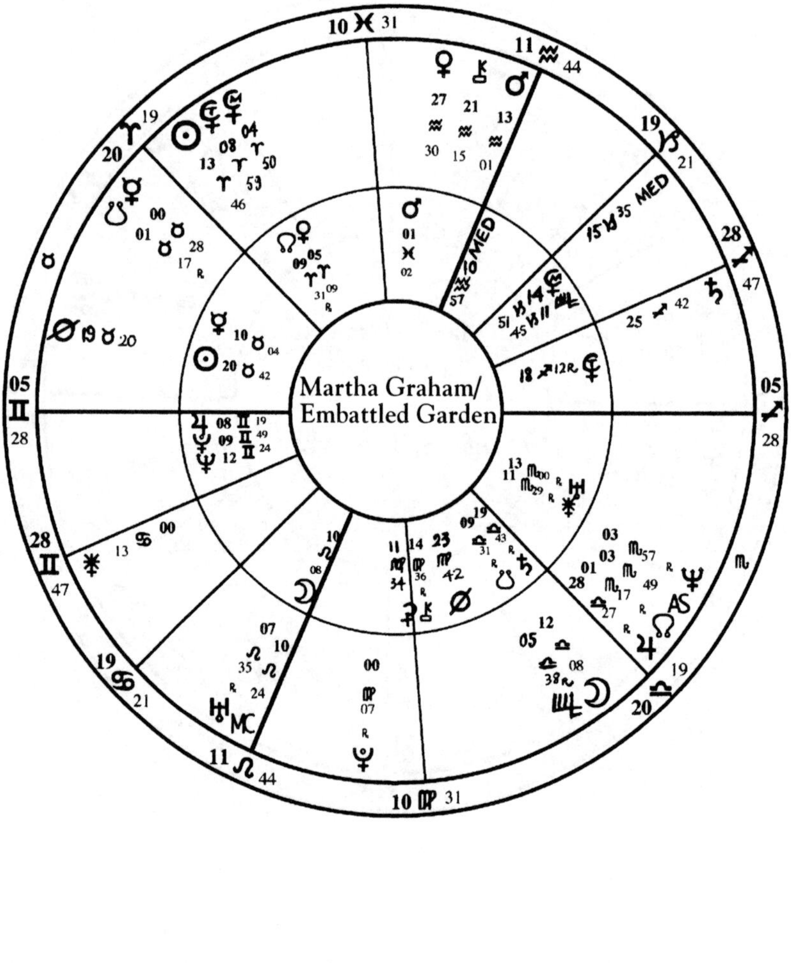

Moon in Taurus was exactly conjunct her Sun. If we add that extra "grace note" of Asteroid Medusa, we see it in the chart of the premiere conjunct Graham's mean Black Moon. Graham's chart shows Medusa on the Midheaven. Her work certainly has a pronounced "look."

Leaving Eden: Lilith as Primordial Mother

In Ann Chamberlin's 1999 novel, *Leaving Eden*, Lilith is the original Mother, ancestress of a Neolithic tribe and mother of the girl who narrates the novel. Adam is her father. She often wonders about her mother. Becoming storyteller of her people, she retells stories she has heard many times. Still she is not sure if her mother is real or myth. "It was no mortal woman, this I conjured, but something rolling on a dust cloud with the wind… in all her divine void."

The people are increasingly disturbed by the new presence of Eve, who has left another tribe to be near Adam. As father of another woman's child, he is not free; he begins asserting new gods and new ways. Lilith returns, for she has felt something out of balance. Mother and daughter are reunited. Even her daughter feels the impersonal nature of Lilith, "Perhaps every soul felt the same in Lilith's presence, chosen — and perfectly loved."

The author draws on the archetypal symbolism of Lilith — the tree and the bird, the wind and wisdom — while offering an original interpretation of her own. Chamberlin attributes the ageless power, wisdom and attraction of Lilith to her unique status as the sole living female from the last race of humans. Her ancient heritage makes her the mother of the new human race. Intimately in touch with nature, she teaches her many children to live in harmony with the ways of nature in their locale on earth. Her magnetic sexual energy is strong when she comes into heat as animals do. All men respond and come to her, yet Adam now resists her. She realizes that the new women, like Eve, have more power over their men because their sexuality is not tied to estrus. However, the rejection of Lilith leads to disharmony with the ways of nature, to the increasing domination of man over nature, and the ongoing struggle for survival. Lilith dies and transfers her power in a magical rebirth rite to her daughter, who then leaves the dying Eden to Adam and Eve.

The Wild Mother

In *The Wild Mother (1993)*, Elizabeth Cunningham gives us another modern revisioning of Lilith, as she who comes from the Empty Land, a Faerie-like otherworld — a Dark Moon Lilith sort of place. Drawn into this world, and exiled from her own by the compulsive will of Adam who seeks to possess her, she loses her connection to Nature and thus her own nature. She leaves, forced to abandon her daughter and son. When Adam realizes that the girl is in touch with her mother through dreams and drawings, he uses his daughter to lure Lilith back and traps her. Lilith re-enters the human world. She trails flowers that come out of the ground under her footsteps, even into the house. For love of Lilith, the children and their grandmother join in a magic ritual to free her — and themselves. Yet again, we encounter the theme of willfulness and dominance over the feminine that leads to repercussions. Adam marries a human woman, Eve, and treats her better because of Lilith.

The Shape-Changer's Wife: Magic and Mystery

Lilith appears as a mysterious central character in Sharon Shinn's, *The Shape-Changer's Wife* (1995), set in the misty days of Druid magic. In this novel, Lilith is a solemn woman with a unique, impersonal and still presence, yet alluring, unusual, disturbing — and passionate about her self integrity." 'I am not like other women,' she said sharply. 'I do not like the things they like or feel the things they feel.' "

As the story unfolds, the fascinated sorcerer's apprentice guesses the secret, that her magician husband had shape-shifted her into a woman in order to possess her. Her true form is a willow tree that lives in the King's sacred grove. A willow tree is associated with the underworld and refers back to Inanna's garden and the Garden of Eden. The apprentice falls in love with Lilith. His desire to serve her happiness accelerates his progress to become a master shape-shifter, able to overpower her husband and return Lilith to her true form, a Tree of Life. "It was the most beautiful, the most awful thing he had ever seen, this transformation of a woman to a tree." Contrasted to the wizard, the apprentice was able to let go of his own possessive desire to honor Lilith, again illustrating the theme of power vs. love in relation to Lilith.

Yakshini

Have you ever seen a woman's shape in the silhouette of a tree at dusk? In Hindu temple sculpture we find the *yakshinis*, voluptuous nature spirits, akin to the dryads of Greek myth. Siren-like, they are beautiful, alluring, somewhat dangerous, whispering in dreams, sounding intimately close, yet ever at a distance. These magical female beings protect hidden treasures of the Earth and grant boons when invoked through mantra and ritual. They live in trees and are often carved with a leg wrapped around the tree, rather like a pole dancer. One arm may be curved up, holding a fruited branch, with the other arm curved down toward or touching the vulva.

Gio is a Tokyo-based musician/producer and popular DJ who founded Dakini Records. *Yakshini* is the title of a 2001 album by his innovative electronic group, Makyo. "I spent two years making this, seeing how deep into the sound I could go," he said. "All I learned is that you can always go deeper." This sounds like Lilith. How about his music? Listen to it at www.dakinirecords.com/

Lilith, the Movie

J.R. Salamanca's *Lilith* was made into a 1964 movie directed by Robert Rossen. An interesting study of Lilith as anima, informed by Jungian psychology, the story takes place at a mental sanitarium named Poplar Lodge, another tree of the underworld. Again we see the tree connection — and the magic. In the film, our first view of Lilith is veiled. She peers unseen through a barred window, playing a flute. "She plays quite magically. She made it herself. It's quite remarkable, isn't it?" remarks a woman patient.

Vincent, the young man who narrates the novel (played by the young Warren Beatty) has been recently discharged from the army. Since boyhood, he has been attracted to the sanitarium, like a dream world on the edge of town. One day he walks through the gates of this "underworld," and starts training as an intern. Assigned to Lilith (Jean Seberg), he becomes fascinated with her; she is beautiful and with a creative zest for living that he does not feel. Lilith draws, plays music, and makes up a language she hears in her inner world, which she calls the real world. She paints with grasses: "My hands move and I follow it. You have to learn to trust if you want them to lead you to the things you love." For Lilith, art and life are one. "You have to demonstrate great courage, a great capacity for joy."

In a clinical conference, Vincent discusses Lilith with the head doctor. Is Lilith trying to seduce him?

"It's much more than that" he replies. "I'm not sure what it is she's trying to offer... She's got some kind of..."

"Rapture," the doctor finds the word. "In Shakespeare's time it meant madness, as ecstasy and innocence often do... When a man devotes himself to studying the nature of rapture he may find himself dispossessed by it... In her case it is seldom possible to tell what is fantasy and what is fact."

"I never try to question her."

"I wouldn't," agrees the doctor. "That is apt to be disastrous."

The intern is pulled toward her, seduced yet conflicted. She questions him, "You think loving me is sinful? You think I have a talent for love? If my talent were greater than you think, would you stop loving me?"

When she becomes involved with another woman patient, it evokes his jealousy and anger. She confronts him, "If you should discover that your god loved others as much as he loves you, would you hate him for it? I show my love for all of you and you despise me."

A male patient (Peter Fonda) is also in love with her. He, too, challenges the intern: "Do you think they can cure Lilith? ... She wants to leave the mark of her desire on every living creature in the world."

Jealousy compels the intern to lie about a gift the male patient has carefully crafted for Lilith, telling him that she didn't like it. The patient kills himself. The disturbed intern confronts Lilith, needing her to say that she wanted him to do what he did, but Lilith has regressed into a catatonic state, withdrawing into her private, "real" world.

The flyleaf of the hardback edition describes the plot as a portrait of innocence corrupted by evil, "an evil so brilliant, so beautiful, so imaginatively conceived that even its violence and amorality have a fantastic splendor of their own." This appears to refer to the intern as the innocent, Lilith as the evil. Perhaps the four decades since this description has given rise to a different perspective when a psychological intern becomes sexually involved with a patient. There is no simple judgment in the complexity of Lilith.

A Jungian perspective would suggest that the psychologically unskilled intern became obsessed by an anima projection on Lilith. An ideal anima figure, the young girl was vital, fascinating, creative, seductive — and mentally ill, living outside the norm both in a sanitarium and in the depths of her unconscious. The intern's own shadow material surfaced, further complicated by the psychotic setting of the sanitarium. The story addressed the depths of the subconscious that are activated in male-female relationships as well as in psychological disorders. As a mental patient, Lilith was compelled by demonic inner voices. She did, indeed, test the intern's motivations and intentions, stirring up hidden depths; yet this was not a simple situation. This intriguing story has many layers, more fully developed in the novel.

Jean Seberg played Lilith. From a famous debut starring in Otto Preminger's *Saint Joan* (1957) to Rossen's shadowy *Lilith* in 1964 was not a big stretch for this Scorpio actress. Born between eclipses, with a Moon/Pluto conjunction in Leo and her true Black Moon at 28+ Sagittarius, her portrayal made the movie memorable and earned her a Golden Globe nomination. Generally not successful in the US, Seberg was much appreciated in France as the epitome of the young, hip woman of the New Wave, supported by the foreign influence of Sagittarius. She also married foreign men. Seberg had a long Black Moon corridor, with the mean Black Moon at 26 Capricorn. With Dark Moon in Capricorn as well, she had double trouble with authorities. Big guns came after her. She was visited by child-killer Lilith, suffering from premature labor and the death of a child, largely brought on by public and deliberately false FBI accusations that the father was a member of the Black Panthers, a group for whom she had political sympathies. Also relevant in the political arena is Asteroid Lilith conjunct Jupiter in Aquarius, square her Sun. This reflects both her radical politics, her New Wave aura and the self-destructive nature of her anti-Lilith tendency to cater to powerful men. Not long after her child's death she was found dead in the back of a car. Ruled a suicide from a drug overdose, some unresolved questions persist.

Warren Beatty, who played Vincent, is a Lilith kind of guy, with Black Moon conjunct his Moon in Scorpio (conjunct Seberg's Sun within a degree) and opposite the Lilith star, Algol. His Dark Moon/Jupiter conjunction in Capricorn lands precisely on Seberg's Mercury.

What does this all mean? See the film and the clues it offers. Lilith weaves her web, like the distorted image of a spider's web that opens the film's footage behind the credits. Who knows what personal issues went on among the cast? Working on such psychological material and Lilithian dynamics would imply personal processing on deep levels. This provocative movie creates a web of mystery and intrigue with an odd overlay of innocence or naiveté. The movie *Lilith* carries on as a cult classic.

Lilith, the Opera

In its three planned performances, the New York City Opera's provocative production of *Lilith* by Deborah Drattell in November 2001 updated the myth in a twenty-first century interpretation. This ritualistic "opera with dance," as the composer called it, drew on Kabbalistic sources, Jewish ritual and Sabbath prayer, as well as Middle Eastern tonalities to tell this ancient, unresolved story.

When Lilith appears at the funeral of Adam, Eve must then tell her children about this shadowy first wife. As the plot unfolds, a seer tells Eve that Lilith is her dark twin, that their souls must be joined to heal them both. A review by retired MIT theater professor, William A. Fregosi, who attended the first performance, outlines the story

> *The ritual begins with Adam's funeral and unfolds as Eve enters Lilith's realm. Now ripe and voluptuous like a Neolithic Venus figure, Eve watches as Lilith, vampire-like, seduces sleeping men to impregnate herself even at the sides of their wives; she returns to the withered Eden and eats again of the fruit. She joins Lilith in the compelling but also strangely joyless acts of reverse rape but cannot commit to a full integration with Lilith's identity. Eve is thrown back into Adam's funeral, again in the guise of the dutiful wife and mother. Her son almost forcibly replaces on her head the veil of mourning as the men fiercely restate the prayer for the cleansing of the soul. Eve slowly disappears and in her place stands her daughter, a new generation to ask the same questions, perhaps to explore the same depths.*
>
> [Review sent to author]

Lilith shows herself in unusual and highly personal circumstances. I can only imagine that those working on the opera production had a profound creative experience and I wonder about any repercussions in their personal lives. I did not see the opera, but I found out about it in an interesting way, choreographed, no doubt, by Lilith herself. Knowing of my interest in Lilith, a colleague emailed about the production, with a promise to send me the New York Times feature. In the meantime, while star gazing at one of the resorts where I live in St. John, Virgin Islands, I encountered William Fregosi, quoted above, who had been an assistant drama professor when I was in college. As we were catching up after thirty-two years, he spoke of attending the opera. He sent me a copy of the playbill and his review. Later that same week (six weeks after the production), I met a couple from New York City who knew Deborah Drattell. Eventually I received the New York Times article from November 9, 2001, entitled "'Lilith' is Made Flesh."

We have a chart for this Opera, which opened at the New York State Theater on November 11, 2001 at 1.30pm. The mean Black Moon was on the Pisces Ascendant, the Dark Moon was on the Midheaven in between Pluto and Chiron in Sagittarius. Chiron was on the Galactic Center degree (26-27 Sagittarius), which might be relevant. The galactic

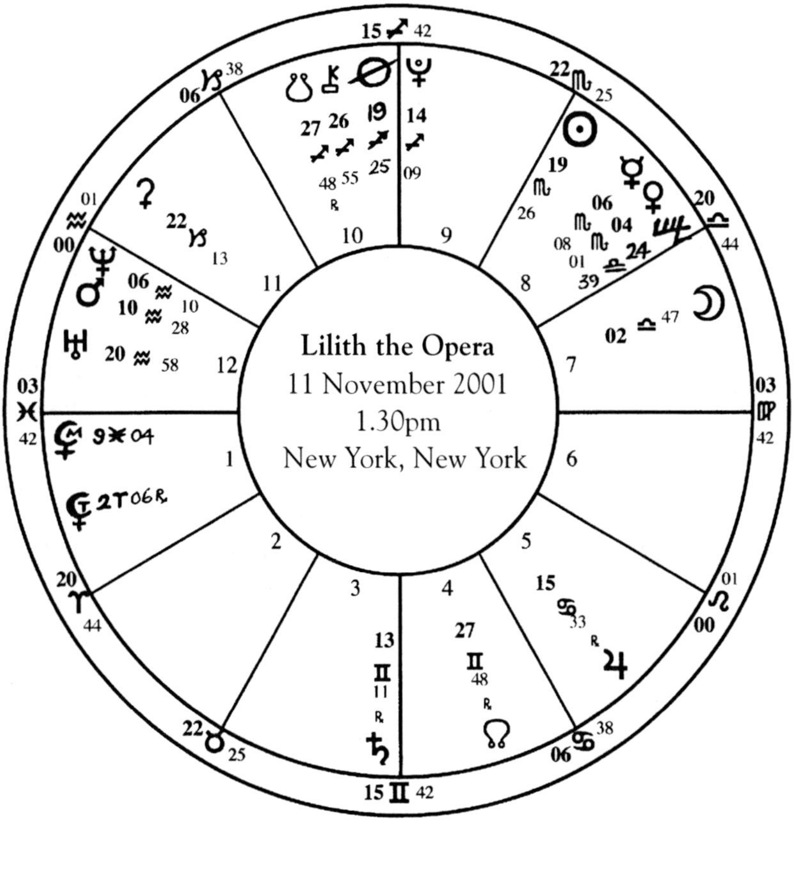

center at the heart of our Milky Way galaxy may be the original Garden of Eden. Maybe Lilith does her dance with the serpent in that supposed black hole in the galactic heart.

In these few artistic examples, we encountered the ambiguous nature and enduring fascination of Lilith. We'll have more examples later. This dark goddess offers great scope for the imagination, as indicated by the breadth of her mythology, literary and artistic presence, and her persistence through the ages. Her stories in literature and the arts are provocative and dark, like herself, full of paradox and psychological complexity, madness, obsession, physical and spiritual transformation, seduction and sexuality, magic and power, love and will. Never wholly abstract, the image of Lilith stimulates the subtle senses and erases easy boundaries of reality and morality.

Lilith is a dark goddess who speaks from deep feminine attunement to the mysteries and the life-death-rebirth cycle of the Great Round. Associated with night winds, many are the names of She Who Sees in the Dark. Living in or descending to the realm of the underworld, the unconscious or superconscious, the source of her knowledge and power is hidden, subtle and sacred. Like a flute player serenading a cobra, she pulls up the energy from deep within the Earth, and pulls us into our shadow selves to meet her. Just inside the threshold stands the Dark Goddess herself, She Who Knows the Way. Inevitably, we follow her.

Lilith Speaks at the United Nations

I continually experience Lilith's personal touch in life and through expressive work in drama, creative writing and visual art. The Sumerian story of Inanna inspired a dramatic exploration by Dragon Dance Theater, an outdoor community theater in Vermont that produces celebratory mythic drama. Over the course of several years, we created a series of plays we called "The Great Round," based on the myth of Inanna. It felt particularly relevant that we started work on this extended project just as the Gulf War began, in the homeland of Inanna. This was revisionist work, taking creative liberties with the original text, seeking fresh relevance for the modern mind. In the play *The Huluppu Tree*, Lilith was "born."

I played Lilith. Working with Lilith lured me into deeper aspects of my self experience, as drama work often does. Exploring this character in a theatrical context underscored other aspects of my life and relationships. The creative work provided a channel through which to process an inner and outer transformation, as I came to recognize some darker emotions and to act more strongly from my personal center. In the creative play of dramaturgy, Lilith taught me through costuming, movement and choreography of events. At times, she seemed to direct interpersonal dynamics in my professional and private lives. I was experiencing a fuller expression of my sexuality and, at the same time, clarifying levels of intimacy in relationships. Lilith challenges both women and men to connect with their instinctive passion for life, for this natural force denied, unfulfilled, caged or exiled, turns destructive.

The experience with Dragon Dance Theater prepared me for further dramatic work with Lilith. From her dialogue in the play, I created a monologue which I have performed a number of times over the years. Woven into it are lines from the Gnostic Gospels, the Biblical Song of Solomon, a 1919 play by George Sterling, and women's chants. [See my book *Black Moon Lilith* for full monologue.]

Playing with this dark goddess constantly stretches my personal and theatrical boundaries. I enjoy allowing the power to move through me and to move my body, yet each time I must overcome some resistance in myself — necessary when working with Lilith! I learn a great deal about myself in the process. I discover how I stay in my power and how easily I can lose it. The intriguing circumstances that occur around presenting this piece continue to educate me in her mysteries. Although impossible to fully articulate the intricate subjective meaning involved, certain situations have been surprising, revealing and, at times, unsettling, demonstrating the archetypal and experiential nature of this dark goddess. One of the most powerful experiences was an invitation to participate in a group presentation at the United Nations in 1993. The Middle East was plunged into Desert Storm. Lilith was angry.

I was not in very good shape as I headed to the Big Apple. I had a migraine coming on so strong I felt nauseous, continuing on sheer will power and desire. I wanted to do this, yet I was in minor panic — performing in NYC was daunting. Mary, who had invited me to be in the performance, had never seen my work. We were going on faith. I found the downtown studio on First Avenue and climbed its labyrinthine stairwell. The musicians were rehearsing. When I heard Mary's song, *Soul Wind*, I knew why I was there.

This was a special presentation at the United Nations by the Humanitas Institute, an organization for cultural therapeutics, promoting creative expression for healing collective wounds. The presentation at the UN was a series of pieces to demonstrate this work. After speaking the Lilith monologue to the small rehearsal group, Mary and her dance partner, John, worked with me. It was great to get feedback from these trained actors. John's male appreciation of the physical grace which I rarely acknowledge in myself (I had been an awkward Sagittarian teen) felt especially encouraging to my female self-esteem at that point. Seeing how ill I was, they encouraged me to be with my body. My stomach felt hollow, sick and sore. I spoke Lilith's words from this empty dark hole, shortening the dialogue to bare essentials. Moving slowly, I put less dramatic force behind my voice and gesture. I began to allow the still power of my body and the words to speak for themselves. Lilith was teaching me — and healing me. At the end of an hour of rehearsal, I felt fine for the first time in two days.

The next day at the UN was opening day of General Assembly. Because of recent threats, security was very tight. It took us over an hour to get our group in. We had no time to rehearse on the stage. The audience was small, but select. UN delegates from Bosnia and Azerbaijan were there. Mary and John's dance, a powerful piece about a woman's inner terrorist, was dedicated to the women of Bosnia. Lilith called for peace in the Middle East. Problems with the lighting kept Lilith in the shadow, until I stepped forward. As the piece ended, a Hindu teacher in the audience put his hands together to acknowledge the presence of Kali-Ma. It was autumn equinox, a day of the balance of light and dark, signaling an opportunity for healing — between spirit and body, male and female, country and country, and humanity with the life-giving power of Gaia-Earth. "Please, call me back," pleads Lilith.

4

The Cosmic Feminine in Wisdom Traditions

Important clues to the potency of Lilith are suggested by images in religious philosophies of West and East. Typically these images are divinities or wisdom-bringers, carrying high-charged qualities that include bliss, creativity, sexuality, transformation, mysticism and/or mystery. We find dark-faced goddesses in many, if not all, mythologies.

Anima

She carries every question into deeper waters. James Hillman

Perhaps it was from the hermetic *anima mundi*, soul of the world, that Carl Jung developed the idea of *anima* to describe the hidden and mysterious nature of a man's inner world in its feminine aspect. Through further exploration by psychologists since Jung, this definition has been broadened to include women's inner experience as well as an inherent aspect of soul, an innate, subjective aspect of the experience of women and men. In *The Pregnant Virgin*, Jungian analyst Marion Woodman defines the word feminine beyond gender identity, as "the part of us… who comes to consciousness through going into darkness, mining our leaden darkness, until we bring her silver out."

Depth psychologist James Hillman associates anima with mirror-like reflection and reverie, interiority and deepening, downward and inward-turning, imagination and fantasy. Aspects of the unconscious that would otherwise remain unknown are reflected in images that personify and personalize interior life into awareness. Anima also reflects on outer experience in a way that gives it personal meaning and feeds the soul. Thus she is the bridge between the inner and outer worlds. In the alchemical view, soul or psyche is more than personal; each is grounded in the larger context of world soul, the anima mundi. Our soul connection to the world is mediated through anima/anima mundi, which gives interior significance to our experience and connects human psyche to Earth and Cosmos.

Anima is so basic as to be almost beyond definition as an archetype. Jung referred to anima as the primary ground of consciousness, living behind our awareness and never fully emerging into the light of consciousness. In *Anima,* Hillman quotes Jung: "Behind all her cruel sporting with human fate there lurks something like a hidden purpose which seems to reflect a superior knowledge of life's laws." Anima dances in the dark, choreographing the movements of the psyche. This dark feminine dynamic leads us in a cosmic tango, revealing our unconscious desires and motivations, stripping away our illusions. It is most often through the irrational chaotic moments in life that deeper meaning is revealed. When we glimpse this meaning, she becomes a bit more gentle. Yet "She" herself is never truly known or fully understood. Like Lilith.

The Black Madonna

> *I am black, but comely, O ye daughters of Jerusalem.*
> *As the tents of Kedar, as the curtains of Solomon.*
> "Song of Solomon," *The Holy Bible*

The miraculous grace of the Black Madonna evokes special adoration in the West. Hundreds of images of the dark-faced mother are found in Western Europe, largely in France, and she is also found in the Americas. As a dark goddess of Western tradition, the Black Madonna in Christianity has older roots. Among a plethora of religious cults, the cult of Isis was a popular one in the early days of the Christian church. Images of Madonna and Child clearly resemble Isis suckling Horus or the Hindu Krishna in the arms of his mother. Egyptian Isis was often shown dark-faced. In *The Great Mother,* Erich Neumann points out the dark face of St. Anne, the mother of the Virgin Mary in Christian art. Ean Begg's study, *The Cult of the Black Virgin*, associated her with Lilith and also with other goddesses from East and West. Her trail may follow that of the Gypsy Rom people back eastward to the Indian subcontinent where she has many names, including Ka-li. Global DNA testing suggests an original ancestress from Africa, whose generations spread out across the Earth in a series of migrations. Lucia Chiavola Birnbaum seeks the implications of this scientific finding in relation to the dark goddess in her work, *dark mother: african origins and godmothers*. The dark goddess is found everywhere.

The Black Madonna is sometimes associated with Mary Magdalene, as a wisdom consort to Jesus. Devotion was given to Mary Magdalene as holder of the holy grail, the one closest to the Savior who was participated in the highest gnosis or revelation. Gnostic sects revered one all-embracing feminine wisdom in the figure of Sophia or Holy Spirit. The popularity of this dark aspect of the Christian feminine was tolerated with suspicion by Church authorities, associated as it was with more personal, imaginal experience and revelation. The Black Madonna contained both the Virgin Mother and "fallen" Magdalene, like the higher and lower Shekhinah, uniting spirit and matter.

The Black Madonna of Czestochowa is Poland's holiest relic and a national symbol, with origins shrouded in mystery. In the lower crypt of Chartres Cathedral, a dark Madonna is secreted in the oldest layers of the building and honored in special services. Notre Dame de Rocamadour, whose shrine is perched high on a rocky plateau in southern France, may date back to the 9th century. In Latin America the Black Madonna is often depicted according to the Biblical Book of Revelations, as the "woman clothed with the Sun, and the Moon under her feet, and upon her head a crown of twelve stars." The black Senora de los Angeles is the patron saint of Costa Rica, a country that dissolved its standing army in 1948. The basilica in Cartago was built over the site where a miraculous black rock in the shape of the Virgin Mary was found. An annual pilgrimage is made in August from San Jose by thousands to see the ornately dressed black stone image.

A miraculous apparition of the Virgin Mary on December 12, 1531 on a hill outside of Mexico City led to the Virgen Morena, the brown-skinned Virgin of Guadalupe becoming the most beloved religious symbol and cultural icon of the Mexican people. The Basilica of Our Lady of Guadalupe is a major Roman Catholic shrine. Her symbolism reverberates on many levels. She represents the fusion of Aztec and Spanish that has created this predominantly mestizo nation. Her unique image is surrounded by a golden, almond-shaped halo and stands on a crescent Moon held up by a young Christ, another version of the Virgin clothed with the Sun. The almond shape is remarkably vulva-like. Mexican Astrologer Luis Lesur has written *Las Claves Ocultas de la Virgen de Guadalupe (Occult Keys of the Virgin of Guadalupe)*, an extraordinary book not yet translated, that explores the occult aspects and astrology of the Virgin of Guadalupe with Black Moon aspects.

Each Black Madonna, wherever she may be, has a specific history that binds her to the people. The miracles attributed to her grace and compassion demonstrate the imminent presence of the Divine Mother who is personally involved with her devotees. "Black Madonnas were considered especially wonder-working, possessing knowledge and power of the hidden mysteries connected to the feminine through symbols of the Moon and serpent," wrote Marion Woodman, connecting the Black Madonna to symbols of Lilith.

Valley Spirit of the Tao

> *When you've cooked the marrow of the sun and moon,*
> *The pearl is so bright you don't worry about poverty.*
>
> Sun Bu-er

The sophisticated astronomy and cosmology of the Chinese is chronicled by star charts inscribed on bronze mirrors from hundreds of centuries BC. The Stein scroll from the Tang dynasty (7-10th centuries AD) is the earliest known depiction of the entire sky of the northern hemisphere, reports Stephen Little in *Taoism and the Arts of China*. The "Chart of the Celestial Patterns," a stele from 1247, the most advanced celestial map in the world at that time, identified over twelve hundred named stars, lunar mansions, Jupiter stations, and showed the Northern dipper as the celestial and seasonal clock.

Taoism, one of the oldest living mystical traditions, weaves through this cosmology. From the everlasting Tao, the empty void of infinite potential, emerged *qi*, vital energy or breath. The light qi rose and formed the heavens; the heavy qi sank and formed the earth. Matter and energy are interchangeable and in a constant state of flux. The shifting patterns of qi are moved by the interaction of yin and yang, female and male, in an interdependent and complementary polarity that creates all within the universe. Yin is represented by a tiger; yang by a dragon. This animal pair is depicted as far back as Neolithic times, around 3000 BC. The familiar black and white yin-yang circle came out in the first millennium.

Lao Tzu, known as the founding teacher of Taoism, lived in the sixth century BC, a time like ours of global paradigm shift. Gautama Buddha and the early Greek mystical philosophers were his contemporaries, all expressing a version of the perennial wisdom that human life mirrors the cosmos. We are born from both the personal mother and the cosmic mother. Our personal, "Moon mother," reflects the eternal cosmic Mother of the Universe within us with her endless stream of life energy. This life force or Tao is often described in feminine terms that suggest potential dimensions of Lilith

The Valley Spirit never dies.
It is named the Mysterious Female.
And the Doorway of the Mysterious Female
is the base from which Heaven and Earth sprang.

Lao Tzu

Women practitioners in the esoteric tradition of Taoism followed their own unique traditions. Thomas Cleary wrote about these *Immortal Sisters*, a title of honor given to revered women adepts of Yin Methodology or Feminine Alchemy, practices of internal regeneration and spiritual development. Such a woman, Sun Bu-er of the twelfth century, became one of the most famous and beloved figures of Chinese folklore. Known as "Clear and Calm Free Human," she attained wisdom and magical powers through these practices. She wrote poetry and teaching texts, such as "Precious Treatise on Preservation of Unity on the Great Way" or "Mind Mirror of the Mystic Pearl." These teaching texts were passed down in the wisdom lineage or as transmissions from visionary beings while in meditative trance.

This "science of essence" and "science of life" combined health practices, psychological self-awareness work, a wide open heart and spiritual meditation to transcend personality conditioning and to realize the ultimate and immortal nature of the human spirit, thereby becoming one of the "Real People."

One known as Old Man of the Blue Flowers sums up this path in a way we can apply to the alchemy of Lilith, "using the emptiness of the light spirit to merge with the emptiness of the great void… uniting with the Tao in reality."

Shakti

Everything in life possesses a force to transform, to become, to be, to expand its inherent nature and grow as it were from within, which is Sakti.

Madhu Khanna, *Yantra*

Sakti or *Shakti* became a central focus in Hinduism during the Tantric renaissance of 700-1300 AD, which especially honored the sacred feminine. Ultimately beyond gender, shakti is considered the female aspect of cosmic energy. As the immense animating power inherent in the universe, Shakti is its multi-dimensional mystery, both abstract and imminent. In an infinity of forms, Shakti generates every aspect of life and plane of existence, supporting and then withdrawing it all back into her invisible body. Her bottomless reservoir of dynamic and potential energy is inexhaustible.

Every goddess carries shakti power. As Leela, Lila or Maya, she takes delight in creating the play of the universe. She weaves webs of illusion where we can become trapped like flies. We are freed by moving through her ever more subtle layers of illusion, duality and time. "The practical difficulty is that the essence of Shakti is terrifying and surpasses human understanding," writes Lizelle Reymond in her powerful little book, *Shakti: A Spiritual Experience*.

In Buddhism it is Prajna-Paramita, the "Enlightened Wisdom of the Other Shore," that brings us "beyond the beyond." Known as Mother of the Buddhas, she is the shakti of spiritual enlightenment, the ultimate reality, the cause, maintainer and directing consciousness of the universe. In his commentary on the *Prajnaparamita Sutra*, Lex Hixon maintained that Prajnaparamita cannot be described. She is beyond any thought, totally indescribable, unthinkable, indefinable, unapproachable and inconceivable. Yet the Reality she represents is "not a void or an absence but is simply more real and more fulfilling than any conceptual or perceptual capacity can convey." The immeasurability and unthinkability of Prajnaparamita is expressed in the cosmos as a whole and in every detail of existence. The illumination and transcendent experience granted by the Mother of the Universe can be sweet and blissful or shockingly raw. She takes one beyond such judgments.

As the prowess, dynamism and vitality of any deity, shakti is sometimes regarded in mythic terms as consort to a god. The universe is inherently erotic and sexual. In the eternal, universal interplay of male-female, every god is paired with such a goddess consort. Shakti and Shiva are the two prime aspects of the universe, with the inherent third factor being their union. Shakti is the power or energy behind all manifestation. Shakti shimmers in each droplet and in each subatomic particle of our holographic universe. Shiva is the creative spark that shapes this power into form. Yet they are ultimately one essence. In the all-pervading stillness before the beginning, Shiva-Shakti are submerged in the invisible sea of nothingness, the void, a state of pure awareness devoid of any particular object, idea or projection. With the love-making of Shiva-Shakti comes the big bang or big bloom, as philosopher Ken Wilbur calls it. In India one sees everywhere images of their union, represented by the god and goddess in sexual embrace, evoking the awakening of the kundalini, or creative life force.

In *Ka*, his delightful and provocative engagement with Hindu philosophy and myth, Robert Calasso dramatizes a high-level inquisition of Vajnavalkya, one of the original Vedic seers. Gargi, the most beautiful and fearsome theologian is on the panel, the high judge. She is like Maya dressed in dark matter, the cosmic weaver who asks questions about how the universe is woven. The seer, Vajnavalkya, found himself looking at her robe. She was draped in an exquisite, sheer fabric, hugging her body like a second skin. "She must have woven it herself," he thought, knowing her renown as a weaver. Then he thought, "Perhaps the excellence of Gargi's thinking was a pastime when compared with her art as a weaver."

Initially playing the coquette, Gargi was, in fact, the most serious inquisitor, relentlessly interrogating the seer on his knowledge of the warp and weft of the universe. More than master theologian, Gargi is portrayed here as the dark mother, herself weaver of the universe and its veil of illusion. That he was looking at her robe, not at the woman herself, indicates that the sage perceived the illusions that she dressed herself in. No one sees her fabrics, but he could perceive her wearing it. He honored the creator in her above the thinker. It is a rare and wise man who honors and answers the unspoken, invisible power of the feminine and gains her respect.

Kundalini Serpent Power

> *The divine power, Kundalini shines, like the stem of a young lotus;*
> *Like a snake, coiled round upon herself...*
> *resting half asleep at the base of the body.*
>
> *Yoga Kundalini Upanishad*

Kundalini, "she who is coiled," is likened to a serpent coiled at the base of the spine, in the lowest chakra — like the serpent in the roots of Inanna's tree. As the basic animating life force, kundalini is another way to say shakti. The chakra centers are whirling wheels or vortices of energy that reverberate from the subtle bodies into the physical. The two large nerve ganglia that wind up and around the central column of the spine to the crown are likened to serpents undulating in a shiva-shakti mating dance, their bodies curving and crossing at the chakras, stirring those cauldrons of energy. Some snakes do mate in exactly such a dance.

In Western culture, the slimy, slippery snake is usually a fearsome symbol associated with evil, as in the Garden of Eden, yet it also winds around the medical caduceus. If Eve hadn't taken the advice of the Lilith-headed serpent, where would we be today? In the East, the Snake or Serpent represents wisdom and transformation. In Hindu mythology *nagas* are serpent kings and queens who personify and direct all the life-giving waters of Earth — lakes, rivers and seas. A serpent-tailed Nepalese sculpture called Naga-Kanya has the upper body of a beautiful woman offering a conch shell. Arching over her head, a five-headed serpent represents her mastery of the five senses.

In the Chinese zodiac, the Year of the Snake comes around every twelve years. Chinese snakes come in colors – silver, gold, blue, gray and purple. Most often considered feminine, they live in cauldrons. What pours out from the cauldron depends on how Snake directs her will power. The Chinese serpent goddess Nu Kua created the first humans from clay. Other serpent goddesses help with childbirth and gift children with special talents. Serpentine princesses have charmed many a wise man and enriched his learning. Like mermaids, they dwell in underwater paradises in pearl palaces, guarding the riches of the sea. They each carry a precious jewel inside their heads which resonates with the cosmic tides.

Like Lilith, Kundalini energy is not something to carelessly play around with. A premature ejaculation of kundalini can seriously disorient one into psychosis or some other form of psycho-spiritual distress, bringing on what has been called a "spiritual emergency."

Dakini, Sky Dancer

> *There is nothing in the world except empty curved space.*
> John A. Wheeler, physicist

Look up into the clear day sky, an immense blue emptiness. Clouds move across like random thoughts drifting through the mind. We daydream on them, yet that luminous field of sky stretches out billions of light years beyond imagination into the cosmic void, an immense black-shining emptiness. On this infinite field of dark possibility, curved like her dark, sinuous body, dances the *dakini*. Dakini is variously described as a celestial woman, she-who-moves-through-space, as fairy, fury or valkyrie, witch or ghoul, beneficent female spirit, wisdom keeper, angel or death-bringer. Basically she is defined as "a semi-wrathful spirit-woman who manifests in visions, dreams, and meditation experiences." [www.khandro.net/dakini.] This sounds like a good working description of Lilith as well.

Derived from the Indian Tantric tradition, dakini became the cosmic feminine in Tibetan Buddhism, describing a complex perspective on the nature of mind and realization. Sky dancing with the dakini is a form of meditative practice to illumine the mind with the pristine emptiness of pure space, the fundamental ground of reality. Personally and collectively, the tide of life arises through us all, creatures large and small. All experience, all phenomena arise as dreams within the vast and luminous space of emptiness. Are we dreaming the world or is the world dreaming us? Shamans, modern physics and the internet highway tell us we are all in this together, an interconnected web of minds and hearts and life force creating a virtual reality, the dream of the world.

Dakini can be a personal link to the impersonal realm, "beyond the beyond." Dakini can manifest through dreams, visions and encounters — with females, in particular. Different than the psychological anima of Jung, dakini is beyond psychological interpretation and symbolic expression, non-existent at the archetypal level. The illumination she represents is an essentially spiritual aspect, from which the more formulated archetypal level arises. Perhaps Jung himself was reaching for this aspect of the feminine. Dakini is as inconceivable as the universe or the most personal inner workings of our secret selves. She will assume whatever form is necessary to take us beyond the delusion, confusion and illusion of our mental concepts of what we think life is — whatever it takes to "blow our minds". It is almost impossible to write about, though some have tried.

In *Shakti Woman*, Vicki Noble notes the trickster dynamic of dakini, evident in encounters or events that upset our routine, get us off track, make us feel out of control. People who play a dakini role in our lives, whether they know it or not, "temporarily embody the purposefully chaotic elements in our environment and give them form." Such encounters wake us up to the larger forces at work in our lives. Dakini may play a sexual role to open kundalini awareness of the male-female energies within and between individuals. As a symbol of a liberated energy and untamed spiritual nature not bound by convention, "She is the Feminine in a much larger sense than any archetypes carried by Western culture for at least the last two thousand years." We could say the same of Lilith.

In their work, *The Feminine: Spacious as the Sky*, Jose and Miriam Arguelles portray the feminine aspect of nature as unborn space, all accommodating, all-pervasive openness, suggesting the original meaning of the word *virgin* as "whole unto oneself." In nature and in the psychology of the mind, the feminine is the ever-empty wholeness. From this spaciousness arises the world of one's subjective experience. All perceptions, emotions, sensations, and physical activity are transitory phenomena. The feminine gives birth to such phenomena and our perceptions of them, as an interplay between the perceiver and the perceived, to reveal the subjective differentiations that define our sense of reality and the inevitable change and impermanence inherent in such limited and limiting perceptions. This subjectivity causes the experience of duality of mind and body, of self and other, of earth and spirit, continually dissolving in the infinite awareness of the cosmic feminine. One of the basic functions of feminine cosmic intelligence is to see beyond the paradox of duality, the separation of spirit and matter, any limited fixations that are barriers to enlightened awareness. This is the awesome, even dizzying, quality of the dispassionate, nonjudgmental, all-embracing feminine. "There is a chilling and primordial sensation that is evoked by this experience of unborn space, yet… one feels strangely at home."

Something in us recognizes the presence of the Great Mother, her dark face of mystery. Facing the unknown, with an alert attention focussed by the desire to "come home," the imagination opens beyond known limitations to radical new perceptions. Many balk at such wild thoughts, wanting to retreat to safe ground and find ways to fit new information into old models. The encounter with the black face of the great mother can be terrifying, as myth tells us, yet once this dark face is seen, there can be no turning back. Disruptive as they are to the current state of affairs, new revelations evoke an excitement, an imminent sense of discovery and opportunity that can be quite compelling and seductive as well as scary. That seductive attraction, that powerful allure is an innate characteristic of the feminine. In Hindu and Buddhist philosophy, the response of the masculine (Shiva) to feminine spaciousness (Shakti) is discriminate and compassionate action. The interplay between the two aspects is inseparable and continual — the paradox of duality that is inseparable wholeness.

In *Dakini's Warm Breath*, Buddhist scholar Judith Simmer-Brown reports on her years of research on the dakini, garnered from interviews with many Tibetan lamas and rinpoches as well as her own Buddhist practice. This book became one of my essential sources for inspiration about Lilith as the cosmic feminine. Simmer-Brown draws a distinction between maternal goddesses who give birth to the material world, and the animating (shakti) power of the universe. In Tibetan Buddhism, nature and the material world are seen as inherently insubstantial and transparently luminous phenomena, as we know from subatomic physics. The cosmic mother principle in Buddhism is of the imminent and immanent unborn emptiness of potentiality, the empty field before any manifestation. She gives birth to pure insight. "There is no space without wakefulness, no wakefulness without space...the sheer intelligence of space, the wisdom qualities of the feminine."

The author describes four levels of the dakini. In this brief summary below, I articulate as best I can my grasp of what she was conveying. As with Lilith, these aspects of the dakini can be intricately and intimately interwoven in our experience.

The dakini's *outer-outer* aspect can manifest through an encounter with a woman or a male acting as a wisdom teacher in some experiential way. This can be a teacher, a lover, even a stranger.

The *outer* aspect of the dakini moves in the energetic passageways of the subtle body, the channels and networks through which consciousness moves in interrelated vibrational patterns throughout the physical body. It constitutes what Simmer-Brown calls "the energetic confluence of the psychophysical human life." She moves through the "winds" of the body in the way prana or life force circulates, and in the subtle interface of aetheric and physical bodies, channeled through chakra centers and meridian points. This outer aspect also involves the internal male-female, shiva-shakti, yang-yin energy and its active expression in both men and women. Therefore it is an active factor in relationship dynamics.

The *inner* aspect of dakini is expressed through images and symbols in the imagination that stimulate spiritual awareness. These images nurture subjective visionary experience in meditative states which awaken the wisdom-mind of the practitioner; therefore personal meditation practice is essential for any real understanding of the dakini aspect. "She represents the most intimate aspects of the spiritual path."

The fourth aspect is a *secret* one, the dakini's dance of emptiness that unravels any concept to open freely into the ultimate awareness and spacious nature of the mind. Not to be imagined as lifeless, "Emptiness is not mere blankness but a mode of being, in which manifestation arises freely, never compromising the power of emptiness," writes Simmer-Brown. "The quintessential dakini is not merely space itself, but simultaneously wakefulness that realizes space." Because of her awakening nature, dakini, like Lilith, challenges the ego's attachments to identity and its conventional interpretations of life. Dakini has a liminal, haunting and evocative quality. "The ambiguous and dangerous nature of the dakini derives from her association not with nature but with phenomena's emptiness, the ultimate ambiguity."

Simmer-Brown discusses how penetrating insight manifests through the intelligence of human women as subtle, pervasive and sharp with a heightened emotional sensitivity, more tuned to dynamics than content.

> *The heat and intensity of women's energy can trip emotional triggers that can create enormous chaos. This can be beneficial when intractable situations present themselves... However, when intense emotionality is indulged, feminine intelligence can become self-serving. When*

> *this happens, feminine wisdom can become wild and even dangerous, subverting its own intelligence.*

This gives great insight into Lilith work, and echoes the caution of Lilith investigators about the necessity to free Lilith's energy from subjective agendas.

Lilith as Dakini

Can we can find any parallels between the four Liliths and these four levels of dakini? It's tempting to want to match the four levels of dakini with the four aspects of Lilith, from Asteroid to Dark Moon to Black Moon to Star. But that is too simplistic — and boring!— for either Lilith or dakini. Plus, we are unlikely to find direct correlations between any two such different systems. There are no easy answers, but we can try to tease out some clues to help us see better how Lilith may have her way with us. I am not a Buddhist practitioner, so my understanding of dakini is not through that path. Please consider this a questing theoretical exploration to evoke possibilities.

If the *outer-outer* aspect of dakini refers to actual people that come into our lives to "blow our minds," a connection to our anti-societal, "hard rock" Lilith seems appropriate. A strong asteroid Lilith might be a signature of someone who publicly challenges the status quo of our collective concepts. This person might be a loner, outside the social norm by necessity or personal preference, or a powerful leader that defies the norm. On the personal level, we find Lilith coming in the guise of a lover, guru, mentor, or even a chance encounter. Perhaps we don't even need to meet in person. No person can BE a dakini, or Lilith, but one can embody aspects of the cosmic feminine.

The *outer* level of dakini is psycho-somatically fluid, moving in the interface between the subtle energy bodies and physicality. Here lives the biological necessity of Lilith. It sounds like this level of dakini breathes us, circulates in the flow of blood, coordinates heart and mind, spins the chakras and dances along the yin-yang spinal nerves. Perhaps she lives in the aetheric body, the lymphatic, chemical and hormonal systems, thus influencing our unconscious and automatic responses to life.

All women carry dakini energy by the very fact that they have female bodies, which are a literal demonstration and experience of dakini energy. Women's wombs are open to Earth energy in a compelling way that men do not experience. There is a participatory vulnerability in female biology that motivates choices and directs experience beyond conscious preference. This Earth energy is not personal, but evokes planet/human co-creativity through irrational and mysterious means, including procreative, sexually-induced DNA combinations. Men are compelled to "plug into" this energy one way or another. There is some evidence suggesting the reality of parthenogenesis, or "virgin" birth, without male-female mating, that may be part of this deep mystery of Earth embodiment and generative creation.

In my mind (at least at the time of this writing), this outer dakini seems to resonate most closely with the Black Moon. It makes sense (not that Lilith always makes sense!) that the Black Moon is connected to the aetheric body, so close to the physical, as the Black Moon is the invisible second focus of the orbit of the Moon, that weaves the physical body. The center of gravity between the Moon and Earth is inside the Earth. Yet the Dark Moon astral influences impinge upon our physical experience too, as uncleared mental-emotional areas certainly affect physical well-being.

The *inner* dakini is an alchemical guide along the intimate inner path, in a way that suggests Dark Moon shadows and highlights. She shapeshifts into images that have deep subjective meaning in our private experience via day and night dreams, animal guides, archetypal images, symbols, mythic stories. These images mirror and move us along on our spiritual path. The Persian mystic Rumi tells a story in which God speaks, saying that He shows up in a specific form and image for each of His servants. "Whatever each of them imagines Me to be, that I am. I am bound to images where God is; I am annoyed by any reality where God is not." [Thackston, Jr., *Signs of the Unseen: The Discourses of Jalauddin Rumi*.] Here is the insistence by both Dark and Black Moon Liliths to cleanse our thoughts and feelings, the dwelling place of God. "See what is more beneficial to you — weeping, laughter, fasting, prayer, or retreat," Rumi advises, according to whichever aspect best promotes spiritual advancement.

God/desses of light and dark, angels and demons, images of our desires and fears, all lead us along our path. Equally, god and goddess images, that of Lilith and her mythic sisters in their various versions, can lead one on, as can the fairies. The many fairy tales and fairy images evoke this inner dakini aspect. Think of Shakespeare's *Midsummer Night's Dream* and *The Tempest* as Lilith-led quests through the world of faerie and out again. In his esoteric fairy tale, *Quest of the Golden Stairs*, A. E. Waite proclaims,

> *Give me the glory of Faerie till I tire of all the images.*
> *Give me the one image, which is love in the heart of all.*
> *Give me the last change of perfect being, when I and my image are one.*

We can also consider connections to inner dakini and the Lilith star, Algol. Stars are consciousness centers of extraordinary light. Humankind has projected stories and qualities onto stars and star patterns for as long as we have been on Earth. Shamans in many cultures glean meaning from the stars through astral travel and altered state communion. There must be something to the image of the demon star that it carries such a charge across cultures, or are we projecting our collective demons onto it? Reverberating on collective as well as personal levels, perhaps the Lilith star has a dakini energy that is experienced by us in an image that forwards the spiritual growth of humanity. As we each are seen by this Eye of Medusa and see through it, we are freed from bandwidths of our collective fears.

All these images lead us to the most *secret* dakini, the Mother of Bliss, Queen of Sat-Chit-Ananda (Reality-Consciousness-Bliss), the wakefulness of undifferentiated space. My thinking about the spiritual dimension of Black Moon Lilith was strongly influenced by this level of Simmer-Brown's discussion. Black Moon, as the invisible second focus of the Moon's orbit around Earth, leads us on a soul journey into incarnation beyond personal agendas, chiding us at any limiting judgment that shuts down our energy. How smoothly and gloriously can we move through this lifetime so the soul can be free to dance in at-one-ness with spirit? Lilith's spirit of atonement is a key aspect of the journey through life. Eventually we shed the four physical elements so that we merge back into the star body of aetheric consciousness and beyond. Perhaps, then, it is the star body of Lilith, Algol, that is most secret. Conclusion-free, we leave this discussion with unfinished thoughts open to the teachings of Lilith as dakini.

Lilith in the Aethers

> *It is as though the moon threw down a black body upon earth visible only to the subliminal senses, which thereby became illuminated.*
>
> Peter Redgrove

Lilith dances in the most subtle dimensions and occult realms. Is she the dark *mater*, the dark mother, that astro-physicists seek in their quest for dark energy and dark matter? We generally experience life through the four elements: earth, air, fire and water. These elements interact in various combinations to manifest the material world. Underlying these four basic elements is the fifth, quintessential element — aether — out of which the other four arise, according to Vedic, Buddhist and Greek philosophies.

A universal primeval substance appears in almost every cosmology. Homer described aether as the pure light of the upper atmosphere where stars live. This aetheric light causes things to be seen in celestial clarity. Anaximander proposed a subtle material of a "boundless nature, from which all the heavens arise and the worlds within them," and into which they again dissolve. This natural philosopher from the fifth century BC, Anaximander, is also the first on record to propose a heliocentric solar system. Aristotle's fifth element was intangible and non-physical, existing in the imperishable world that lies behind the world of appearances. In Hindu philosophy, aether is the fifth element, activated in human beings as our capacity for self-reflection and God-realization.

Hindu and Buddhist traditions distinguish physical and pre-physical aether, like the light and heavy qi of Taoism. Pre-physical aether is a spacious "sea of consciousness," a unitary, a-logical state of consciousness that is pre-existent to physical duality. Physical aether (perhaps the dark matter or energy of modern cosmology) is the homogeneous plenum in which space/time exists. Spiritual aether is the absolute brilliancy of super-consciousness, subtle divine light without luminosity, a continuum of eternal consciousness that flows through all dimensions of existence. This spacious aetheric consciousness perceives beyond self-consciousness, beyond conceptual frameworks of duality to illumine the true essence of reality.

The Black Goddess and the Unseen Real (also published as *The Black Goddess and the Sixth Sense*) by Peter Redgrove is evocative Lilith reading. Among many intriguing things, he wrote of a "dark knowing, which he calls 'synaesthesia,' gained through our subliminal senses which perceive subtle energy. Redgrove refers to our invisible, radiant, astral or "star-like body" as the chief organ of spiritual intuition that synthesizes and imagines meaning from data gathered by the five sense organs of sensation.

Lilith draws us inexorably into the realm of invisibilities, beyond the known. No wonder she is suspect and given a demonic reputation. "Yet," writes Redgrove, "there is a persistent rumour that she herself is the Messiah, come to redeem the divided souls of women, by virtue of her ability to circuit the sky and traverse the depths of the abyss."

In mythology, philosophy and literature, the cosmic feminine demonstrates her essential being against the powers that seek to shape her into something apart from Her Self. Lilith speaks in elusive whispers, like the serpent in garden, through the sweet, wild dakini winds of our star bodies.

As anima in the Jungian sense, the dark goddess mediates soul-making, as she opens a psychic awareness that links personal with transpersonal dimensions, with the origin of life and consciousness. As Black Madonna, she embodies the mystic mysteries in the heart of religion. As Valley Spirit, she is the doorway to immortality. As Shakti, she brings us into relationship with the heart of the universe. She leads us in her sexy cosmic dance, with cyclic rhythms of creation and destruction. As Kundalini, she undulates up our spinal columns, the conduit between the heights of heaven and depths of earth. As the Dakini sky dancer of Tibetan Buddhism, she lures us toward the void, that threshold singularity from which the Big Bang bursts into materiality and through the black hole at the center of the galaxy. Dressed suggestively in veils woven from the infinity of dark matter, the unseen energy of consciousness that is the fabric of our universe, she undresses us from the dark coverings that hide our naked beauty.

5

Lilith on the World Stage

Some examples of people with strong Lilith placements at birth will illustrate her themes. In my research I have found that the four Liliths cannot be clearly dissected and isolated into distinctly separate parcels. Let's hope not! Nevertheless, let us start simple and keep an ear tuned for the particular voices of Lilith. Archetypally reflecting the "whole-sum" quality of the feminine, Lilith offers various facets that resonate, with a glint in her eye of multi-dimensional experience. We will only find suggestive clues here, as the subjective depths of living with Lilith cannot be truly known from an outsider's view, just as no third party can really know what is going on in any relationship.

As we explore facets and faces of Lilith as she appears on the stage of life, let us focus first on the Asteroid Lilith and its social challenge to the status of women and gender issues, or other generally disenfranchized groups. Then we will look more intently on the two Liliths that are related to the Moon, the Dark Moon and the Black Moon, bringing us to a liminal edge where the subjective, personal reactions of the Moon are challenged, turned inside out, even transcended. We'll head out briefly into the starry realms to look into the baleful eye of Medusa and the Lilith star.

Asteroid Lilith

British Suffragettes: The Pankhurst Women

One of the themes of Asteroid Lilith is a challenge to socialized gender role models. In this regard, women suffragettes come to mind. On the British suffrage front, the leading figure was **Emmeline Goulden Pankhurst**. She was born for involvement in revolutionary social causes with **Asteroid Lilith in Libra** as part of a grand trine in Air, including

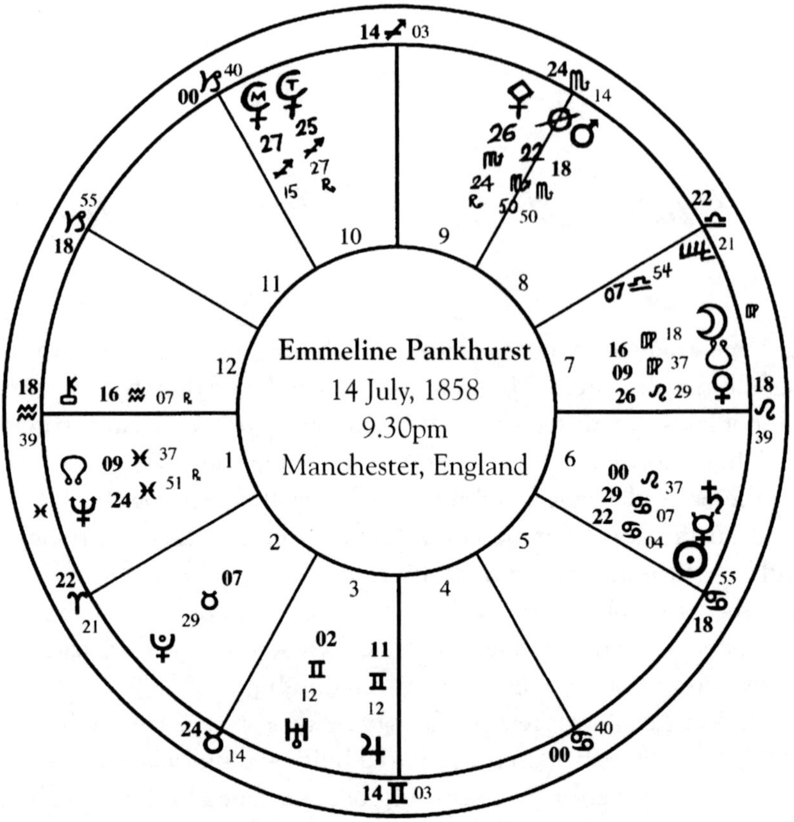

revolutionary planet Uranus conjunct Jupiter in Gemini and Chiron in Aquarius (on her Ascendant if the given birth data is valid). Note the continuing presence of Chiron in the Asteroid Lilith signature in this family. Emmeline first founded the Women's Franchise League, her work interrupted due to the death of her husband, Dr. Richard Pankhurst, a lawyer, pacifist, socialist, and women's rights advocate, who had helped draft legislation to extend women's property rights. With Lilith in Libra, it was important for Emmeline to share agendas with her partner. Unfortunately, I could not find birth data for him, but we can assume Asteroid Lilith is active.

In 1903 Mrs. Pankhurst started the **Women's Social and Political Union**. This organization became militant, breaking windows and starting fires, leading to repeated arrests of members, and even a death of a woman trampled by a horse during a suffrage protest. The WSPU chart shows **Asteroid Lilith in Capricorn** close to Chiron and squaring the Libra Sun. The WPSU provided an organizational platform for the work, but one with Chiron wild-card tendencies. If Asteroid Lilith challenges and seeks changes in relation to the societal context, the maverick centaur Chiron often takes a different route. Asteroid Pallas, North Node and Mercury are also in Libra in the WSPU chart, conjunct Pankhurst's Lilith, and making a grand trine in Air signs, like her own, but with Moon in Gemini and Saturn in Aquarius.

Mrs. Pankhurst was largely aided by her daughters, particularly **Christabel Pankhurst**. A co-founder of WSPU and militant instigator, she was nicknamed "Queen of the Mob." Her **Asteroid Lilith in Scorpio** was joined by the Dark Moon, both opposite Neptune/Moon/Chiron in Taurus. She was pulled in deeply to her mother's energy, ready and willing to push the agenda, fight passionately for the cause. Her Asteroid Pallas and Mercury matched that of the WSPU, with Mars added. She defined the perception of the organization as much as her mother, initially through an arrest and highly publicized trial. Arrested numerous times, she spent two years in Paris to avoid prison. Jailed again upon her return, she engaged in a hunger strike which shortened her prison time. She joined her mother in fervent support of World War I, promoting national service by all men and women. After the War, with women's vote won, she spent a decade as an evangelist in the US. She died there after a short return to England, where she was appointed Dame Commander of the British Empire in 1936.

Sylvia Pankhurst, the youngest daughter, was a member of the WSPU for several years, splitting with her mother and sister due to her anti-war stance. With **Asteroid Lilith in Aries** she stood by herself, willing to go her own way. Important to note, she was born with her Taurus Sun closely conjunct the Saturn/Uranus conjunction of her time, along with Mercury, Chiron and, later, Pluto. She continued on by setting up the ELFS, East London Federation of Suffragettes and its newspaper, "Women's Dreadnought," which evolved to a more expanded organization. She pursued a life-long path of activism in support of labor, peace and the broader European leftist communist movement, involved in the Italian Socialist Party. She became a supporter of Haile Selassie and published extensively on Ethiopian culture. Her independence showed in her relationships. She was long-time lover of Keir Hardie, Scottish socialist, peace activist and Labour Party leader, until his death. She later lived with Italian socialist revolutionary Silvio Corio, with whom she had a child out of wedlock at age 45. Her mother never spoke to her again. She died while living with her son in Ethiopia, by special invitation of Haile Selassie, and was given a full state funeral there.

Adela Pankhurst Walsh was a multiple Gemini, with Sun plus five planets in that sign. **Asteroid Lilith in Sagittarius** opposed Chiron most closely, along with Mars, Pluto and Mercury, taking her across the world. Initially involved in WSPU as a teenager, she emigrated to Australia in 1914, during the year of her first Saturn return, estranged from her family and for the sake of her health. Her Sun was conjunct Saturn and square Uranus (and possibly her Moon). She was a life-long activist, working for women's rights and peace with the Women's Peace Army. Her husband, Tony Walsh, was a fellow anti-draft activist. Briefly involved with Australian communists, she became disillusioned and eventually founded the anti-communist Australian Women's Guild of Empire, a conservative patriotic organization raising money for working class women and children, advocating industrial cooperation and the value of British citizenship.

American Suffragettes

Lucretia Mott, Elizabeth Cady Stanton and Susan B. Anthony were the front-line suffrage leaders in the United States, largely responsible for the 19th US Constitutional amendment that gave women the right to vote. Previously disenfranchised, women were then able to participate in political choice. We would expect Asteroid Lilith to have a strong presence in the charts of such promoters of women's rights in society – and it does.

Lucretia Mott published *Discourses on Women* in 1850, giving an overview of the educational, economic and social restrictions on women in western Europe and the United States. Like Emmeline Pankhurst, this American pioneer for women's equality had **Asteroid Lilith in Libra,** hers exactly conjunct Asteroid Pallas. Named for the goddess of wisdom, Pallas Athena is associated with a creative flair and mental acuity that expresses a particularly feminine wisdom. Asteroid Pallas plays a large role in the women's movement as well, but Lilith gives more audacity

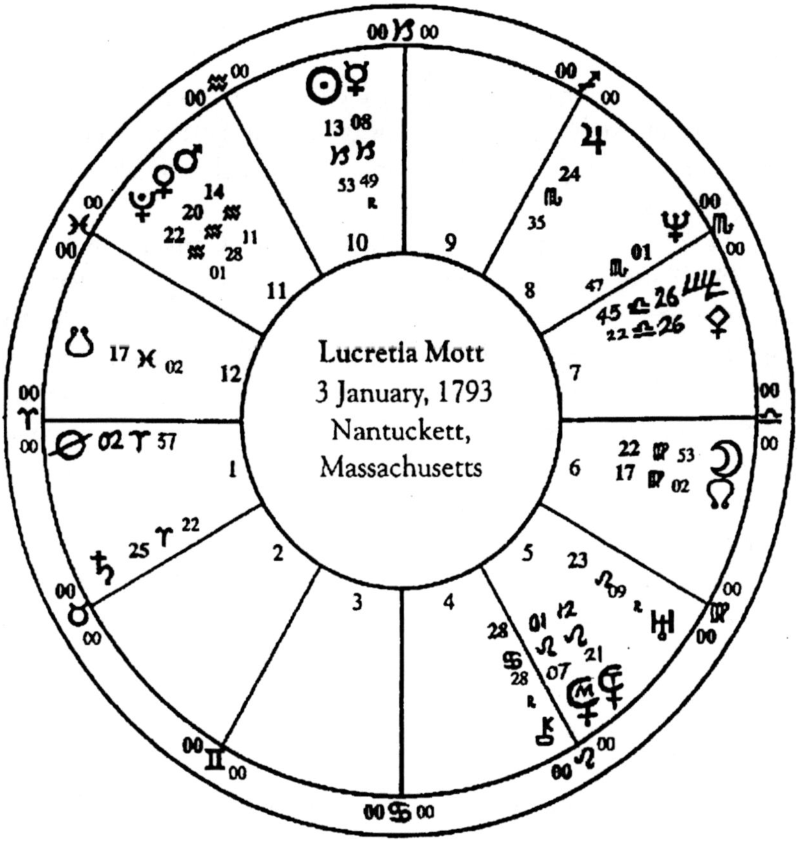

and a radical stance in the quest for equality. Asteroid Lilith will impact the direction of Pallas's creative intelligence into strident action for women's rights. A Quaker by birth and later a minister of that faith, Lucretia Mott married young. With Lilith in Libra, a sign noted for its concern for quality, fairness and justice, she worked in partnership with her husband, fellow Quaker James Mott. His chart also has Asteroid Lilith conjunct Pallas — in Virgo, sign of service.

The Motts met abolitionists **Elizabeth Cady Stanton** and her husband, Henry Stanton, who were spending their honeymoon in London to attend the 1840 World's Anti-Slavery convention. When the women were not allowed to be seated, they became more interested in women's rights issues. The birth chart of Elizabeth Cady Stanton shows **Asteroid Lilith in independent Sagittarius** conjunct freedom-loving Uranus, reflecting the radical nature of her vision for women, her stand for legal rights and her fiery pen. The Sagittarian truth-seeker shows in this statement: "The moment we begin to fear the opinions of others and hesitate to tell the truth that is in us, and from motives of policy are silent when we should speak, the divine floods of light and life no longer flow into our souls."

These two women called the **Seneca Falls Convention** for July 19, 1848 in Seneca Falls, New York. Cady Stanton wrote the "Declaration of Sentiments," a radical statement for women's rights written in the form of the Declaration of Independence. A call for women's right to vote was included, a stand so radical that it was a sticking point that pushed beyond the reasonable limit for many of the attendees. The chart for the Convention shows a very tight Mercury-Venus-Sun conjunction with **Asteroid Lilith in Cancer**. It was an excellent time for networking, communication and public awareness connected to women's issues. The Asteroid Pallas and the dwarf planet Ceres, Earth mother, are on the Virgo ascendant, describing the character of the event as related to women's wisdom and practical outcomes. As reported by the "Seneca County Courier" of August 4, 1848, the convention was well-ordered, even while the doctrines espoused were unprecedented, startling and radical for the time.

Soon after the Convention, Cady Stanton met Susan B. Anthony, beginning their decades-long partnership. On the surface, these two women could hardly be more different. Cady Stanton, a passionate Scorpio, had a strong commitment to home and family, her husband and five children, while Aquarian Anthony remained single and was the more public figure. Yet, both with asteroid Lilith conjunct Uranus in Sagittarius, they shared strong beliefs and convictions about women's independence.

Susan B. Anthony had the **Lilith/Uranus conjunction in Sagittarius** in a dynamically interactive square with an exact Venus-Pluto-Chiron conjunction in Pisces, reflecting her passion, personal sacrifices and devotion to the cause of women's empowerment. We'll see those three factors — Venus, Pluto and Chiron — back up the Lilith quality in more charts as we go on. A Quaker like the Motts, Anthony was active in the temperance and abolitionist movements before becoming an indefatigable spokesperson for women's suffrage.

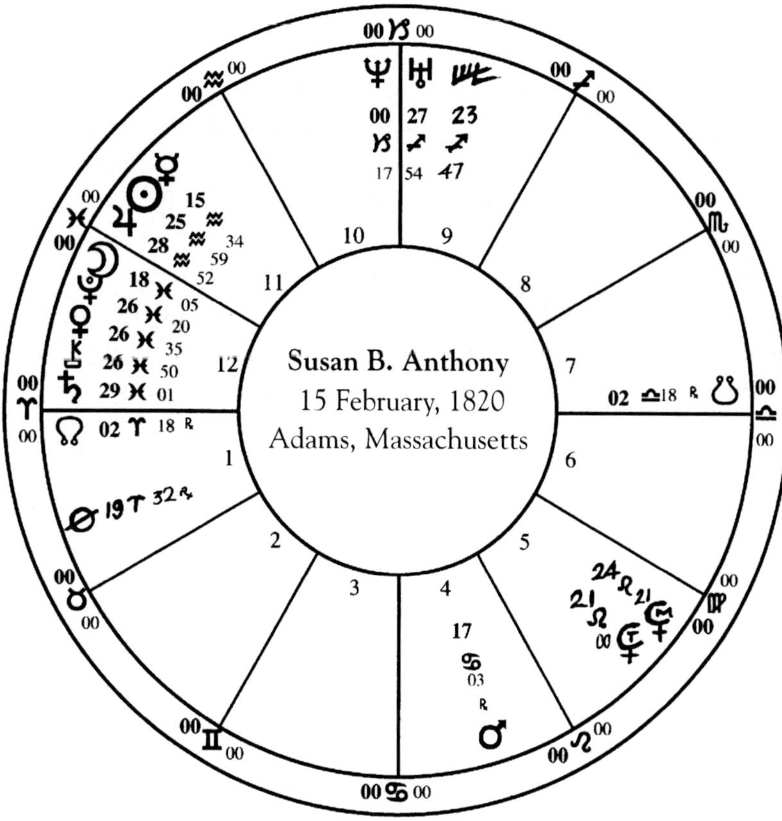

Temperance was an original feminist concern of the times, as it addressed the abuse of women and children by alcoholic husbands, a continuing social problem.

"Woman must not depend upon the protection of man, but must be taught to protect herself," Anthony believed. "Men their rights nothing more, women their rights nothing less," was the motto of "The Revolution," a weekly paper she published about the suffrage movement. Unmarried, she traveled almost constantly on the Sagittarian lecture circuit for thirty years, tirelessly criss-crossing the States to promote the ratification of the 19th amendment that gave women the vote. A notable public figure, often vilified and ridiculed by opponents, she was a driving force behind the formation of national and international women's suffrage associations.

None of these three pioneering women lived to see this amendment passed. The 19th Constitutional Amendment was passed on August 26, 1920, with Tennessee voting it in by one slim vote. The chart for that day shows Asteroid Lilith at 21 degrees Sagittarius, matching its sign placement in the charts of these two leading women and putting into effect a law (Sagittarius) granting a new legal freedom to women.

Women's Liberator

Born within a year of the passing of the US Constitutional amendment that gave women the vote, **Betty Friedan** became a major voice for the women's liberation movement in the United States in the new century. Her ground-breaking classic, *The Feminine Mystique*, published in 1963 and still in print, documents contemporary women's dissatisfaction with the idealized "happy housewife" role that discounted feminine intelligence and short-circuited career aspirations outside the home. "What is missing from the image that mirrors and creates the identity of women in America today?" she asked.

Her questions — and answers — set off a national debate about women's roles as she revealed the extent of women's discontent in the narrow confines offered by social expectations: the "mystique." The choice, she spelled out, is "between adjustment, conformity, avoidance of conflict, therapy or individuality, human identity, education in the truest sense, with all its pains of growth" — a classic Asteroid Lilith quote.

A challenging Moon-Pluto-Venus/Chiron T-square pushing and pulling at three corners of her birth chart reflects a compelling interest in women's issues. But it is the close conjunction of her Sun with **Asteroid Lilith in Aquarius** that put her on Lilith's path and placed her in the radical forefront of the modern women's liberation movement as a powerful voice calling for redefinition of social expectations of women. Betty Friedan's revolutionary work came out of her personal reclamation of feminine power and illustrates the Lilith archetype that breaks through socialized gender dynamics.

Cherokee Chief of Her People

With a name like hers, one might expect **Wilma Mankiller** to have a prominent Lilith. She does. The first female chief of the Cherokee Nation, from 1985-1995, she worked to restore their philosophy of gender equality in the practice of *gadugi*, men and women working together for the common good. "I've run into more discrimination as a woman than an Indian," she remarked. A role model for her Nation, especially young Cherokee girls, **Asteroid in Scorpio** accompanies her Sun and Pallas, echoing the socially radical, creative intelligence reflected in several charts of the suffragettes. She had a strong belief in education: "Whoever controls the education of our children controls our future." Her female power is also shown in a dynamic T-square, similar to that of Betty Friedan, involving Venus/Black Moon in Scorpio, Pluto/Mars in Leo and the Moon in Taurus.

Lilith Spokespersons: Mercury with Lilith

A woman needs a man like a fish needs a bicycle.

With the Mercury conjunct **Lilith in Pisces, Gloria Steinem** has given voice to Lilith in her writings and as editor of Ms. magazine, a pioneering publication for feminist awareness. "In my heart, I think a woman has two choices: either she's a feminist or a masochist," she asserted. Less stridently, she equalizes the field with this Pisces-type statement: "A feminist is anyone who recognizes the equality and full humanity of women and men."

The first Black US Congresswoman, **Shirley Chisholm** was born with Mercury and ruling Jupiter conjunct **Asteroid Lilith in Sagittarius**, sign of the Truth-seeker and truth-speaker. "My greatest political asset, which professional politicians fear, is my mouth," she once said. The Asteroid/Mercury/Jupiter conjunction formed a close and potent T-square with Dark Moon in Pisces and Black Moon in Gemini. She was also the first woman to seek the Democratic party presidential nomination.

Literary pioneer **Virginia Woolf** helped women find *A Room of One's Own*, living and dying on her own terms. She had Mercury/**Asteroid Lilith in Aquarius** squared by a hefty Taurus stellium of Saturn/Uranus/Jupiter/Chiron.

Romantic poet, **Percy Bysshe Shelley,** had his **Asteroid Lilith in Virgo** conjunct Mercury in its rulership. Its square to the Dark Moon in Sagittarius made him even more outspoken, even strident in his idealism. One of his first major works, *Hymn to Intellectual Beauty*, is a good title for this Virgo placement. A major Romantic poet, he wrote philosophical and political as well as poetical works. He spoke out for social justice and vegetarianism and was often criticized for his views and his works. Lilith the child stealer played a large part in his life. He was not able to gain custody of his children from his first marriage, and three later children died. He himself died during his first Saturn return in a sudden storm while boating. There were some questions surrounding the event.

With his **Asteroid Lilith in Leo** joining a serious to-the-degree Saturn/Mercury conjunction in Leo, South African leader **Nelson Mandela** knew what to say as he showed the leadership quality that it takes to bring consensus to a seriously racially-divided nation.

Lady Diana Spencer, Princess of Wales had **Asteroid Lilith in Cancer** conjunct both Mercury and her Sun in the 7th house of marriage. This trio made one corner of a grand trine in Water signs that included Neptune in Scorpio and Chiron in Pisces. She was very sensitive. The Cancer placement reflects her problem with eating disorders. Her life path was to speak out, which she did more frankly than the royal family would have preferred about her marriage and divorce. She was actively involved in charity causes and was an outspoken advocate for banning landmines. Of course, Asteroid Lilith in the 7th house speaks to her famous marriage and divorce.

Record-Maker and Breaker

With **Asteroid 1181 in Gemini** conjunct her Sun, Canadian-American singer-songwriter **Alanis Morissette** lives the Lilith life. Starting a recording career at age 13, her third album, *Jagged Little Pill,* released when she was 18, became the highest selling international debut album of all time with a series of hit singles that kept it in the Top 20 for over a year. She has won twelve Juno and seven Grammy awards. Her Sun-Lilith are in a T-square pattern opposite Neptune in Sagittarius, square Ceres, Juno and Jupiter in Pisces, showing music, film and image to be natural mediums for her socially-challenging agenda. A classic Gemini, she has a twin brother, dual citizenship, and has had bi-sexual experiences. "I see my body as an instrument, rather than an ornament," she once said, a hard-earned statement as she healed from trouble with panic attacks, anorexia and bulimia.

In part to prove that a woman could do it, she took over much of the production of her music to wrest creative control from the pressure of the music industry. Her songs address her inner dilemmas, often expressed through scathing and explicit lyrics and her strident, haunting voice. She also challenges the censors in suggestive videos and once hosted a Juno awards ceremony in a bathrobe that opened to reveal a flesh-colored body suit. Even her hair, a la Leo rising, has been a statement, ranging from long, wavy locks to shaved bald in political protest. *Flavors of Entanglement*, a Lilith-flavored title, features the song, "Underneath," part of the 2007 Elevate Film Festival, a celebration and creation of consciousness-raising via the medium of film. Her songs give a good musical sense of Lilith.

Lilith's Fairest

Sarah McLachlan, another Canadian songstress, created the highly successful Lilith Fair movable music festival, featuring all women musicians. Does she or doesn't she? Yes, she does have a strong Asteroid placement, appropriate for such an innovative and risky venture by the music business world. **Lilith is in** late **Sagittarius**, conjunct by degree but across cusp to Venus in Capricorn. A most interesting thing about this Lilith is that it is right on the 26-27th degree of Sagittarius that marks the Galactic Center. She channels the song of the Goddess in the heart of the galaxy, "fumbling towards ecstasy" and "Building the Mystery." This Lilith also sits at the hub of a T-square, dynamically interacting with an opposition of Chiron in Pisces and Uranus/Pluto in Virgo. The Uranus/Pluto is the signature conjunction that made the 1960s. Many have the Chiron and/or Saturn opposition as well. She sings for her generation and for the cosmic feminine. Listen to "Building a Mystery," free on YouTube, and "Mary Walks" from her *fumbling toward ecstasy* album.

Actor and Advocate

Michael J. Fox, another Canadian-American, has **Asteroid Lilith in Gemini** conjunct Sun. This highly popular film and television actor has won multiple awards and honors, including Emmy, Golden Globe and Screen Actors Guild Awards for his two hit television series, *Family Ties* and *Spin City*. He is a devoted family man. His four children include twin girls. Diagnosed with rare early-onset Parkinson's Disease, a degenerative neurological disorder that affects movement (Gemini issue), he founded

The Michael J. Fox Foundation to promote research through embryonic stem cell study. His fame has allowed him to become a strong advocate and educator about this illness. He has that eternally youthful look of Gemini, yet with the Parkinson's he says, "I love the irony. I'm perceived as being really young and yet I have the clinical condition of an old man."

Actor and Activist
True Black Moon on his Sagittarian Ascendant accounts for the rugged cowboy charisma of actor **Brad Pitt**, but it is **Asteroid Lilith in Sagittarius** conjunct his Sun that accounts for his activism. With a strong interest in green architecture and design, he is walking his talk, like a good Sagittarian. He has raised multi-millions to put his vision into practice while helping to rebuild New Orleans after Hurricane Katrina. He has also adopted children from several countries with his partner, Angelina Jolie (mentioned below).

Playwright and Social Commentator
With a close Sun/Venus conjunction in Leo, **George Bernard Shaw** had a natural dramatic flair, strong aesthetic nature and appreciation of the feminine. Theater critic turned playwright, it was his **Asteroid Lilith in Taurus** conjunct Moon/Uranus that filled his art with big doses of critical social commentary and acerbic wit. He was a prominent member of the Fabian Society, a progressive socialist think tank, still influential today. Radical in theatrical style and content, he authored powerful, provocative dramas that challenged moral and political territory of the times. He was awarded the Nobel Prize for Literature in 1925. Earlier I mentioned his play, *Back to Methuselah*, citing the scene in which the serpent tells Eve about Lilith, the first one in the garden.

Dark Moon Lilith

Continuing to explore the facets and faces of Lilith as she comes into embodiment, we now focus on the two Moon-related Liliths — the Dark Moon and the Black Moon — bringing us to a liminal edge where the subjective personal reactions of the Moon are challenged, turned inside out, even transcended.

A number of fantasy writers and poets suggested themselves to

Dark Moon research, as they seem to tune in to the shadowy realms of otherworlds, the realms of Faerie and worlds of "as if." They don't all inhabit the same other worlds, however, some are darker than others, some are drug-crazed, others more redeeming. We start with them, then consider an artist and a couple of rock stars. Scorpio is over-represented in this brief selection, which seems more or less than reasonable.

The Brooding Romantic Dark Moon

The waves were dead; the tides were in their grave,
The moon, their mistress, had expir'd before,
Darkness — She was the Universe.

from *Darkness*, 1816

George Gordon, Lord Byron, still today cuts the quintessential, larger-than-life figure of the Romantic hero, with his **Dark Moon in Aquarius** closely conjunct his Sun. A solitary, shy boy born with a painful club foot, possibly sexually abused by his nurse, he came into his title from his great-uncle, the "wicked" Lord Byron at the age of ten. He lived with his mentally unstable mother in the ghostly ruins of his inherited estate, Newstead Abbey, for some years before moving to London, where he dissipated his monies in profligate living and trips to the Continent. An unrequited love moved him to write melancholic verses which resonated with the mood of the times. He was only twenty-four when his *Childe Harrold's Pilgrimage* was published, creating an instant sensation, expressing the disparity between the real world and the romantic, otherworldly ideal; a Dark Moon haunting.

He spent the rest of his life exiled from his homeland, moving around in Europe, especially Italy, seducing ladies, some married, and publishing satiric commentary and poetry on the state of the world. Both of his daughters, by different women, died in childhood. He enjoyed a stimulating friendship with fellow poet Percy Bysshe Shelley, until Shelley drowned in suspicious circumstances at the age of 29. Byron also died young, from a fever in Greece, while aiding the Greek army in the resistance against Turkey. He was just 36 years old. The Romantic melancholy and guilt, accompanied by a yearning for nobility of spirit — "half dust, half deity, alike unfit to sink or soar" — characterized his life and work, which continued to influence later generations of writers.

Dark Moon Fairy Tales

Can that be true that loves the night?
The darkness is the nurse of light.
Can that be true which mocks at forms?
Truth rides abroad in shapeless storms.
from *The Shadows*

George MacDonald wrote the novelette, *Lilith*, mentioned above, but he is best-known for his fairy tales. Such stories as *The Princess and the Goblin*, *The Light Princess* and *At the Back of the North Wind* have become classics in children's literature. Born with a rich Celtic heritage from a leading clan from the Scottish Highlands, he was well-acquainted with the fairy realms of nature. Raised a farm boy, he became a minister, then Professor of Literature at London University, but MacDonald was first of all a storyteller. He wrote many stories for his eleven children. Although a true Sagittarian, he had a great deal of Capricorn energy, a sign most attuned to nature kingdoms and fairy realms.

MacDonald had Uranus/Neptune and Mars/Venus conjunctions there, as well as an exact conjunction of Asteroid Lilith and **Dark Moon at 2 Capricorn**, with his North Node at 0+, right on the Sagittarius-Capricorn cusp. I call this the "Unicorn cusp," using an image that combines the one-pointedness of Sagittarius in the single horn of a mythical earth beast, akin to the Capricornian sea goat. Pluto at 2 Aries squares the Liliths and colors the Dark Moon a little darker, with a fire of originality that pulls up fresh images that reverberate with meaning for the collective consciousness. Some of his stories are more appropriate for adults than children, spiced with humorous and indulgent commentaries on social behavior, as befitting the Asteroid Lilith placement, and a serious undertone that evoked the mystical and magical with a Dark Moon-tinged double meaning. *Lilith* is such a story, discussed earlier, and so is *The Shadows*, another mystical allegory, with Dark Moon depths that can almost be Dark Moon definitions.

The Shadows is written about a man whose illness sends him into a dream state between worlds, where he has been named King of the Fairies. He is approached with a petition by beings called the "Shadows," who "go through the unseen, and only by a passing chill do men recognize an unknown presence." They are powerful in the moon's light and shapeshift in firelight and starlight, from humanoid to grotesque forms. Their existence is in danger, they say, because of increasing use of artificial light. Such unnatural lights "blind the eyes by which alone we can be perceived." Their petition is "to restore us to our rights in the house itself, and in the hearts of its inhabitants." Their purpose is not to cause fright, unless it is for the good, they assure, but rather "to make people silent and thoughtful; to awe them a little," to make common things reveal the wonderful through shadow games, and to disclose the truth behind the appearances with a light touch of a wavering shadow.

A friend of Charles Dodgson (a.k.a. Lewis Carroll of "Alice" fame), MacDonald was also an inspiration to C. S. Lewis *(The Chronicles of Narnia)*. MacDonald may not have reached the fame of these two men, but he had a rare genius, an ability to invent fairy tales that open windows into other worlds that shine with delight, letting in a special magic spark that tickles the soul. Maybe that's the Dark Moon Unicorn.

Through Lilith's Looking Glass

Speaking of Dodgson, better known as **Lewis Carroll**, this author of the much-beloved "Alice" classics was born a few years later than MacDonald and had his Black Moon on that Unicorn cusp! His chart shows his intellectual brilliance with Sun/Uranus in Aquarius sextile Moon in Sagittarius, accounting for his mathematics and writing. But the Sun/Uranus/South Node conjunction is also the hub of a dynamic T-square, involving **Dark Moon in Scorpio** opposite Chiron in Taurus, requiring an active engagement with the shadowy realms. This certainly influenced his quirkiness, and influenced the subject matter of his writings which were, inevitably, a creative engagement with his own psycho-spiritual journeys, talking in *Jabberwocky* and hunting the *Snark*.

One of the finest Victorian photographers, Dodgson leaves a portfolio of many well-known persons of his age and of children. Myths about the man have circulated, distorting modern perceptions of his life. Questions about his sexuality, especially toward young girls, use of hallucinogenic substances, and questions about missing diaries have given ample room for misunderstandings over time. Astrologically fueled by Asteroid Lilith in Libra square Neptune in late Capricorn, our modern questions may tell us as much about the differences in the social standards between the centuries as about the man.

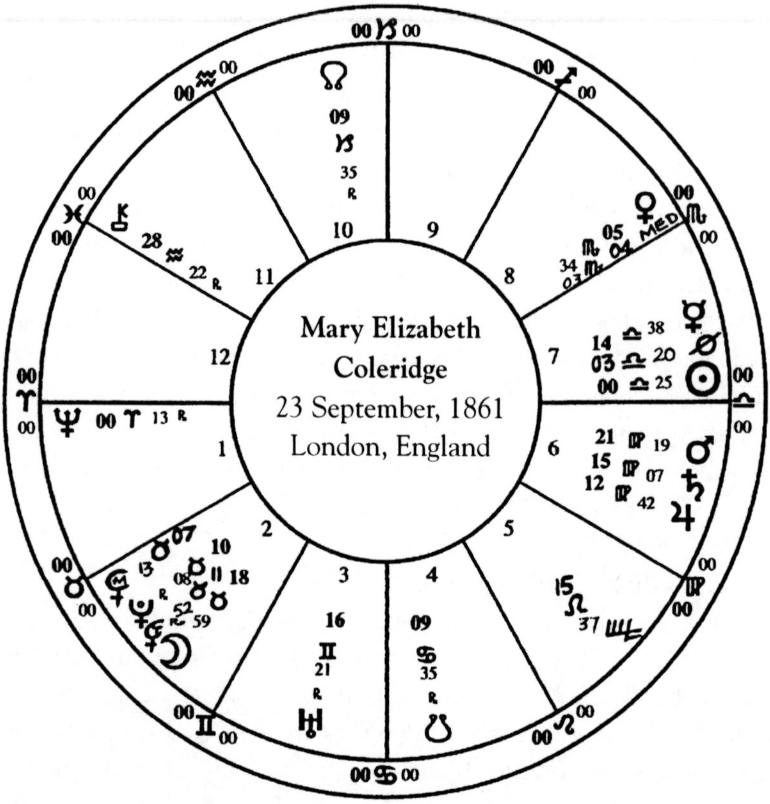

The Other Side of the Mirror

The vision of a woman, wild
With more than womanly despair…
Made mad because its hope was gone…

Born on Fall Equinox with **Dark Moon in Libra** conjunct her Sun, this novelist and poet **Mary Elizabeth Coleridge** was the great grand-niece of Samuel Taylor Coleridge. We heard from her poem earlier, when discussing Algol and the Medusa connection. Closely connected with the artists and poets of her time, Coleridge wrote poetry under the pen name Anodas, taken from George MacDonald. *The Other Side of the Mirror* expressed the anguish of the repressed female of her age, seeing herself as Medusa. The Asteroid Medusa conjuncts her Venus as a nuanced level of the Lilith signature, very pronounced in her chart. See how the Black Moon conjuncts Moon/Pluto and squares Jupiter/Saturn/Mars, even aspecting Venus.

Otherworldly Poet

There is a tideless ocean in her eyes,
There is a serpent soul that sways and swoons...
With witchery of unremembered moons.
from *She*

Poet Mary Maud Dunn must have known Lilith well to take her pen name of **Lilith Lorraine**. The lines from the above poem, **She**, prove that with just this small sample from her rich poetry. Her **Dark Moon Lilith in Pisces** opposite her Virgo Moon accounts for this writer's early-felt dreamy dissociation from the mundane world. A poet from age ten, she became America's first female science fiction poet, writing award-winning, star-infused poetry and futuristic stories of otherworlds. A member of the Poetry Societies of Texas and England, she was also founder and editor of a number of poetry magazines: *The Raven, Different, Challenge* and *Flame*. These titles and those of her books of poetry articulate themes of Lilith: *Beyond Bewilderment, The Day Before Judgment, Wine of Wonder, And Ever the Pyres of the Dead Burned Thick, With No Secret Meaning*.

In her collection called *Let the Patterns Break*, she tells a story of her marriage: as a young man, her husband fell in love with an unknown teenager whose love poem blew across the trail where he was riding his horse. Years later on their honeymoon, his confession of this early love led to the remarkable realization that she was the author of that poem, *The Greater Love*,

There's a love that builds in darkness, shaping heavens ever new,
From the wreck of lesser passions —that's the love I have for you.

This is a fine example of the potential of a Lilith relationship.

Dark Moon Visions

The bleeding sun's phantasmagoric gules,
Are fungus-tapers of the twilight witch
(Seen by the bat above unfathomed pools)
And tiger-lilies known to silent ghouls....
A Wine of Wizardry

Bohemian fantasy poet **George Sterling** wrote *Lilith: A Dramatic Poem*, first published in 1919. The storyline tells of Tancred, the everyman hero, who is seduced by the irresistible witch to kill his father, betray his wife to her death, and become a martyr himself. Lilith seared him to the soul, challenging his morals, beliefs and sanity. "Thy heart is colder than the light between the northern ocean and the moon! Thou art evil!" he cries.

Sterling was a romantic poet in high vogue in the golden age of the Bohemian art scene of early twentieth century San Francisco. A protégé of Ambrose Bierce, he wrote visionary poetry of unique power and lyricism, often compared to that of Keats, Shelley, Baudelaire and Edgar Allen Poe. "A *Wine of Wizardry*" is one of his most-lauded works, recently republished in *The Thirst of Satan: Poems of Fantasy and Terror.* His personal favorite was *The Testimony of the Suns*, a poetic paean of vast sidereal vision. He knew astronomy, if not astrology.

Sterling sought to experience the world behind the physical, using opium and possibly other narcotics to that end. He died in 1926 at the Bohemia Club after drinking cyanide. His **Dark Moon in Scorpio** was most likely conjunct his Moon, evoking deep shadows of quicksand. Moon/Dark Moon was opposite Jupiter/Pluto/Asteroid Lilith, one indication of the Bohemian artistic life style on the fringe, yet influencing society. Black Moon conjunct Neptune in Aries, quincunx Moon, suggests use of alcohol and narcotics — and poetry — to an impulsive extreme.

Dark Moon Despair

Major Swedish poet **Karin Boye** knew Lilith well. She wrote a poem, *Lilith's Song*, and made two watercolors of a wraith-like Lilith among trees. Her Moon/North Node in early Sagittarius was opposed by the **Dark Moon in Gemini**, significantly conjunct the South Node. An early morning birth time could push that Dark Moon back into Taurus. Yet the Gemini position seems likely, because of her life-long involvement with education, study of languages, and sexual ambivalence with lesbian leanings. Nodal conjunctions indicate significant karmic issues that carry over from lifetime to lifetime (if one believes in reincarnation), deeply embedded in the path of destiny. Spiritually, even mystically inclined, influenced by Buddhism then Christianity, she wrestled mightily with life's pain and suffering, with personal sacrifice and selfishness, freedom and determinism. Along with the Dark Moon pattern, her Black Moon in Libra indicated relationship difficulties, including failed marriage,

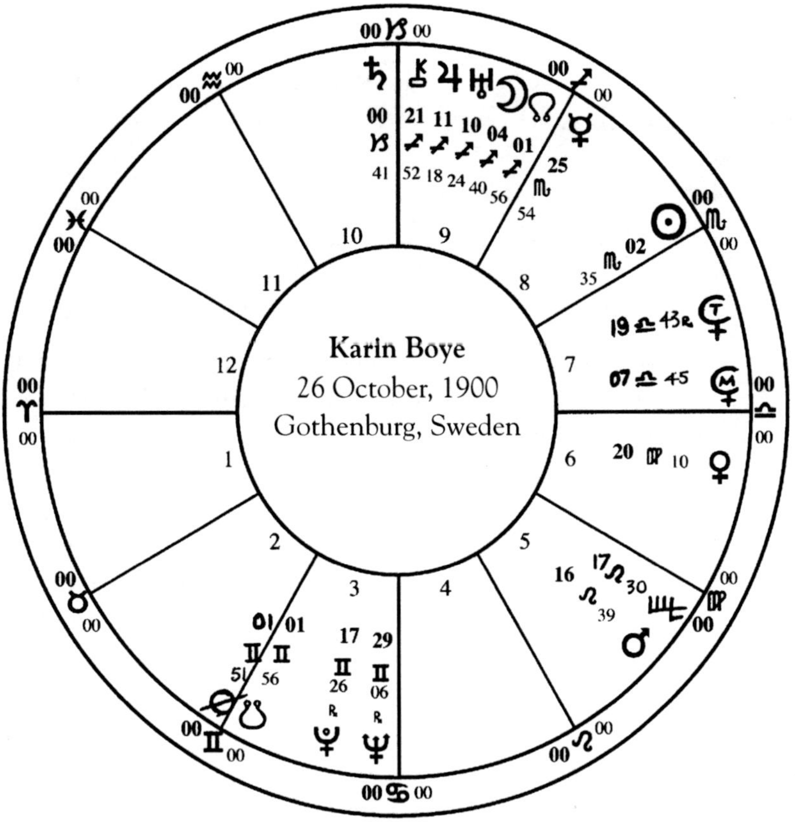

lifelong unrequited love and burdensome co-dependency. Deep psychological despair led to suicide at age 40. [You can read her poetry and see the watercolors at www.karinboye.se/verk/index-en.shtml.]

Far Memory

Some would call it fantasy fiction, but author **Joan Grant** called it "far memory" and wrote esoteric fiction, or reincarnational autobiography. She was able to recall and write about numerous past lives. With **Dark Moon Lilith in Aries** sandwiched tightly between her Moon and Sun, surely she crossed between worlds. Though not within active orb of influence, Grant's Black Moon/Jupiter/Neptune conjunction in Cancer, the sign of memory, contributed to her timeless perception. Her first book, *Winged Pharaoh*, was an instant hit, followed by several more, as well as books on esoteric matters. She may have died in 1989, but she is still publishing! An anthology edited by her granddaughter, *Speaking from the Heart: Ethics, Reincarnation and What it Means to be Human*, was published in 2007.

Dark Moon Psychologo-Fantasy

> *She just brought me to a place in a fairy tale where I needed to be most...*
>
> from *Solstice Wood*

If you want to go on a Dark Moon journey, any book by **Patricia McKillip** will take you there. An award-winning fantasy writer, McKillip beguiles with her psychologically subtle stories that dissolve the borders of reality into the otherworlds. McKillip has a fluid grand trine in Water — Sun in Pisces, Moon in Scorpio (close to Chiron) and **Dark Moon in Cancer** — which gives her a natural affinity to dream in these other realms. Her works evoke elusive yet primal universal memories. Her colorful worlds and characters engage with magic, mystery and musical prose interlaced with intricate psychic weavings. Honoring the power of Nature and without denying the dangerous undertones of the astral realms, her stories are of rapprochement, redemption, healing and love. Her wizard hero and heroine in *The Riddle Master* trilogy epitomize fictional Dark Moon characters.

Several covers of her books feature the evocative art of Kinuko Craft, a master painter of fantasy. I was unable to find birth data for her beyond the year, but I postulate a strong Lilith signature featuring an active Dark Moon. I suggest the same for fantasy artists Brian Froud and Wendy Froud, who live both in Devon, England and in Faerie.

Dark Moon Artist

> *Shadow is a colour as light is, but less brilliant.*

A highly sensitive, brooding and troubled man, **Paul Cezanne** was haunted by memories, sensual ambivalence and an oppressive father. Ahead of his time, he was ostracized and ridiculed much of his career. Beyond innovative, his unusual perspective, palette and emotional tone were outside the understanding of his age, even among most fellow artists. He generally isolated himself, working in solitude. A Capricorn, he drew from the Old Masters in spirit and from some Impressionists in technique, but pushed aesthetic vision into new territory in a highly subjective way, impelled by deep inner motivation to transcend his inner demons. His style is unique and his legacy continues, as his work dares artists to seek radical expressions of the relationship between art and life.

Prone to sudden tempers, he experienced a profound emotional betrayal by his childhood friend, Emile Zola, who portrayed him as a neurotic failed artist in a novel. Cezanne had a Uranus/Moon conjunction in Pisces, joined by both **Dark Moon and Asteroid Liliths in Pisces,** probably in the 5th house of creativity. Dark Moon suggests the shadowy family emotional distemper, Asteroid Lilith the social ostracism. He spoke from his own experience when he said, "Genius is the ability to renew one's emotions in daily experience."

Dark Moon Stars on the Silver Screen

Mary Astor (nee Lucille Langhanke) had **Dark Moon in Taurus** conjunct her Sun (and Black Moon) in a grand trine with Virgo Moon on the Midheaven and Uranus in Capricorn. Her parents were ambitious German immigrants, constantly entering her in beauty contests. She was discovered by a Hollywood agent at age fourteen. Her super starlet status began with the silent film *Beau Brummel*, playing opposite John Barrymore. She successfully transitioned to talking films, appearing in over one hundred Hollywood productions, in New York theater, and on numerous television shows in a career that lasted well into the 1960s. She won an Oscar for Best Supporting Actress in 1941 for her role in *The Great Lie* and is best remembered as the irresistible villain in the classic, *The Maltese Falcon*, with Humphrey Bogart. Her career faltered at times due to personal problems, such as scandals, drinking, health and family issues. Her first husband died in a plane crash. There were three divorces, custody battles over her daughter and a suicide attempt. Her parents, who lived a lavish life off her earnings, sued her for support (Taurus issue). She wrote two books about her life that became best sellers. She wittily summed up the five stages in the life of a Hollywood actor: "Who's Mary Astor? Get me Mary Astor. Get me a Mary Astor Type. Get me a Young Mary Astor. Who's Mary Astor?"

Julia Roberts has **Dark Moon in Virgo** conjunct her Venus/Pluto (with Uranus close by), adding an extra nuance of sensuality to the chart of this immensely popular actress. Otherwise remaining hidden in the aethers, a grand trine in Earth is revealed when we add this Dark Moon to her Mars in Capricorn and Black Moon in Taurus (opposite her Scorpio Sun). Nominated several times, her 2001 Best Actress Oscar was earned for her title role as Erin Brockovich, a woman who became a legal activist. Roberts herself is an active supporter of UNICEF and other charitable organizations. Now a producer, she wields more star power than most, as her films have made her the highest grossing actress in history. Not that she would ever be called gross — not with that special conjunction in Virgo.

With **Dark Moon in Sagittarius,** charismatic **Angelina Jolie** (nee Voigt) emerged on our screens as a martial arts action star, bringing to life the *Tomb Raider* videogame as Lara Croft. This agrees with her extra dose of Aries — Mars and Jupiter surround her Moon (exactly conjunct Eris), and Chiron trines Dark Moon. She has had a fascination with knives and went through a phase of self-harming in her teens. She has earned multiple acting awards, including an Academy Award for Best Supporting Actress in *Girl, Interrupted.* Deeply interested in international issues, Jolie is official Goodwill Ambassador for the UN Refugee Agency. She has adopted several children from countries in Asia and Africa. That Dark Moon is in her fifth house and opposite Mercury. You can find her famous partner Brad Pitt in the Asteroid section. Her Dark Moon is conjunct his Sun/Asteroid in Sagittarius.

Dark Moon Rock Star of Today

> *...there are colours and feelings and emotional terrain that we occupy that is ours and ours alone.*

Lead singer **Bono** (ne Paul Hewson) of Ireland's U2 exudes a strong hint of Lilith from behind his shades, with **Dark Moon in Scorpio** cranking up his already enigmatic Moon-Neptune conjunction, and exactly opposite Mercury, Venus and Sun in Taurus. It is largely his aura that makes the band U2 extra-ordinary. Ambitious though he is with Saturn conjunct his Capricorn Ascendant, personal success is not enough for this man. There is a strong sense of compassion and sacrifice from both Neptune and Dark Moon, so that he travels the globe (9th house placement), using his fame to gain entrée to world leaders and to promote positive world politics. Bono founded DATA (Debt, Aid, Trade for Africa). "As a rock star, I have two instincts, I want to have fun, and I want to change the world. I have a chance to do both."

Dark Moon Rock Star of Yesterday

An iconic figure, **Elvis Presley**, "King of Rock and Roll," exuded a sexual charisma that challenged social censure of the Fifties and opened the doors to the Sixties revolution. Certainly his Uranus-Venus-Pluto T-square accounts for some of his radical impact on the collective consciousness. The **Dark Moon in Aries** adds an additional tone, conjunct Asteroid Lilith, closely opposed Mars in Libra and squaring his Sun in Capricorn. He created an original, trail-blazing fusion of musical influences — pop, country, gospel, blues — that defied categories, stretching across the racial divide and ushering in a new era of American music.

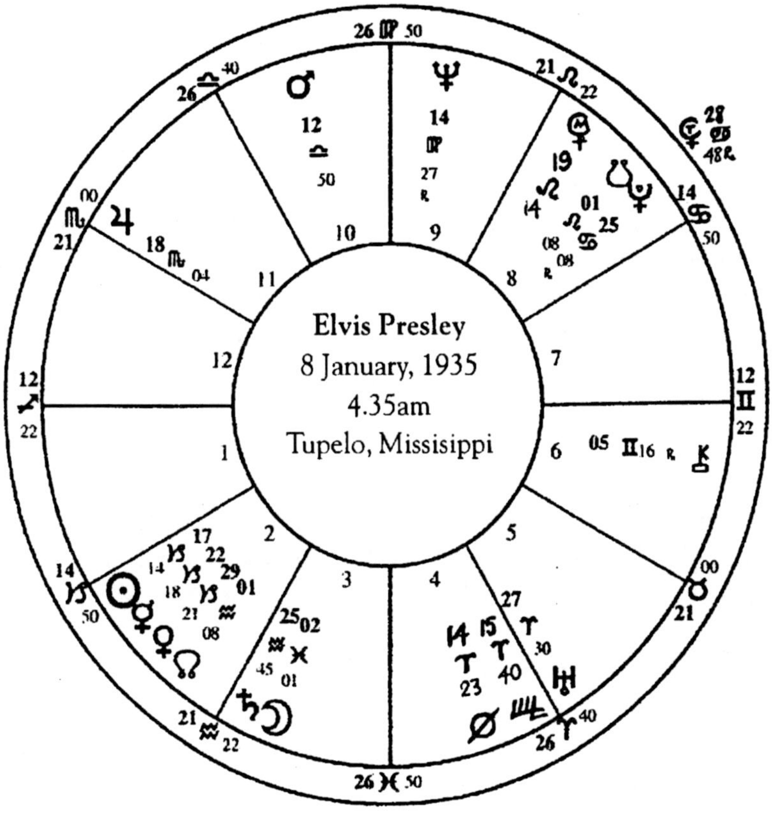

From impoverished beginnings to megabucks, his life was full of extremes. With the Dark Moon memory of a stillborn twin that likely haunted his life on some subliminal level, he overcame early shyness, peer ostracism and an inferiority complex to express uninhibited, censurable sensuality in his artistry. With his high sexual charisma, no one would question the intensity of his masculinity except, perhaps, himself in his search to define his personal authentic manhood on his own terms. The Lilith-infused T-square hints of a personal struggle to balance public life with private. He died in 1977, during his mid-life Neptune square, supposedly from long-term prescription drug abuse or maybe he drowned in the glamour of public projections.

Black Moon Lilith

Black Moon Rock Stars

Rock Stars come in Dark Moon and Black Moon flavors, like different brews of coffee. **John Lennon** and **Paul McCartney** formed a song-writing partnership that created most of the music for the ultra-famous Beatles, the phenomenon on the vanguard of the 1960s "English invasion" of the rock world. This was a Black Moon liaison. Lennon's strong personality was indicated by **Black Moon in Aries** conjunct South Node, very close to his Ascendant. The opposition to his Libra Sun reflected the strong partnerships and their confrontational aspects. His songwriting partnership with Paul McCartney produced dozens of well-known songs. His marriage to Japanese artist Yoko Ono effectively broke up the Beatles and led to his solo career. The couple staged a publicized sleep-in to promote peace, a radical way to say "Give Peace a Chance." He was shot by a former fan.

With a Sun/**Black Moon in Gemini** conjunct a ruling Mercury, McCartney possesses rare talent. With and without Beatles partner John Lennon, Sir Paul has composed endless numbers of popular songs, as well as classical works. Post-Beatles he formed the group Wings, joined by wife Linda who died of cancer.

Mick Jagger, lead singer of the legendary Rolling Stones, is one of many 1943 Leos who share a dramatic stellium of **Black Moon in Leo** conjunct Sun/Jupiter/Pluto/Mercury/North Node in the sunshine sign. Still rolling and rocking after 40 years, Jagger's theatrical, Leonine presence is an essential part of the act, along with long-lasting songs and sound. His daughter, Elizabeth Scarlett Jagger has a Moon/Black Moon/ Mercury conjunction in Pisces in the fourth house, a clear indication of Black Moons in the family.

Grammy Award-winning musician **Eric Clapton**, considered one of the greatest guitarists of all time, is also a singer and composer who spans a range of musical styles. **Black Moon in Libra** is opposite his Sun and squaring his Nodes. If the generally used birth time of 8.45pm is correct, Black Moon is close to his Ascendant. Clapton made artistically fruitful collaborations in his career, but has also had a rich solo career. He first reached popular heights in the US as a member of Cream. With Derek and the Dominos, he made the classic song, *Layla,* one of Lilith's alternative names. He had a visitation from Lilith as child killer on March 20, 1991, when his son tragically died at age 4, inspiring one of his most enduring songs, *Tears in Heaven.* On that day, his Black Moon was being opposed by Mercury, and squared by an opposition of Chiron in Cancer and Uranus/Neptune in Capricorn.

On the other side of the world, and not so much rock as R&B, Japanese "forever idol," **Seiko Matsuda** (nee Kamachi Noriko) made a record of 24 consecutive #1 hit singles in her 1980s heyday. She has a close conjunction of Pluto/**Black Moon in Virgo** straddling her Ascendant. She embodies the Japanese *burikko,* an woman who acts like a cutesy girl to be attractive. This image did not translate well in her US attempts. One of the most influential artists and media magnets in Japanese pop history, she has been alternately reviled and praised by the press and feminists. Married and a mother, she pursued scandalous affairs, and eventually divorced, a rare event in Japan, especially criticized when initiated by the woman.

The "White Lady of Soul," with **Black Moon in Aquarius, Dusty Springfield** (nee Mary O'Brien) became one of the all-time biggest solo singers in a career than spanned four decades. Early on she was deported from South Africa for refusing to perform for an apartheid audience. One of the first British performers to successfully cross the Atlantic and make an impact in the US, she moved from folk into the Motown Sound, then into the Nashville scene, equally adept at jazz, blues, rock-and-roll and popular music. A combination of emotional insecurity, perfectionism and stardom led to eccentric behavior, substance abuse and self-harming.

Queen Elizabeth conferred on her the Order of the British Empire just before her death, and shortly thereafter she was named to the Rock and Roll Hall of Fame. Bi-sexual, she quipped, "Basically I'm a drag queen myself."

Black Moon Actors

With **Black Moon in Aries** sandwiched between Sun and Moon, actor **Gary Oldman** has created an astonishingly odd, often villainous array of movie characters, from musician Sid Vicious of the Sex Pistols to Dracula, Beethoven, a pimp, terrorist, corrupt and sadistic officials and, recently, Sirius Black in the Harry Potter movies. He invents a new accent for each role. He wrote, directed and produced the largely autobiographical and highly praised film, *Nil by Mouth*. Abandoned by his own father at a young age, he later found himself the single father of two young sons.

With **Black Moon in Gemini** conjunct his Moon, exactly square Mars in Virgo, actor/producer **Hugh Jackman** is extraordinarily versatile and talented, equally for acting, singing and dance. He made a big impression in the London stage version of the classic American musical *Oklahoma!* and on Broadway in *The Boy from Oz*, virtually a one-man show about the life of composer Peter Allen. He has high charisma and a healing light. Best known as a film actor, his famous role was Wolverine in *X-Men*, with a set of knives for a hand — very Black Moon in the "handy" sign of Gemini! As was his role in *The Prestige*, a movie of magic and illusion, where he played a character competing against a pair of twins in increasingly dark acts. *The Fountain* is an esoteric movie, challenging perception, in which he plays three lifetimes of one character, one of them played at the foot of Lilith's tree of life, death and rebirth.

Black Moon Composer

With **Black Moon in Cancer** opposite his Moon in Capricorn, beloved composer **Frederic Chopin** gives us another example of the heightened emotional sensitivity that Lilith in Cancer and in concert with the Moon can lend to artistic sensitivity. Chopin's Black Moon was part of a grand trine in Water signs, including Uranus in Scorpio and his Sun in Pisces flanked by Venus and Pluto. He had a tempestuous relationship with female writer, George Sand. He died at age 39 of tuberculosis, leaving a rich and extensive legacy of some of the most moving piano music ever written. His tomb at Pere La Chaise cemetery in Paris is topped by a sculpture of a sorrowing muse and always decorated with flowers, candles and other mementos of appreciation.

Black Moon Empress

The powerful Empress, **Catherine II**, "The Great," exemplified **Black Moon in Taurus**. Taking the throne in a coup from her incompetent (and reported impotent husband,) she became a tyrannical monarch and expanded the borders and political power of Russia. A true Taurus patron of the arts, literature and education, she established the Russian Ballet, a school for girls, and corresponded with leading thinkers in Europe. She herself was a writer. A typically highly-sexed Taurus, she was generous to her many lovers, but distrusted her son and kept him semi-confined. The Russian word for money, *babki*, means "old women" and refers to her picture on old ruble bills, appropriate for Taurus.

Black Moon Scientist

Winner of two Nobel Prizes, the famous scientist, physicist and chemist **Marie Curie** had **Black Moon in Capricorn** on her Ascendant. She worked with her husband Pierre, investigating chemical structures and isolating radium and ultimately died from its poisonous effects. In spite of her stature in the science world, she was denied entrance into the French Academy because of her sex. She and her husband lived a rich family life. After his sudden, accidental death, she caused a scandal by having an affair. Not the accepted way for a female scientist to behave!

Sisters of Mercy

Do you know the Leonard Cohen song, *Sisters of Mercy*? He sang of compassionate women that helped him at a difficult time. Whether or not these were the sisters that Cohen found, the Sisters of Mercy are indeed "not departed or gone," but a continuing service order of nuns founded in Ireland on December 12, 1831. Several years earlier, on the Feast Day of Our Lady of Mercy, a group of women, led by Catherine McCauley, opened the House of Mercy to offer religious, educational and social services for women and children. As it was too unusual for lay women to be doing such social service work, several of the women became ordained as nuns and founded their religious order. This took place early in the morning, for they did not stay to breakfast at the Church, it is said, but went on home and back to their work.

Today the Mercy International Association spans the globe with strong centers in Ireland, Australia, Great Britain, New Zealand, Newfoundland, the Philippines and the Americas, with a membership of ten thousand sisters serving the needs of the poor in these countries. Because their founding date is the tri-centennial anniversary of the Apparition of the Virgin of Guadalupe in Mexico, the Sisters find a special welcome in Latin America.

The chart of the founding of the Sisters of Mercy has the Sun conjunct the mean **Black Moon in Sagittarius**, both squaring the Moon in Pisces. The oscillating Black Moon is in practical Capricorn, conjunct Mercury and in a grand cross with Asteroid Lilith in Libra, Pluto in Aries and the Dark Moon in Cancer. Originally ahead of their times in the social services, we would expect the Asteroid to be strong, and it is super-supported by the two Lilith Moons as well. [My sincere thanks to Sister Cynthia for telling me this story.]

Black Moon/Moon in Scorpio

This is a very powerful signature with depth of psycho-spiritual processing and extraordinary regenerative capacity. Having secured his place in the top echelon of tennis history, **Roger Federer** has a driven Moon/Black Moon/Uranus conjunction in the third house, all square Sun/Mercury and opposite Chiron. A class act of quiet intensity, high charisma and generosity, he was early on subject to a fitful temper and has done a good amount of psychological work on himself, an ongoing process for Scorpio, especially with this combination of factors. His family helps run his business, which includes a foundation that supports innovative projects operated by local relief organizations in selected countries. Perhaps his Dark Moon/Neptune conjunction in Sagittarius, the sports sign, also has something to do with the foundation work and his oft-noted athletic ability to make the extraordinary look ordinary.

One of the foremost teachers of women's psycho-spirituality, **Marion Woodman** started her career as a Jungian therapist working with women suffering from eating disorders (Moon connection). Her writings and experiential workshops tap into unconscious images that evoke healing. Her Scorpio capacity for regeneration led her to dance her way out of a wheelchair. Tumors on her spine had weakened her so that she was bound to a wheelchair — for life, said the doctors. At a musical party, delighted to hear the lively Polish music from her childhood, she stood up and a dancer swept her onto the dance floor. Later surgery on her spine was successful. It is from such depths that she wrote her many books, including *Dancing in the Flames: The Dark Goddess in the Transformation of Consciousness*. From her closely bound Moon/Black Moon, she exquisitely expresses the empowerment and regeneration that come through the feminine attention to body and embodiment in relation to the Earth.

Black Moon Myth Makers: Black Moon in Sagittarius

Hans Christian Andersen, internationally beloved writer of novels and travelogues, was best known for his slightly dark fairy tales. He had mean Black Moon one degree from his Ascendant in the storyteller sign of Sagittarius and the true Black Moon exactly conjunct Neptune in Scorpio opposite Algol. Socially awkward, he had a difficult early life, raised in poverty by mentally disturbed relatives which left him with phobias and scars of inferiority. Yet his sincerity, wit and talent won him friends. Such stories as *The Ugly Duckling, The Emperor's New Clothes, The Little Match Girl* and *The Little Mermaid* remain classics beyond childhood.

Steven Spielberg, a most successful film maker, directed some of the greatest mythic movies ever made. Sagittarius is the sign of story, myth and imagination. With the conjunction at 26-27 degrees, the galactic center point, he tunes into outer space and meaningful images that stimulate collective consciousness. Such movies as *E.T., Close Encounters of the Third Kind, Raiders of the Lost Ark* and *Jurassic Park* are among these. He won three Academy Awards: two for *Schindler's List* and one for *Saving Private Ryan*. He is a co-founder of the Starlight Starbright Children's Foundation, that uses entertainment and technology to enrich the lives of children with illnesses.

Let's take a deeper look at two Black Moon people of rare talent. These two extended portraits of a poet and an artist who lived and expressed Lilith to the full pull us further into the dark heart of Lilith, her living mythology and hidden mysteries.

Black Moon Poet

> *I love the dark hours of my being.*

The poetry and letters of **Rainer Maria Rilke** exquisitely express the visionary potency of the Black Moon in **Sagittarius**, dripping with soul mysteries and invisibilities. His Sagittarian Sun was conjunct the mean Black Moon, while Venus exactly conjoined true Black Moon, at the last degree of **Sagittarius** on the Unicorn cusp. In addition, Venus/true Black Moon squared the Dark Moon at the edge of Pisces/Aries and trined Neptune at the cusp of Aries/Taurus. The aesthetic, artistic nature of Venus was colored by Neptunian mysticism and lyricism, brought to a deeper edge by the Lilith connection — and the cusps! He was altogether a cuspy man.

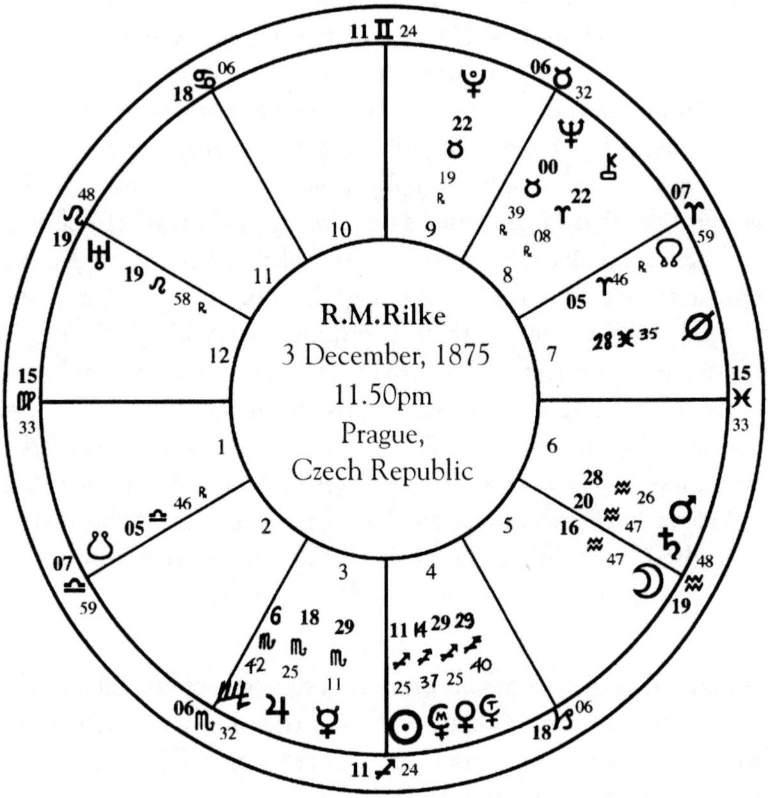

His chart deserves fuller consideration than this brief look. One can't ignore the dramatic aspects which beleaguer the Moon (Moon conjunct Mars/Saturn, square Pluto in Taurus, for starters). Rilke endured a difficult childhood, first dressed as a girl by his highly devout mother grieving the loss of an earlier daughter; then, at age ten, sent to a rigorous military school for five years. He turned inward to illness and to poetry to offset the outer pressures. His internal conversations with God became love poems that ruthlessly explored intimate experience of the spiritual, toward an extreme often urged by Black Moon Lilith, so eloquently evoked in his writings.

He fearlessly wrestled with angels, asking the biggest Sagittarian questions about the meaning of human life in its depths of anguish and heights of exhilaration. "If I cried out who would hear me up there among the angelic orders?" Thus opens the *Duino Elegies*. Rilke flung his Sagittarian imagination vast distances, toward far reaches of the universe. "I live my life in widening circles, That reach out across the world" (from *Book of Hours*).

Rilke traveled extensively, as Sagittarians are wont to do — to Russian, Italy and Spain, Denmark, Sweden and Egypt. He never really had a home base, but Paris was a center of creativity, where he worked early on for Auguste Rodin and developed his new style of lyric poetry. Yet he suffered in the city, witnessing the poverty and cruelties of life and society. With Venus/true Black Moon on the Unicorn cusp, he appreciated Nature, its lovely nuances, visible and invisible presences.

> *For the sake of a single poem you must see many cities… know the gestures which small flowers make when they open in the morning.*
> (from *The Notebooks of Malte Laurids Brigge*)

Needing a great amount of independence and solitude, relationships were often short-lived for Rilke, or lived from a distance. A Sagittarian Sun and Aquarian Moon personality would typically need space, in this case made urgent by the interactions of the lights with rigorous, inward-pulling processes suggested by the Black Moon and the impact of the complex T-square on the Moon. His first love, who remained a major influence in his life, was the beautiful Russian countess, Lou Andreas-Salome, formerly a lover of Nietzsche and sixteen years older than Rilke's twenty. He later married a young sculpting student of Rodin when she was pregnant. They separated to pursue their respective arts, leaving their child to be raised by his wife's parents. Wealthy patrons, mostly women, hosted him at their castles, villas or city apartments.

Intimately aware of the mystical element that lives beyond death in a secreted place beyond worldly concerns — the aetheric realm, perhaps — Rilke could write to his old lover or to each of us

> *Silent friend of many distances, feel*
> *How your breath enlarges all of space...*
> *In this immeasurable darkness, be the power...*
> (*Sonnets to Orpheus*, sonnet xxix)

With fiery Sagittarian creativity, he invented language, employing freely-flowing images and metaphors to convey his vision of life and death intertwined. He wrote his own epitaph before his death from leukemia at the age of fifty-one, instigated by the prick of a rose thorn that would not heal

> *Rose, o pure contradiction,*
> *Desire to be no one's sleep*
> *Beneath so many lids.*

Black Moon Artist, Frida Kahlo

I paint self portraits because I am the person I know best.

In photographs and in the numerous paintings of **Frida Kahlo**, we see the living face of Lilith, her exotic, sensual look and signature thick-knit eyebrows. Kahlo's birth chart shows the true Black Moon conjunct Pluto/Venus at the end of **Gemini**, opposite Asteroid Lilith in late Sagittarius. The Dark Moon is earlier in Sagittarius, in wide orb. Meanwhile mean Black Moon is conjunct her Sun/Neptune/Jupiter in **Cancer**, opposite Uranus/Mars, both retrograde. That's a mouthful of a condensed Lilith signature.

One of Mexico's best known and innovative artists, Kahlo experienced extreme physical trauma in her life. A victim of polio at age ten, she then suffered a horrific traffic accident when she was seventeen that crushed her foot, twisted her spine, broke her already lame leg and pierced her body from back to front through her vagina and, oddly, left her dusted all over with a shimmering patina from an artist's packet of gold leaf. These extreme injuries caused chronic physical suffering, multiple miscarriages and over thirty operations, yet drove her to art.

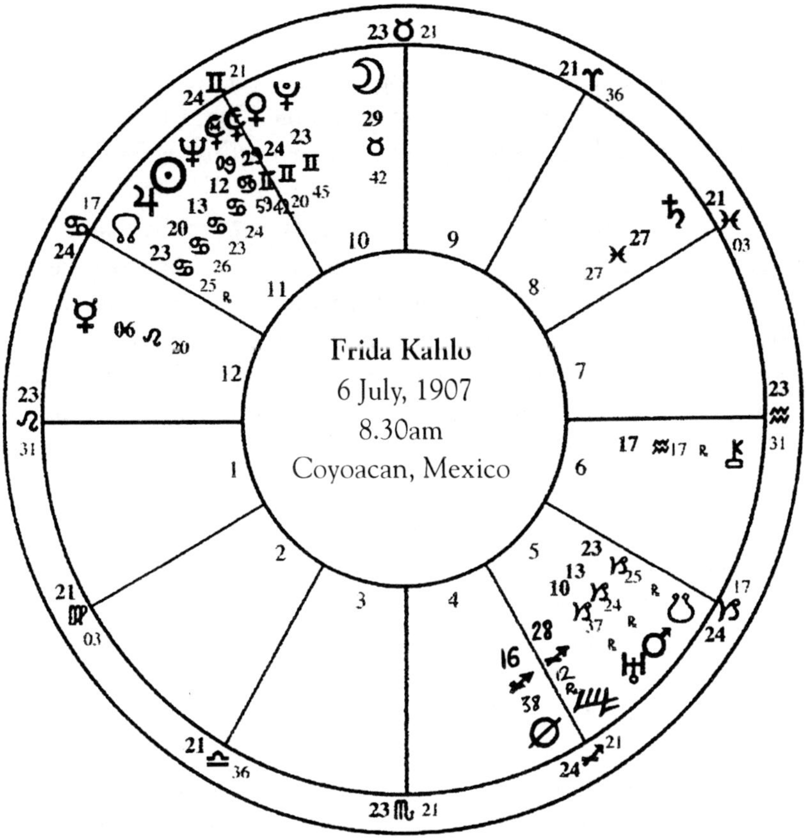

Painting, reading and writing were things she could do in bed. Her paintings chronicled her outer and inner worlds. In her youth, she had started into pre-medical studies. Like a shamanic dismemberment, she often showed her body turned inside out, x-rayed, dissected and punctured.

The Gemini Black Moon heightens the dilemma of duality experienced, in part, by the deep split between her joint European and Mexican mestizo heritage, depicted in numerous works, most famously *The Two Fridas*. Born of a Jewish Hungarian father, a photographer, and a highly devout Catholic Mexican mestizo mother, she sought to join her dual heritage in a nation seeking the same. The opposition of the Gemini stellium to Asteroid Lilith infuses this personal identity crisis with social implications. Mexico is a country unique in its high mestizo population, fusing the Spanish and Indian. An ongoing dialogue about national identity was indelibly impressed upon Frida, born on the eve of the anniversary of the 1910 revolution. Her Cancer Sun/Neptune/Black Moon retained bloody impressions from early life. The revolution became part of her life and her identity, up to her death. Days before she died, she attended a political rally.

True Black Moon is conjunct Venus, planet of the arts, and Pluto, transformer of the collective consciousness. Gannit Ankori's excellent study, *Images of Her Selves: Frida Kahlo's Poetics of Identity and Fragmentation*, explores "the complex multilayered meanings of the many selves she comprised." Kahlo's diary documents her last decade, a rather shocking chronicle of the process of transmuting pain into beauty, demonstrated through her person and her art in a distinctly personal yet archetypal language of images. The mythic and shamanistic flavor of her work opens out to an incredibly broad vision, constantly reminding us of the basic human duality of spirit and body. The style of her work drew from the *retablo* of Mexican religious art, small votive pictures on wood or tin, often framed behind the church altar. Another major artistic influence was surrealism, though she never identified with this art movement: "They thought I was a Surrealist, but I wasn't. I never painted my dreams. I painted my own reality." She sometimes called her work "revolutionary realism."

She was conscious of her persona, dressing in traditional garb, evocative and symbolic, decorating her broken body as a work of art, expressing timeless feminine beauty, revolutionary commentary and personal connection to her ancestry. Her charismatic presence, a trademark of Lilith people, was eloquently described by Mexican writer and diplomat Carlos Fuentes in his introduction to *The Diary of Frida Kahlo: An Intimate Self-Portrait*. Fuentes once saw her at a concert, and eloquently testified to her extraordinary presence, jingling jewelry and silent magnetism, evoking a vision of Aztec, Indian and Spanish goddesses, and her own self, "moonlike headdresses opening up her face like the wings of a dark butterfly."

Political themes, religious threads of Christianity, and indigenous paganism overlap in her intensely autobiographical work. We find goddess images of the holy mother, La Llorona, Hindu images and an original amalgam of Nerfertiti and Isis. The fixed star, Sirius, was in close alignment with her Sun/Neptune. This brightest of stars, the hot, bright, "scorching" or "shining" one, the Egyptian star of Isis, imprints a high priestess signature. This Cancer Sun/Neptune can suggest a life of sacrifice and spiritual transcendence.

The additional presence of the Black Moon in Cancer often makes a connection with the Great Mother. She often felt orphaned, that she had failed her parents. Desiring yet unable to have children, experiencing the child-killer face of Lilith through several miscarriages, she became an artistic Mother of her country, and of her husband, whom she often referred to as her child. Her marriage, divorce and remarriage to Rivera was tumultuous and passionate. He was not sexually faithful, and Frida also took lovers of both sexes, including the Russian politician Leon Trotsky. Rivera's affair with her sister led to their brief divorce, yet theirs was a deep, abiding loyalty and protection. The hermaphroditic images in her art sometimes referred to their relationship, the desire to fuse. The Gemini factor can seek a twin experience.

Kahlo's first solo show was in New York in 1938. The only solo exhibit of her work in her native land was in 1953, the year before her death. Bedridden, she had herself carried to the opening. With her larger than life persona and remarkably original artistic oeuvre, she was a woman of her time and beyond, expressing the imminence of the goddess that leads beyond, beyond... beyond the pain and suffering of the physical to the release of spirit. As she wrote in her diary, "The anguish and the pain, pleasure and death are no more than a process."

The Lilith Star, Algol

The fixed stars move very slowly backwards through the zodiac along with the Precession of the Equinoxes. It takes about 72 years for a star to move through one degree. The current zodiacal equivalent of Algol is 26-27 Taurus. In these Algol examples, we also see some extended Lilith signatures.

Algol-Sun Conjunction

Everyone born May 16-18 in this past century has Sun conjunct Algol. Do you have the Eye of Medusa? Here are some prime examples that have an extra dose of Lilith.

Ho Chi Minh was born on the day of an Algol New Moon. This Vietnamese revolutionary became the first Prime Minister and later President of the Democratic Republic of Vietnam (North Vietnam), after defeating French rule. If born at dawn, he is a triple Algol, with Sun, Moon and Ascendant conjunct the star.

Flamboyant, award-winning musician **Liberace**, with signature candelabra on piano, was known as "Mr. Showmanship." A tight Sun/Mars/Algol conjunction squares his Saturn at 21 Leo.

Famed prima ballerina **Dame Margot Fonteyn** (nee Margaret Hookham) had Sun/Mars conjunction on Algol square Moon in Aquarius. The Mars factor reflects that she experienced this dynamic largely through her husband, Dr. Roberto Arias, Panamanian politician and once ambassador to England, who attempted a coup against the Panama government in 1959. He was later paralyzed by an assassination attempt. Dame Margot continued to dance and retired late because of his high medical expenses. "Life offstage has sometimes been a wilderness of unpredictables in an unchoreographed world," she once said.

Transformed from criminal drug dealer to Black Muslim minister **Malcolm X** (ne Malcolm Little) founded the Organization of Afro-American Unity. This influential man was assassinated at the age of 39. His Algol-Sun conjunction was square Asteroid Lilith at the end of Aquarius.

Argentinean investment banker Máxima Zorreguieta Cerruti became **Princess Maxima** when she married Prince Willem-Alexander, Prince of Orange, heir to the Dutch throne, in 2002. She has an exact Sun/Saturn conjunction on Algol square her Aquarius Moon and square Dark Moon Lilith in the royal sign Leo in the 9th house (foreign countries), and trine a very close Asteroid Lilith/Pluto/Black Moon conjunction in Virgo in her 10th house. She is a Lilith lady to keep a Medusian eye on.

Algol-Moon Conjunction

With Moon exalted in Taurus, this combination is potent. Many natives convey public trends in a personal way.

Even with conflicting birth time, **Madame de Pompadour** (nee Jeanne Antoinette Poisson), beautiful and accomplished mistress of Louis XV certainly lives up to the close Moon/Neptune conjunction on Algol.

She has become a popular cult figure and is often depicted in film.

Ariel Sharon, known as "The Bulldozer", rose into power as a controversial military leader to become Prime Minister of Israel.

Call girl/model **Christine Keeler** was the focus of the Profumo affair, a sex scandal that toppled Great Britain's Conservative government of Harold Macmillan in 1963 and made sex a hot political potato. Her Taurus Moon was closely conjunct Uranus and Algol with a Mars/Saturn conjunction just a few degrees earlier. She also had a prominent Black Moon.

Algol Ascendant

Famous Pre-Raphaelite painter and poet, **Dante Gabriel Rossetti**, created *Lady Lilith*, among other paintings and poetry glorifying the feminine. With 4:30am birth time, he was a double Taurus with the Lilith star on his Ascendant and his Sun a few degrees earlier.

With his archetypal name, Hollywood actor **Harry Carey Jr.** specialized in Westerns, appearing in over ninety movies, many alongside John Wayne. His dozens of television appearances ranged from *The Lone Ranger* and *Wagon Train* to *Bonanza, Gunsmoke* and many others. He had Algol/Sun — and Ascendant, if born at dawn, as indicated. Not one of the top names, he was rather invisible to the public, but with a consistent presence that helped define an archetypal genre.

The controversial theories of **Carl Sagan** about the nature of the planet Venus proved to be correct. With the Algol connection, he must have had a special insider's track with the Goddess. Sagan became a well-known astronomer and prolific writer, accessible to the public mind. His book *Contact* was made into a movie, in which Jodie Foster went to the star Vega. We know he was not astrology-friendly, but he knew something significant.

American school teacher and civilian astronaut **Christa McAuliffe** was killed with the rest of the Challenger crew when a faulty seal blew out during take-off. She and her fellow astronauts were honored by asteroids named for them. She is number 3352, a Near-Earth Asteroid discovered on February 6, 1981. The discovery chart shows McAuliffe at 25 Gemini, opposite Neptune and Asteroid Lilith at 25 and 27 degrees Sagittarius. McAuliffe's 'McAuliffe' was at 24 Sagittarius. The discovery Mercury was in Pisces conjunct her mean Black Moon and opposite her

Moon in Virgo, all at 5 degrees, with her Sun at 11 Virgo. This is one of those confirmation asteroid factoids. Thank you, McAuliffe.

Algol-Pluto Conjunction

When the outer planets contact the degree of a star, there is outpouring of related themes and experience. Uranus will conjunct Algol every eighty-four years, Neptune every one hundred sixty-five, and Pluto every two hundred forty-eight.

The highly elliptical orbit of Pluto causes it to move through the signs at different speeds for various periods of time. At aphelion when in Taurus, it takes its time plowing through this slow, but steady sign that can be most resistant to change. It will, therefore, spend an extended period of time in any degree and conjunct Algol on and off for several years. The last time Pluto was in Taurus was from 1852 to 1884, birthing some persons who made a lasting impact on the collective.

Carl G. Jung, father of psychoanalysis and archetypal psychology, had Pluto within a few degrees of Algol, opposite Black Moon at 29 Scorpio.

Exotic dancer and courtesan to many military officers in Europe during World War I, **Mata Hari** (nee Margaretha Zelleamous) was accused of espionage and executed. She dressed in style for the event. Efforts have been made in recent years to re-examine the case. For many years her embalmed head was kept in a museum, then disappeared. The lost head remains a mystery. She had a fixed T-cross with Pluto conjunct Algol, square Uranus/Mars/Mercury/Sun in Leo, and Jupiter in Scorpio. Her legend lives on.

Modern dancer inspired by ancient Grecian culture, **Isadora Duncan** also had Pluto very close to Algol, in a fixed cross with her Moon at 26 Scorpio 24, Mars at 24 Aquarius and Uranus at 21 Leo. She died when a long scarf caught her around the neck (Taurus) and choked her, a version of Algol beheading.

Ground-breaking Cubist visionary artist **Pablo Picasso** shocked the aesthetic taste at the turn of the 20th century. Drawing from African art and other unusual sources of inspiration, his multi-faceted images tapped into an earthy, chthonic feminine energy that redefined art. He had Pluto at 28 Taurus 37®, a little past the Algol degree, but pulled back into mid-point play through Jupiter at 23 Taurus 34 ® opposite Mercury at 24 Scorpio 15.

Other Algol Natives

Vincent Van Gogh, original, colorful, yet mentally unstable artist with a vision way ahead of his time, had Black Moon very close to the Lilith star — a double Lilith. He famously cut off his ear.

Rising to be the powerful President of the American Teamsters' Union from 1957 to 1971, labor leader **Jimmy Hoffa** had purported ties to the Mafia and organized crime. After serving limited prison time, he mysteriously disappeared in 1975, presumed murdered. He has become a popular icon, referred to in various artistic contexts. An exact Moon/Saturn conjunction with Algol closely squared Black Moon, Sun and Mercury in Aquarius. Perhaps he was beheaded?

"I have a dream!" **Reverend Dr. Martin Luther King** famously proclaimed shortly before his death. It was a dream many shared, black and white, as he carried a collective destiny with his North Node on Algol. His 1968 assassination did not dispel his power, as his name continues to be celebrated beyond the US national holiday in his honor.

Also born with North Node right on Algol at 26 Taurus, and opposite Jupiter at 24 Scorpio, **Stephen King** is a best-selling author of horror novels. He tapped another collective chord and gives the public a chance to confront the face of fear.

The Venus/Algol Connection

What do **Al Gore**, **Johnny Depp** and **Prince William** of England all have in common? Apart from being uncommonly good-looking men, they all have Venus conjunct the Lilith star Algol. Come to think of it, the Algol connection may be an integral part of their charm and charisma. Venus conjunct Algol gives them a rare connection to the feminine.

Perhaps it is in part the influence of this star that informs the environmental awareness and activism of politician **Al Gore**. With a name that sounds like the star, Al Gore has Venus conjunct Algol at 26 degrees, with Ceres, the ecology dwarf planet, nearby at 21 degrees. The conjunction is in a grand square with Chiron opposite at 25 Scorpio and Black Moon in Aquarius opposite Pluto/Saturn/Mars in Leo in the mid-range degrees. Lilith had different ideas for him than being U.S. President. His interest and research on global warming and climate change led to a book and documentary film, both titled, *An Inconvenient Truth*. The film, which he narrates, won two Academy Awards. Gore was awarded the

Nobel Peace Prize in 2007 for focusing the world's attention on this critical issue. Though there may be cosmic forces, like heightened solar flare activity, contributing to climate change, his educational work has helped set the collective agenda for the Pluto in Capricorn era.

Full-Bodied Lilith

Even while focusing on the various Lilith positions, we have seen that more than one of the factors of the Lilith signature are often woven intricately into a chart. Let's look at a few charts with a strong interwoven Lilith signature. Al Gore got us warmed up (globally), with his Lilith-charged grand cross. Let's look more 'Depply' at the charts of the last two men, Johnny Depp and Prince William, good examples of full-bodied Lilith-type men.

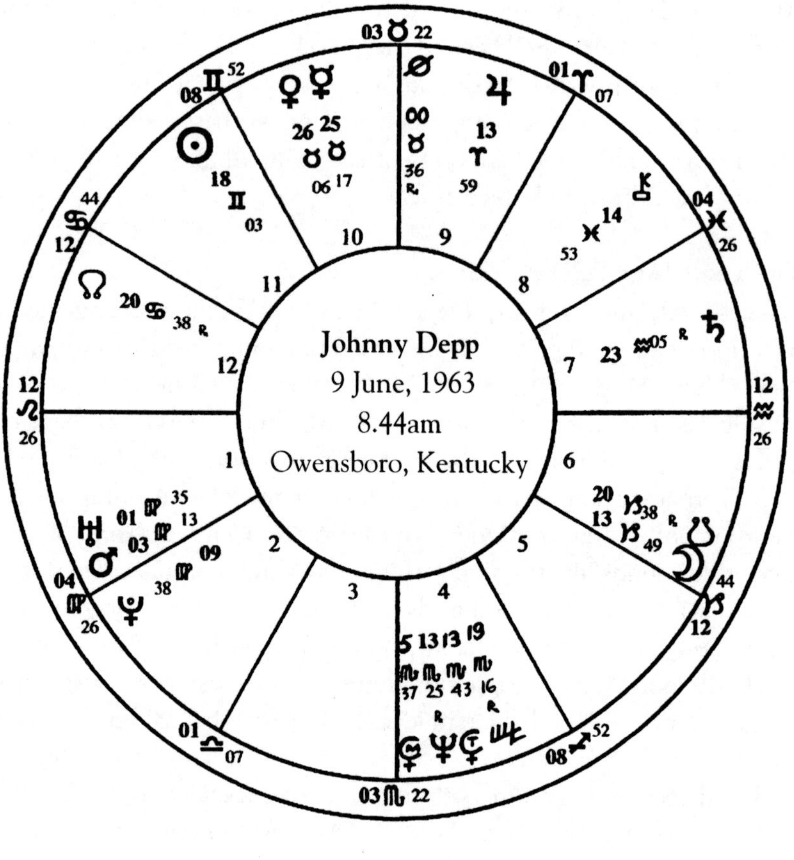

One of the highest paid actors in the world, **Johnny Depp** has created a roster of unique characters that often reveal a subtle feminine essence. He has Mercury and Venus conjunct at 25 Taurus. The full Lilith signature of this Algolian reveals Scorpionic undertones that we see in so many of his characters. Certainly Sun square Pluto accounts for quite a bit of that, but the Liliths push the dark energy to elusive and shadowy places that he explores in his special way that mysteriously reverberates on screen.

Whereas Bono has Dark Moon with Neptune in Scorpio, Depp has the others; both Black Moons and Asteroid Lilith accompany his Neptune. Particularly the Asteroid opposes his Mercury/Venus on Algol, reflecting his anti-Hollywood attitude and unusual film choices, and evoking further subtle currents of the feminine in his life and work. Neptune is in the same degree as true Black Moon, more than suggesting the potential for extremes in drug and alcohol use, as well as charisma and filmic genius. The Sabian symbol for 14 Scorpio reads: "Workers push a telephone line across forbidding ranges." Depp certainly scaled a number of unusual peaks and valleys. Dark Moon is right on his Midheaven at the early edge of Taurus, opposing mean Black Moon. The Taurus/Scorpio polarity is Lilith's territory in this chart, a private and secreted well of energy that fuels his star-power with legendary ripple effects.

With his royal heritage and mother's tragic death, it remains to be seen how **Prince William** expresses this deep connection to feminine power. He has an exact Chiron/Venus/Algol conjunction along with an otherwise strong Lilith signature. His North Node is aligned with Sirius, the Star of Isis, another strongly feminine star of destiny. There was an eclipse at high noon on Summer Solstice, 1982. This Prince charming was born nine hours later, as the sun was setting and the Black Moon rising. Very close to his late Sagittarius Ascendant, and less than a degree apart, the true Black Moon is in Sagittarius with the mean Black Moon just across the Unicorn cusp into Capricorn. That cusp is more and more intriguing. Taking a look at the Sabian symbols, using Dane Rudhyar's version, we find two leadership images:

30 Sagittarius	The Pope is holding audience in a hall of the Vatican.
1 Capricorn	Indian Chief claims power from the assembled tribe.

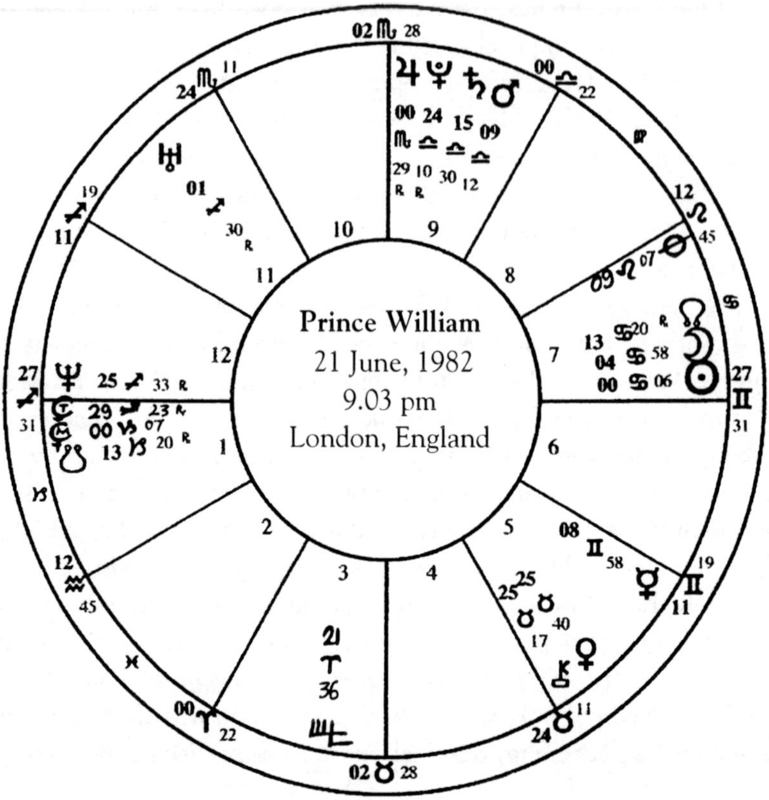

These are certainly apt images for a prince and possible once and future king. Later we will look at some characters who are both spiritual and temporal leaders of their people. This is the original concept of the divine right of kings, as the embodiment of power that is God or Goddess-given.

In addition, these Black Moons are opposite his natal Sun/Moon union, fresh from being eclipsed. This is mythic stuff. The mean Black Moon is within one minute of precise opposition with the Sun, just a few minutes into Cancer. The North Node is nearby, aligned with Sirius. This is "Sirius" stuff for the ruling Moon in Cancer. Oppositions imply relationship, further indicated by the Sun/Moon on the descendant. For him, this means not only personal relationships (Moon signifying family and mother), but his relationship to his nation and the world. He was fifteen when his mother, Princess Diana, the Queen of Hearts, died in a car crash, effectively eclipsed. Her Sun was also in Cancer, conjunct Asteroid Lilith. His father, Prince Charles, is first in line to the English throne; William is second. It is early yet to tell how he will live this powerful energy, how he will carry the royal legacy forward into this new millennium.

With Dark Moon in Leo, he is cosmically called to kingship, not for his own glory, but for the sake of the people or in a way that empowers others as well. Certainly he has had a sense of being special from day one. This position carries a strong Will, to be aligned with divine will rather than self will. This is challenging as the whole world will watch him deal with the expectations of others of his own self expression. Asteroid Lilith in Aries can be a bit headstrong, especially opposite a Saturn/Pluto conjunction. Again, this suggests learning how to find the best balance between his own desires and what others want of him. He is willing to blaze a new trail. Like Johnny Depp, he has Black Moon conjunct Neptune, but in Sagittarius. This is a strong influence on his Ascendant and could suggest self sacrifice to a cause. His birth as a prince is such, but with three Liliths in Fire he will find his own original way to live the role, perhaps through the particular personal causes he takes on, or even via the arts. The Venus/Chiron conjunction on Algol also suggests the arts may play a role, certainly relationships with women. And also suggests the call to honor the feminine. Lady Diana had her Venus conjunct Algol as well. The death of his mother was not only a personal grief but a collective one. We will see what the Prince's personal grief and the memory of his mother continues to mean through how he lives his life and what he gives to the world.

Lili Boulanger and her Asteroid

Marie-Juliette "Lili" Boulanger was the young French composer for whom Asteroid Lilith was named. Her chart lives up to the name, with an active Lilith signature beyond the Asteroid at the end of Libra sextile her Sun. Her mother was a Russian princess. Her father, a professor at the Paris Conservatory, died in her arms when she was six. Lili's Sagittarian Moon was conjunct the Black Moon Lilith and opposite both Dark Moon Lilith and Pluto in Gemini. That is a very deep and dark opposition. Her works, inspired by myth, poetry and psalms, were largely impacted by the lingering grief from her father's death.

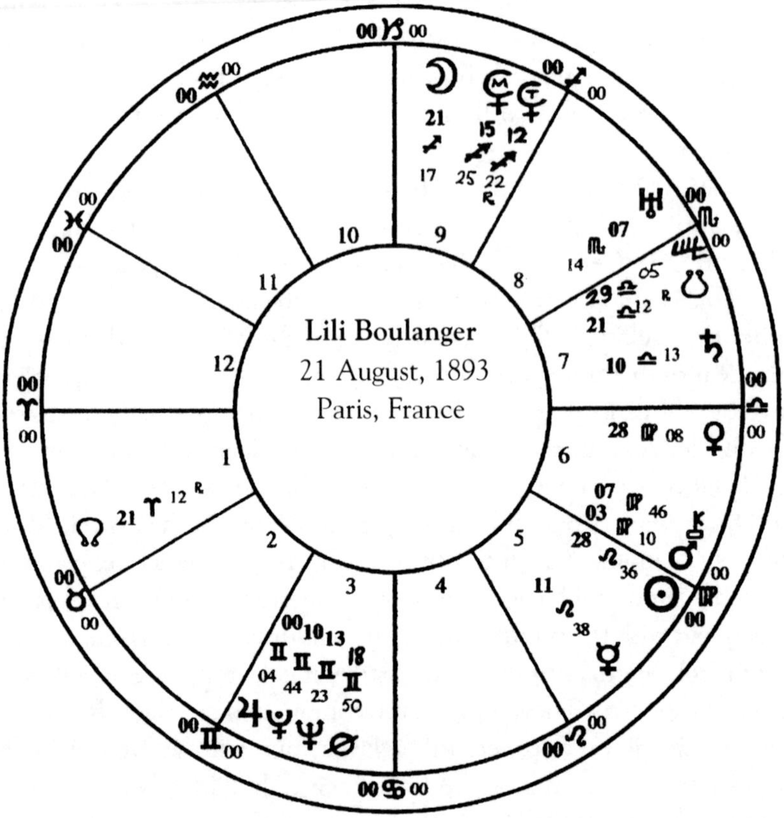

This young musical prodigy was skilled on piano, violin, organ, cello and harp by her teens. At age 19, Lili became the first woman to win the Prix de Rome for her cantata *Faust et Helene*. Of frail health, she died of Crohn's disease at age 24, leaving an innovative musical legacy, including an evocative, Lilith-sounding piece called *Les Sirenes*. Aware of her approaching death, she wrote her masterwork, an extraordinary musical translation of Psalm 130, *Du Fond de L'Abime*, "Out of the depths have I cried unto Thee, O Lord." Her sister, Nadia, initially her teacher, cared for her and was dedicated to Lili's work. After the death of her sister, she became the most influential music teacher of the 20th century and the first female conductor of several major international orchestras.

The **Asteroid Lilith discovery chart** has an airy Aquarian Sun and Gemini Moon, yet a strong watery Piscean flavor with a close Mercury/Jupiter/Venus conjunction early in the sign and Uranus later

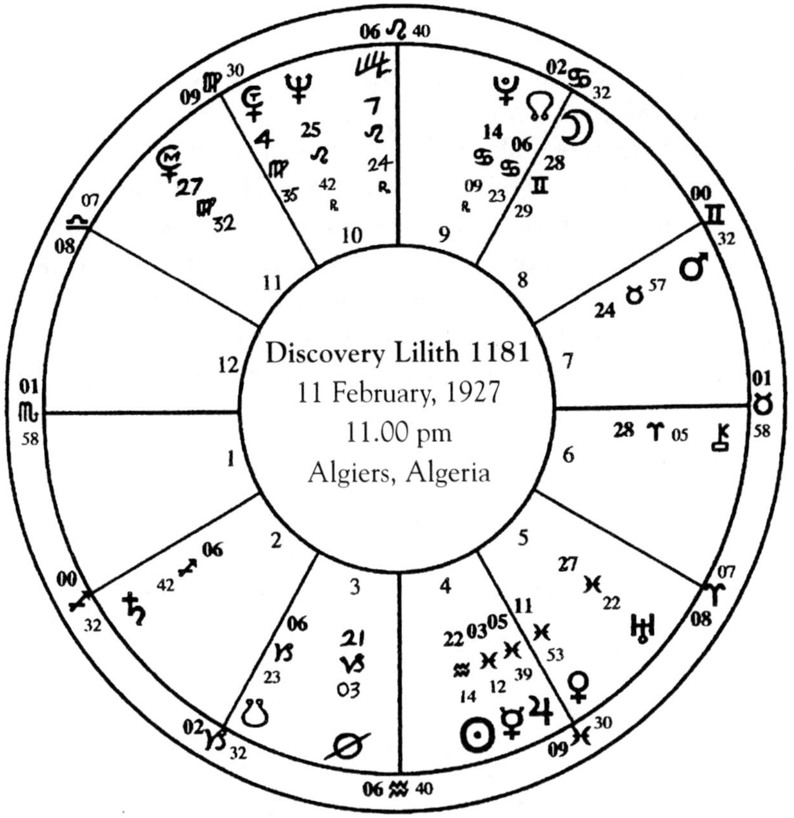

on. Jupiter is a ruler of Pisces and Venus is exalted there, empowering the trio, with an extra power punch from true Black Moon opposing from Virgo. At the far end of Virgo, mean Black Moon is opposite Uranus and also squares the Moon. The Black Moon is in on the action, supporting this entrance of Asteroid Lilith into our collective consciousness. The Dark Moon in Capricorn squares Chiron in Aries and becomes the hub of a yod by making quincunxes with the Gemini Moon and Neptune in Leo. One purpose of this asteroid, then, is to bridge worlds, through spiritual or creative expression and a sensitivity to subtle energy fields. The several Pisces planets and the Leonine Neptune love the arts. And artists love Lilith, as we have seen. The Asteroid 1181 itself is at the 8th degree of Leo, again showing how Lilith is to be expressed. Artists are fascinated and encouraged by Lilith. We see ourselves in our creations and in the mirror of life as we live it. The highest arts are living and loving. This placement also coincides with Lili Boulanger's Ceres/Mercury conjunction. The Gemini Sun of the discovery chart is conjunct her Dark Moon and directly opposite her Moon/Black Moons.

The Dark Moon also makes a subtle grand trine in earth signs with Mars in Taurus and Black Moon in Virgo. This asteroid participates in the communion with anima mundi, with Gaia. The Moon's nodes reinforce the strength of Earth and Water, with Capricorn at the tail and Cancer at the head. The Sabian symbol for the North Node gives a clue as to the meaning of the asteroid's presence on the stage of life: "In a moonlit fairy glade two little elves are dancing," reinforcing the Lilith connection to the realm of Faerie.

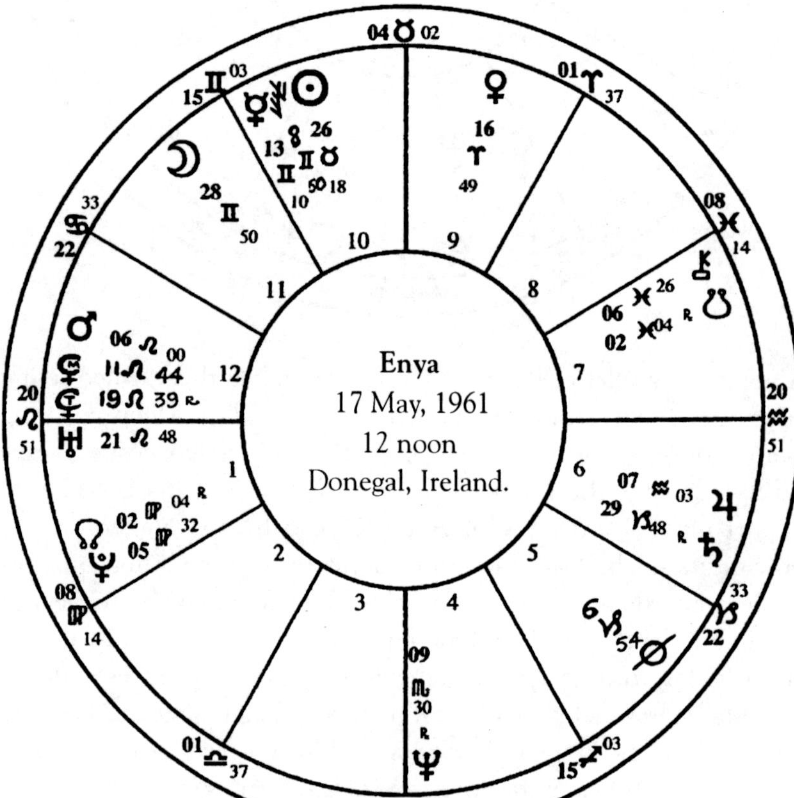

Music from the Heart of Lilith

One of Ireland's best-known musicians, award-winning singer-composer **Enya** (nee Eithne Patricia Ni Bhraonain) is one of the biggest selling female artists in history. Her evocative presence, voice and music create an ethereal, other-worldly, heart-opening effect. Enya has a strong Lilith signature. In addition to an exact Sun-Algol conjunction, she has true Black Moon on her Leo Ascendant with Uranus (at 19, 20 and 21 degrees) and mean Black Moon earlier in Leo conjunct Mars and opposite Jupiter. She is a Royal High Priestess. Her Dark Moon in Capricorn is in the sign of the standing stones and elemental faerie folk. Her Mercury/ Asteroid Lilith conjunction in Gemini articulates themes of the cosmic feminine and is demonstrated in the triple group identity (she collaborates with Nicky and Roma Ryan) that makes up the musical phenomenon that she gives her name to. She has stretched the world music scene, making best-selling music with a spiritual tone. She keeps a very private life.

Lilith in Fiction and Diaries

Sensuality is a secret power in my body.

Born the same decade as Frida Kahlo, French fiction writer **Anais Nin** is especially known for her provocative Diaries, which give some real-life background to her erotic, psychologically penetrating and surreal scenarios of relationship, love and desire. It is hard to draw a clear line between fact and fiction, even in her Diaries, as Moon opposite Neptune confuses hard reality with the imagined. Black Moon and Asteroid Lilith conjunct the Moon in Capricorn fall to the Nadir like a plumb line dropped down from the Dark Moon and Neptune in Cancer at the top of the chart. The various Liliths in opposition to each other bring extra layers of complexity to relationships. She uses imagery and elusive dream-like sequences in her writing to explore the anxieties and confusions that arise in sexual experience and the search for love. Her fiction and prose poems were very original, creating a new genre, which Black Moon in Capricorns are particularly capable of doing. *The Diaries of Anais Nin*, in several volumes spanning 1931-1974, were similarly innovative, delivered in a clearly feminine voice.

Conjunct her Moon at the nadir, Black Moon suggests deeply

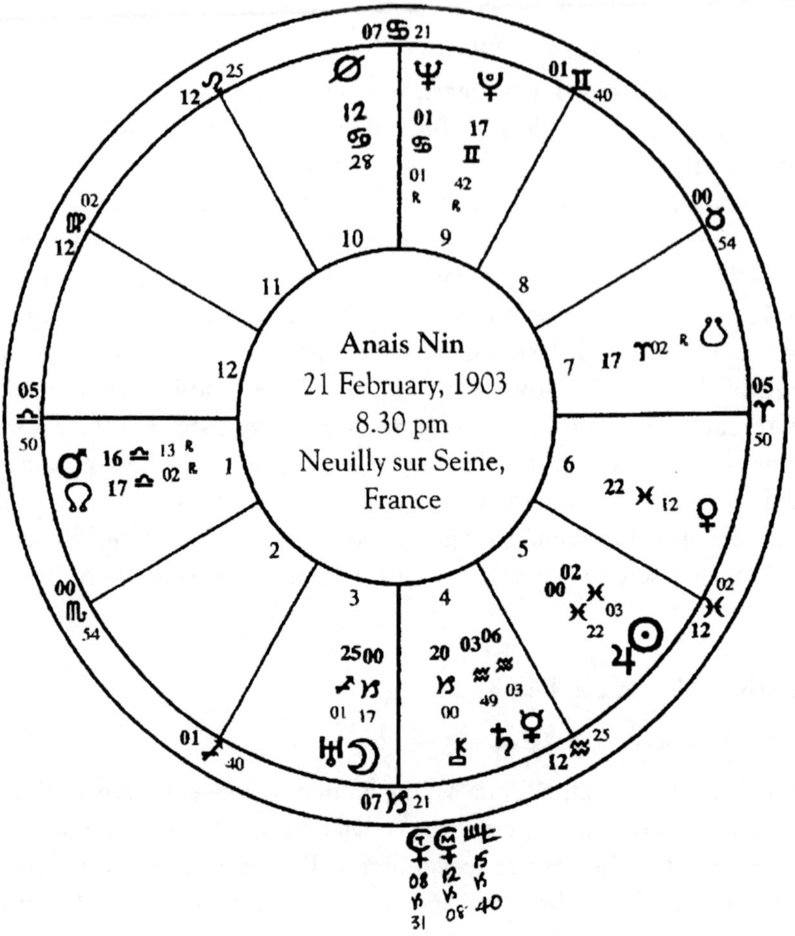

disturbing family and home issues. She wrote of incest with her father, Cuban musician Joaquin Nin, later in life. He had abandoned the family when she was eleven. She lived in France and the US, had husbands in New York and California. Numerous lovers, men and some women, included writer Henry Miller and his wife, as well as psychologist Otto Rank. She worked as an analyst for some time and studied astrology. "I once loved astrology but some fatalistic predictions harmed me (I would die at stillbirth, I would never achieve recognition) and I turned away from it. The symbolism still fascinates me" [note to author].

Her first publication was *D.H. Lawrence: An Unprofessional Study*. Interestingly, Lawrence had Black Moon in Capricorn as well. Nin was a popular lecturer in the academic world in the 1970s, with circles of women gathered around her, but she was not interested in feminist politics. Asteroid Lilith presented its unconventional leanings in her life style and in her work, each feeding the other. All of her Lilith positions square North-Node/Mars (retrograde) in Libra near her Ascendant.

A character named Lilith appears in several of her stories. In *The Voice*, Lilith is a kind of alter ego, a little girl self engaged in psychological analysis with a father figure and in dialogue with her woman self. Says this fictional Lilith, "I feel I have created this personage and that I sit outside of her, lamenting because they are worshipping a sort of image… fear compels me to continue acting." Lilith finally sees the pattern that swings back and forth from neediness to control (Cancer-Capricorn), resolves it and can join with the woman for a whole self.

Anais Nin articulates an essential theme of Lilith: the neurotic dimension that undermines wholesome living, denies and frustrates emotional health; but, when attended to, offers soul growth through responsibility to the greater whole. "I have made myself personally responsible for the fate of every human being who has come my way."

Lilith Starlets

The Lilith charisma can be recognized in some memorable stars of the silver screen, who lived in the aura of glamour.

Marvelous Marilyn Monroe

I have too many fantasies to be a housewife. I guess I am a fantasy.

Norma Jean Mortenson carried true Black Moon on her Leo Ascendant. Her persona glows with solar radiance and Lilith's seductive charm. Neptune adds more than a little of its own glamour conjunct the mean Black Moon later in Leo, still in her 1st house. Thus she became Marilyn Monroe, Playboy's Number One sex star of the 20th century. Her extraordinarily magnetic persona had an ethereal beauty, a radiance that raised her to icon status. She became a symbol for something greater than herself. "If I'm going to be a symbol of something, I'd rather have it sex than some other things we've got symbols of," she once said. Yet she found it a heavy load to carry, often feeling fragile and misunderstood. The circumstances surrounding her death by drug overdose are still in

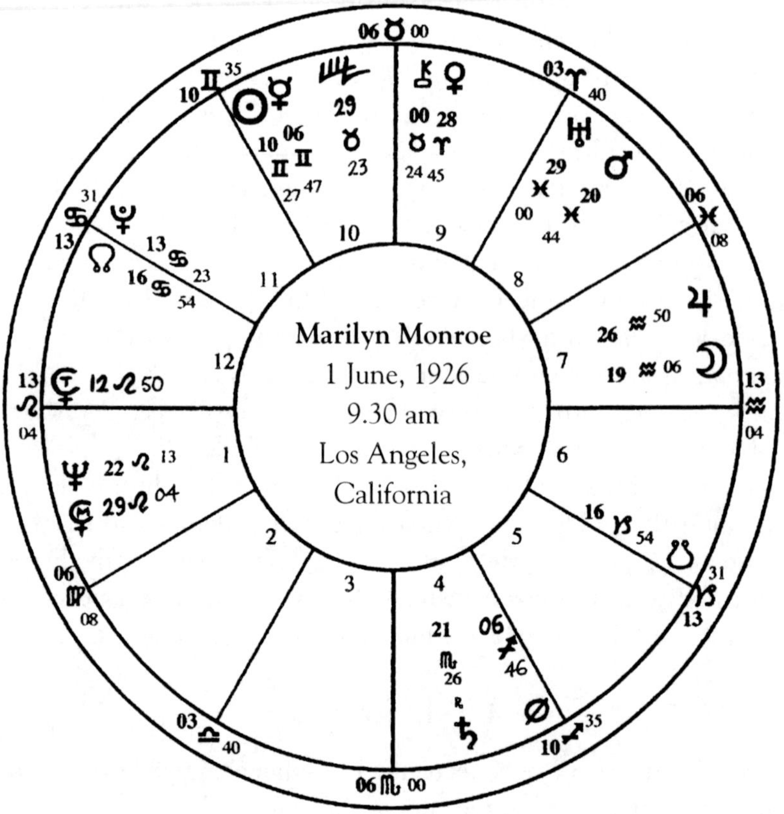

question.

The mean Black Moon/Neptune in Leo opposes her Moon/Jupiter conjunction in Aquarius, a big load for the Moon to carry. Asteroid Lilith at the end of Taurus was conjunct the Lilith star Algol and square mean Black Moon at the end of Leo. The Dark Moon was opposite her Gemini Sun/Mercury. Those are strong, interwoven Lilith placements.

When her mentally unstable mother (Moon opposite Neptune) was "put away," the child bounced around between foster homes, family friends and orphanages until she was sixteen, when she married the boy next to one of those doors. While he was away at war in the South Pacific, she was discovered and became a model. The marriage dissolved when her husband returned in 1946 and objected to her career. Asteroid Lilith in her 10th house was not going to give it up for marriage. Never having belonged anywhere, she now belonged to the public. That very year she made her national magazine debut on the cover of *Family Circle*. In August of that same year she signed with Twentieth Century Fox. Her progressed Ascendant had reached her mean Black Moon and transiting Mercury, Mars and Pluto were conjunct her Leo Lilith Ascendant. The movie *Niagara* made her a star in 1953.

The asteroid placement also indicates her ambition to be more than a sex symbol. Serious about acting, she went to New York City in 1955 to study with Lee Strasberg at The Actor's Studio and formed her own production company in 1956. She had the rare creative talent that often comes with Black Moon in Leo, in both drama and comedy. Becoming an actress and pursuing that talent was a Leo quest for self. Through that personal process she was able to express something so quintessential from inside herself, an indefinable magic and charisma that reached beyond the screen and evoked a feeling of pure womanhood. Such deep inner journeys no doubt evoked Lilithian undercurrent of resistance, of self-questioning or self-denial and emotional vulnerability, all showing through her characters.

With Dark Moon opposite her Sun, relationships were not easy. She was married to baseball star Joe DiMaggio and playwright Arthur Miller and reportedly had a liaison with John Kennedy, among possible other political figures. Miller wrote the role of Roslyn Taylor in *The Misfits* for Marilyn. It was her last film and also the last one Clark Gable made. The social misfit Asteroid Lilith was at the far edge of Taurus in the 10th house, square her mean Black Moon. This earthy placement added to the sensuality that made her a sex star: "Sex is part of nature. I go along with nature." Yet the challenge of living it in society often set her apart. Men would avoid her for fear of offending their wives, and "the ladies would gang up in a corner and discuss my dangerous character."

The Great Greta Garbo

> *The story of my life is about back entrances, side doors, secret elevators and other ways of getting in and out of places....*

The "Divine" Garbo, the "Sarah Bernhardt of Films," had mean Black Moon in Aries and true Black Moon in early Taurus. Asteroid Lilith was 16 Virgo, widely conjunct the Sun. Dark Moon, strongly placed conjunct

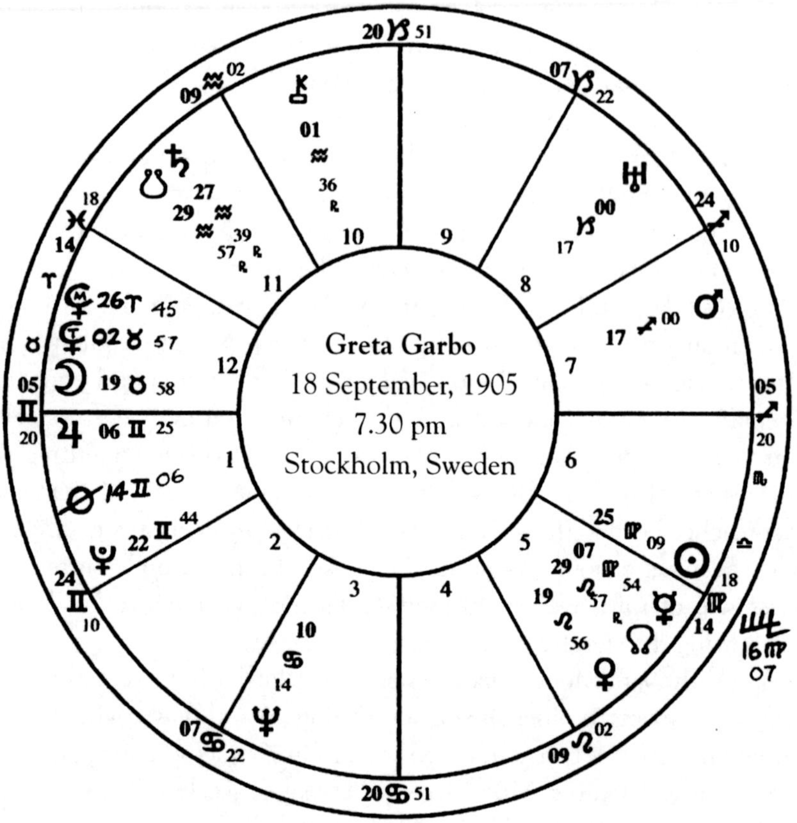

Jupiter on her Gemini Ascendant, is the dark light behind her persona. For Monroe it was the Black Moon Ascendant; for Garbo the Dark Moon Ascendant.

Interestingly, the connections between the charts of Greta Garbo (GG) and Marilyn Monroe (MM) were very strong, suggesting a kind of passing of the baton. GG's Jupiter/Dark Moon Ascendant was conjunct MM's Sun/Mercury. GG's Venus/North Node conjunction encompasses MM's Ascendant/Neptune and two Black Moon placements. MM's true Black Moon conjunct GG's North Node to the degree. GG's Black Moon placements straddle the Aries-Taurus cusp with MM's Venus/Chiron. GG's Saturn/South Node were conjunct MM's Jupiter. There were truly some resonances, particularly including the Liliths, Venus and Jupiter.

Greta was given the name Garbo, meaning "spirit" in Swedish, by Martin Stiller, a major figure in the Swedish film industry, who noticed her in the Drama School of the Royal Theater in Stockholm. He saw that elusive "something" and took her with him to Hollywood in 1925 when MGM invited him over. Not initially interested in Garbo, who remained "unseen," like the Dark Moon, for a short time, MGM eventually signed her on and dismissed him. He died two years after returning to Sweden, a shock to her, cutting more ties to her homeland, as her father had died when she was fourteen and her sister during Garbo's first year in the US.

With the invisible Dark Moon on her Ascendant coming through her persona, and the Black Moon with the exalted Taurus Moon in the reclusive 12th house, she was a very private person, a la her famous line, "I want to be left alone" from the movie, *Grand Hotel*. Dark Moon in the first house naturally flavors the persona and the influence of early life on self-consciousness and self-projection. The personality carries a larger-than-life aura. In the first house, Dark Moon creates "an inexhaustible drive for personal identity and a recognition this one feels strangely denied of," wrote Dark Moon researcher Delphine Jay. "Self-projection is necessarily more impersonal and the major talents are expressed." With Lilith's seductive mystery, she became a major sex symbol, exuding an aura of sensuality with a hint of otherworldliness with impeccable Virgo earthiness.

With the Dark Moon extrasensory awareness, the 12th house sensitivity, and strong mutable signs, she would have had a heightened sense of what was going on around her that could be distracting. "I am always nervous and restless when I am making a picture… I tremble always, all over," she revealed in a rare interview with Ruth Biery in 1928 for *Photoplay Magazine*. While making her scenes, she would have no one watching, creating a kind of 12th house alchemical laboratory to be able to let emotion come through purely. "If I am by myself my face will do things I cannot do with it otherwise." Her haunting expressions spoke beyond words, inviting the viewer to imagine what is left unspoken. With Asteroid Lilith conjunct her Virgo Sun, she refused to live up to social expectations of a movie star. Garbo left the set promptly at 5.00pm daily, signed no autographs, allowed no interviews, attended but one premiere of her many movies, answered none of her 90,000 fan letters per week (80% from women). Even the studio did not have her home phone number. Only seven photographers were officially authorized to take portraits. She sometimes disguised herself as "Miss Harriet Brown."

Her private life was kept very private, though smoky rumors of liaisons with her leading men and beautiful women piqued the public's interest. She almost married one favorite leading man, John Gilbert, but left him waiting at the altar. "I have never had an impulse to go to the altar. I am a difficult person to lead" — an essential Lilith statement, especially with Black Moon in Aries. Yet she was loyal enough to Gilbert to insist upon firing Lawrence Olivier from her film *Queen Christina*, so that Gilbert could co-star and revive his career. He did not move as well from silent film to sound as she did.

Such a stance reflected her iron fist in velvet glove will, an Aries Black Moon trait, that allowed her to maintain artistic control and get her way when she wanted it. She was the most highly paid woman in the US at the height of her stardom, the 1930s decade. A true Virgo, she followed a healthy diet, though she did smoke (Gemini seems to be a smoker's sign) and liked her cocktails. "Gimme a visky with a ginger ale on the side — and don't be stinchy, baby" was her first speaking line, in the 1930 movie *Anna Christy*. In 1941 she took a break during the war. Afterwards, an attempted project failed and she never went back to films. What kind of regrets she may have had for an abrupt retirement, we can only guess. She lived quietly for almost fifty years in a luxurious apartment in New York City, collecting art and traveling. She died on her Uranus return.

One of her best friends, Jane Gunther, experienced her otherworldly Lilith nature this way: "She has a poetic magic, so difficult to describe, and all one knows is that one wants this in one's life."

Glamorous Gloria Swanson

> *I have decided that when I am a star, I will be every inch and every moment a star.*

A classic example of Lilith's flashy side in Leo, Gloria Swanson flaunted her movie stardom and lived it to the hilt, spending lavishly with several luxurious homes. She brought the word "glamour" into popular usage and helped invent the definition of "movie star." Born just after midnight, she had mean Black Moon in Leo, as did Marilyn Monroe, as well as Dark Moon. Swanson's true Black Moon was in late Cancer with Mars.

She liked men and married six of them, including a French marquis. She had an affair with Joseph Kennedy (father of JFK). With Asteroid Lilith conjunct her Venus in Aquarius, she was an unconventional, free-thinking woman. Her career was at a peak in the 1920s, but she played a memorable role in 1949 as Norma Desmond in *Sunset Boulevard* and as herself in the 1975 *Airport*. She earned several Oscar nominations and was the first actress to have her own talk show. Passionate about the health food movement, she developed an organic cosmetics company. At the age of eighty-one, she published a well-received autobiography.

Haunting Jean Harlow

> *Underwear makes me uncomfortable and besides, my parts have to breathe.*

Jean Harlow, nee Harlean Carpenter, made an indelible mark on the silver screen in her very short life; she died at the age of twenty-six. A Dark Moon lady, like Garbo, "Platinum Blond" Harlow was a smoky, charismatic Pisces with Sun closely conjunct the Dark Moon, thus her "laughing vamp" image. Pisces Dark Moon is extra-sensitive to energy fields. It couldn't have been healthy for her in the Hollywood world. This conjunction was part of a grand trine in Water signs, formed by Neptune in Cancer and Jupiter/South Node/True Black Moon in Scorpio. That Black Moon complex produced a deep undercurrent with self-defeating compulsions. Her Pisces-Neptune signature being strong, she was alcoholic and died from liver failure. "I'm drinking only because I have to have something to keep me going," she said. Her life was never normal. She ran away from home at age sixteen and got her start in movies in Howard Hughes's epic *Hell's Angels* in 1930. She played well with Clark Gable, making six movies with him. In between movies she ate a lot, gained weight and would have to diet before the next picture.

The mean Black Moon was conjunct Asteroid Lilith in Sagittarius. She had a "mouth" and a wry sense of humor. "When you lie down with dogs, you get up with fleas." Fiery, her Aries Moon and Venus got a little feisty at times. Venus, especially, worked with her Sagittarian Lilith factors to make such anti-star comments as, "I like to wake up in the morning feeling like a new man," and "Must I always wear a low-cut dress to be important?"

She was not your every day, garden variety Hollywood actress.

She could admit, "I'm not a great actress and I never thought I was. But I happen to have something the public likes" — her seductive Dark Moon aura.

Supergiant Star and Master Actor

> *I beg you to believe my reputation. I am a constant soldier, a some time poet and I will be King.*

Those introductory lines from film debut in *The Lion in Winter* (with Peter O'Toole and Katherine Hepburn), were prophetic for Welsh actor **Anthony Hopkins**, who has become one of the finest of our time. All four Liliths actively represented at the time of his birth, his Dark Moon is conjunct Algol, suggesting a deep personal engagement with some compelling and fearsome collective issues. His 1991 Academy Award

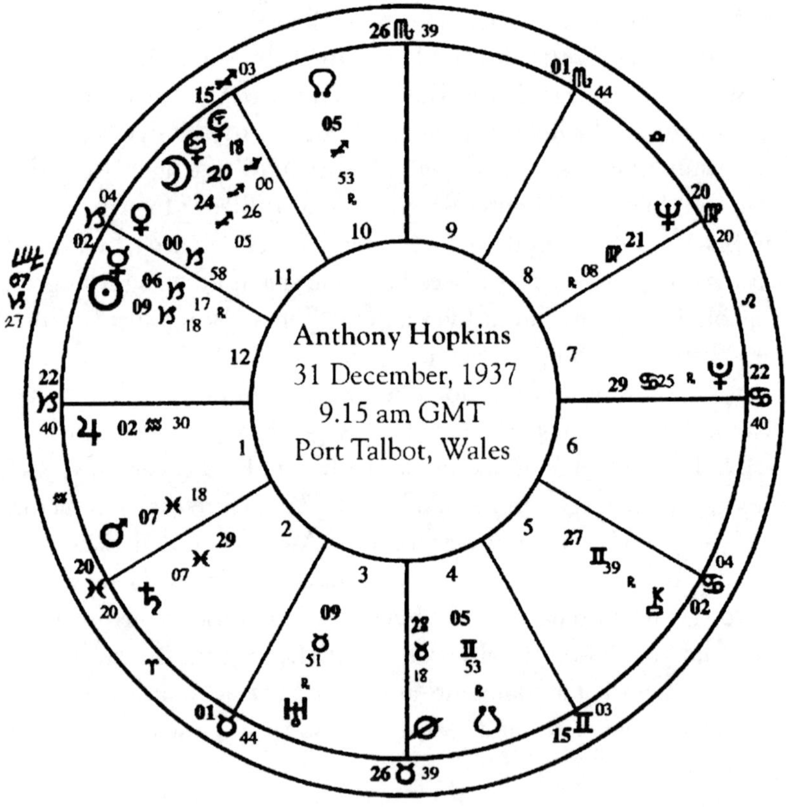

winning role, serial killer cannibal Hannibal Lektor, caught the public's attention, requiring a sequel and a prequel. He is not someone you would want to look in that Eye. He has collected numerous other awards and nominations.

Asteroid Lilith is closely conjunct both Sun, Venus and Mercury retrograde, all in Capricorn. As a youth, he did not fit in well, being both dyslexic and a loner, more interested in art than studies. He is a hard-working actor, preparing rigorously for his roles. His Black Moon in Sagittarius is closely conjunct his Moon, that most difficult of conjunctions. This Sagittarian flavor shows in *The World's Fastest Indian*, in which he plays Australian legend Burt Monro, an aging Aussie loner who rebuilds race cars and competes, reportedly the actor's favorite role. Now a US citizen, he lives in California with his third wife. The Sagittarius Moon/Black Moon conjunction is enough to suggest early and continuing family issues, but it is only one hub in an unusual and closely knit grand cross, composed of Saturn in Pisces across from Neptune in Virgo, and Chiron in Gemini. His skills are rare and highly nuanced. Recovered from severe problems with alcoholism, he is active in philanthropic causes, and has spoken for whales as an active member of the environmental activist organization Greenpeace. He released a love song called *Distant Star* that reached up in the music charts. Perhaps it is channeled from Algol. [Listen to it on www.youtube.com.]

World Leaders

The following men have very strong Lilith signatures, connecting them to the cosmic feminine at a profound level. As leaders of their people, both spiritual and temporal, they demonstrate the ideal potential to embody the spiritual in the mundane.

Catholic Pope

The only Polish Pope and the first non-Italian Pope since the early 16th century, **Pope John-Paul II** (ne Karol Jozef Wojtyla) served from 1978-2005, the second longest pontificate in modern times. The Moon in early Gemini was just pushing away from the Algol/Sun conjunction. His feminine astro-signature was largely enhanced by an exact Venus conjunction with the Dark Moon, along with South Node, Ceres and

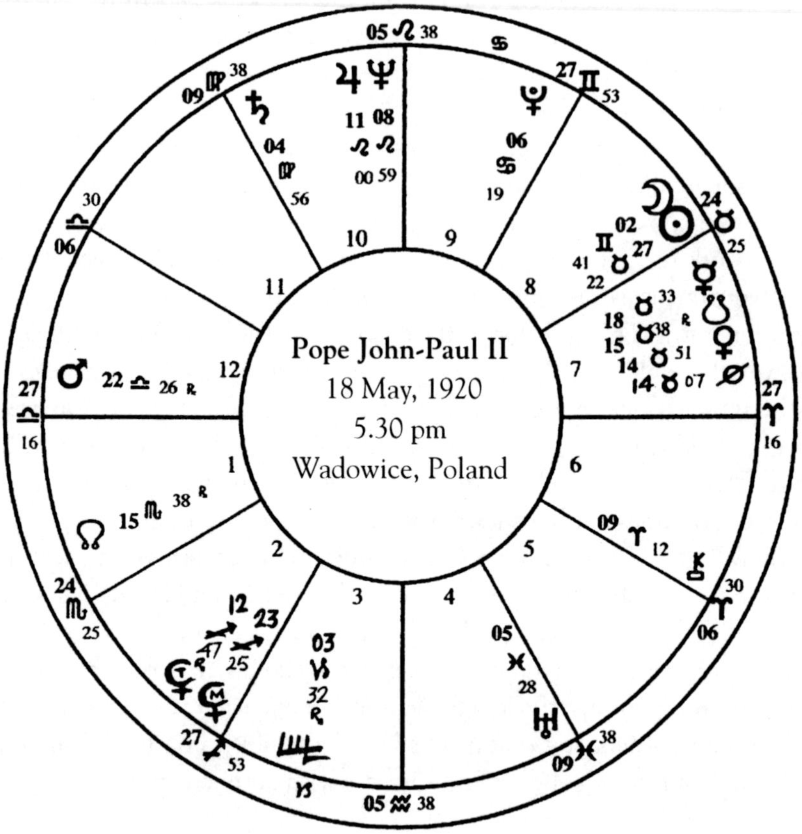

Mercury all closely bound in Taurus. With Venus in its ruling sign, this conjunction stimulated deep, sometimes darkly held issues in relation to the feminine.

His natal Black Moon was Sagittarius, a sign most often associated with a pontiff. His election at 5.15pm on October 16, 1978 took place when the Dark Moon, exactly conjunct Eris, was on the Aries Ascendant — and his Chiron. His spiritual rule was not without controversy. At that time he was having a Jupiter return in Leo. The transiting Black Moon (mean and true) were flanking natal Jupiter/Neptune on his Midheaven with Chiron in Taurus squaring them. Chiron was closing in on his early stellium and, more exactly, Uranus was exactly on his North Node with Mars/Venus all in Scorpio opposite his Taurus planets.

Natally his Chiron was the hub of a T-square with Pluto in Cancer and Asteroid Lilith in Capricorn. He had a tricky time between conservative stances and innovative stands, making some bold moves yet holding a strong Church line on key social issues such as contraceptives, abortion and divorce.

This Pope was a life-long devotee of Mary, starting at his mother's death when he was eight. He created an institute for dialogue between Catholic theology and contemporary science. Statues of the Virgin stand in every campus of the institute world-wide. He was particularly devoted to the Black Madonna of Czestochowa. He believed that the Virgin of Fatima saved his life from an assassination attempt in 1981 on May 13, the anniversary of her first appearance in 1917. He made three significant Consecrations. In 1984 he consecrated the world to the Immaculate Heart of Mary. In 1999 he consecrated the Americas to Our Lady of Guadalupe and the Third Christian Millennium to Our Lady, auguring the importance of the feminine divine in the new era

> *To you, Mother of the human family and of the nations,*
> *we confidently entrust the whole of humanity, with its hopes and fears.*
> *Do not let it lack the light of true wisdom.*
> *Guide its steps in the way of peace…*

Tibetan Dalai Lama

His Holiness, the 14th Dalai Lama, Tenzin Gyatso, exiled spiritual and political leader of Tibet, is the fourteenth incarnation in an unbroken living spiritual lineage going back over six hundred years. The title *Dalai Lama* means "Ocean of Wisdom." The Black Moon, both mean and true positions, are appropriately and closely conjunct his Moon and Neptune in Virgo. In part, this reflects his spiritual heritage and embodiment of "compassion, forgiveness, tolerance, contentment and self-discipline" cited on his website as human values and secular ethics to which he is committed. Dark Moon is right there as well, all of these factors within 5 degrees, and opposition Saturn, the authority figure, in Pisces, at its best a compassionate and spiritual sign.

The Asteroid is in the same degree as his Sun, 13 Cancer, a potent indicator of his life path, to promote religious harmony among the various world's traditions, and as the free spokesperson for people of Tibet under Chinese rule. In exile, he made a dramatic escape from Tibet in 1959 to elude Chinese pressure and continue to lead his people from afar. As a result, he has become a global ambassador for Tibetan Buddhism and

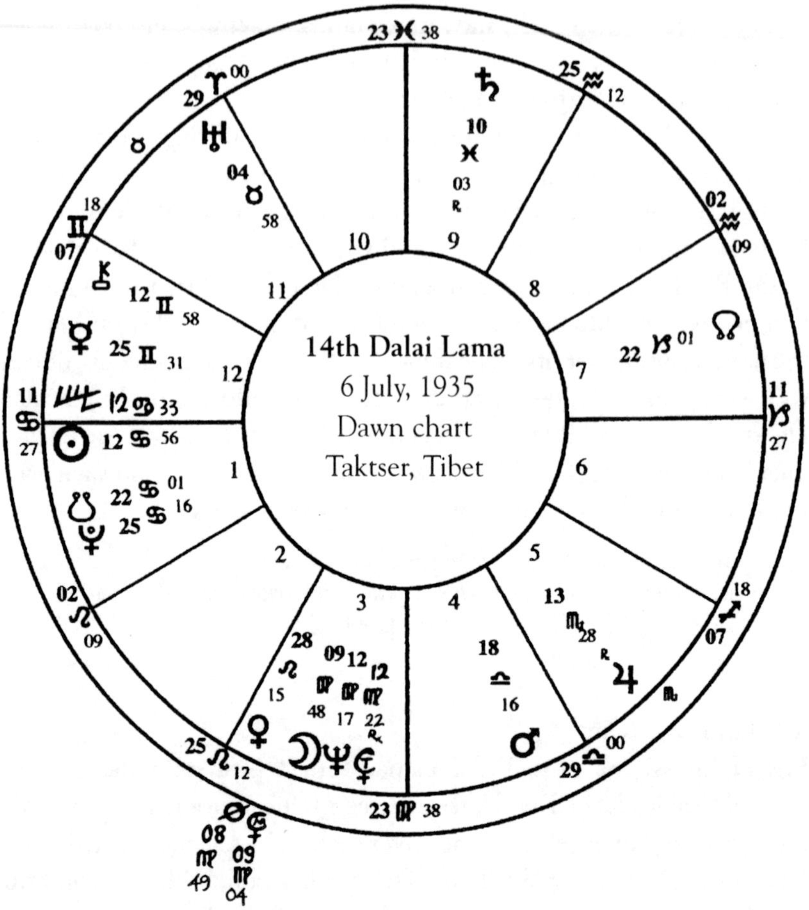

culture and seeks an integrated solution to the melding of Chinese and Tibetan cultures. He was awarded the Nobel Peace Prize in 1989, one among many honors and awards. It is significant that his Sun is the degree of the fixed star, Sirius, the Egyptian Star of Isis, another strong focus of the cosmic feminine. The Sun/Asteroid Lilith make a grand water trine with the Saturn in Pisces and Jupiter in Scorpio. Yet, as Saturnine and Siriusly serious his chart may be, he has an infectious sense of humor and has been known to sprinkle chuckles through interviews about weighty matters.

The Algol degree is not occupied by any obvious factor, but is squared by his Venus in Leo, aligned with the royal star Regulus, which marks the Heart of the Lion. Truly, His Holiness has the royal heart of a Tibetan Snow Lion.

Third Millennium Leader

Barack Obama, the 44th President of the United States, was a globally-celebrated leader at the moment of his election. Though a political rather than spiritual leader, he offered an uplifting message of hope that resonated with the spirit of the feminine divine in the new millennium. Like the Dalai Lama, Obama was born under the light of the Lion Heart star, an African lion in his case. With a Kenyan father and American mother, a childhood spent in Indonesia and Hawaii, and a Harvard education, this rare man broke racial barriers and created a vision of hope that rippled around the world. So why was I surprised when I saw how strong his Liliths are? Obama has an exact conjunction of true Black Moon with Mercury in Leo, making good use of Lilith's intellectual acuity. He was elected editor of the Harvard Law Review on his Saturn return. Not someone to be pigeon-holed, his Saturn is authorative in its own

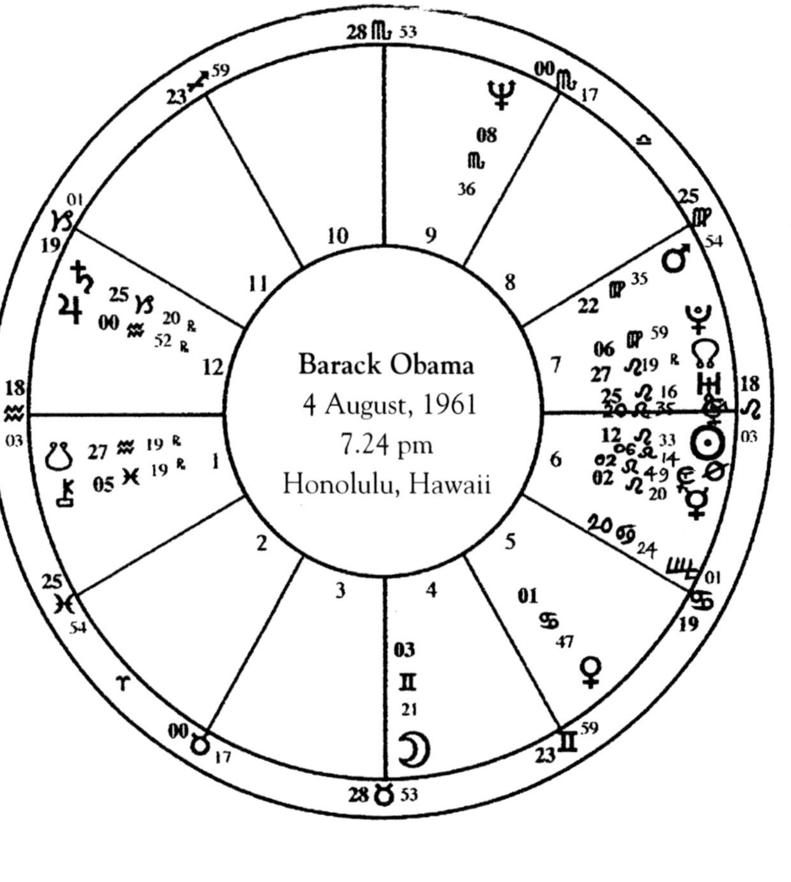

sign of conservative Capricorn, yet opposite the Asteroid Lilith in Cancer, close to the US Sun, and ready to reset the standards. But the real Lilith hub in his chart is his Sun, adding more Lilith in Leo radiance with Dark Waldemath Moon and mean Black Moon conjunct on either side. Mean Black Moon also conjuncts Uranus and the North Node, which is aligned with the star Regulus, Heart of the Lion and the Star of Kings.

Obama had a Jupiter return in January 2009, the month of his inauguration. On that day, January 20, the mean Black Moon was conjunct Pluto almost to the minute. Lilith has a lot to say to and through Barack Obama. His First Lady Michelle has a Moon/Venus conjunction on the early cusp of Pisces squaring mean Black Moon in Sagittarius. A Harvard-educated Capricorn lawyer herself, the dress she wore on election night was a shrewd Lilith power statement in red and black. Fashion is not the only statement she will make at her husband's side.

6

Interpreting Lilith

Development of the Feminine

The four aspects of Lilith in the chart offer personal access to the cosmic feminine. The Lilith complex takes us beyond the more familiar feminine dimensions of the Moon and Venus. We can start to work with Lilith in an astrological context as a developmental factor in relation to the feminine aspect of spirituality.

The Moon, Venus and the four Liliths, significantly supporting each other, are all important factors in feminine consciousness in both men and women. We are nurtured in the womb of the Great Mother and the personal mother. As newborns, we are still largely in touch with the transpersonal life source. Life experiences and relationships soon start to shape our self-identity. The Moon indicates our emotional foundation, how we are impressed by our mother's feelings and by the environment. Our automatic responses are set, like grooves in a record, by family patterns, particularly relationships with, and between, our mother and father. Object relations theory and other psychologies explore the creation of such basic self-identities and ego structures. The initial conditions and impressions may be reconstituted karmic situations that we carry with us into life. Lilith puts her two cents or more into this mix, largely through her Dark Moon influence.

As a child moves into puberty, the Mars and Venus factors wake up along with hormones. During our teen years, social, relational and sexual values are explored. In part, gender role expectations mold this development, inviting the participation of Asteroid Lilith, with strong images and messages coming from familial, social and cultural input. Sports for Mars and fashion for Venus are two major influences. Generally there is little educational support for development of emotional intelligence, social and aesthetic values, and self-esteem — all in the realm of Venus. Many studies have been done on the subtle repression and redirection of leadership and creativity, with girls especially. Ideally, education for teens should support the personal integration of the Mars and Venus factors: physical fitness (not only competitive sports) and sex education to develop Martian strength and confidence; and, for Venus, aesthetic values and social skills. Modern educators are now starting to address a broader range of intelligences — emotional, social, mathematical, artistic, etc. Astrologers know that not all women are from Venus nor men from Mars. We also know that each planet has its own intelligence.

Consider the Moon and Venus positions in your chart to think about your experience as a woman or with women. See how they are placed and related to each other. Venus trine or sextile the Moon suggests a smoother emotional ease with the feminine, with oneself and in relationship. A Moon/Venus conjunction may need to be explored to discern the difference between Moon "mothering" and Venus "lovering" to successfully combine them. Moon square Venus often indicates a tension between mother and daughter, with a difference in values and emotional satisfaction. A woman with this placement often seeks a different expression of her female self than the way shown by her mother. A man is likely to be in touch with his emotional and creative nature, and may well be happier in relationships with women who are different from his mother. The opposition of these two feminine factors highlights the dualities inherent in feminine expression and relationship. The Moon/Venus placements are primary considerations in our emotional development and impact our confidence in how we "do" Mars.

Lilith hovers inside all of this development, like a good and bad angel sitting on either shoulder. As Lilith denies specific outlets of satisfaction, she promotes emotional growth through an evolving understanding of the creative process. She pulls us into very deep spaces, at times disconcerting. She tugs our psychic strings in the most touchy places and private circumstances. It is impossible to fully describe the impact of Lilith moments, as their multi-layered richness in subjective details would mean little to someone else. Writer Margaret Drabble puts it so well in her novel, *The Waterfall*, "Fate was so sensitive to the details of my fears and desires that it had paid more attention to their underlying patterns than to their surface appearances."

When we place our four Liliths in relation to Moon and Venus, we get a more complicated and revelatory picture of our feminine side. Does one Lilith placement have a stronger connection to the Moon or Venus? Some charts show a dynamic interaction between these factors that brings the path of feminine consciousness to the fore in a compelling way. It may not mean smooth emotional seas, but rather an exploration of uncharted waters.

Knowing our intimate secrets, Lilith in all her guises drags out our most personal and subjective responses built from ego structures and seeks to unravel them, to free them into fuller realization and soul expression. Lilith lives on the edges of the highly personal and the ultimately impersonal. She directs her penetrating gaze beyond the generational issues and agendas of the outer planets that engage the collective consciousness. Lilith is a midwife of spiritual life and can be a great guide along that path. Perhaps she creates an aetheric pathway beyond the solar system — a cosmic birth canal. Rather than the personal Moon's mother womb, Lilith pushes us through to a cosmic birth at a whole other level.

Rabbi Lynn Gottlieb, author of *She Who Dwells Within: A Feminist Vision of a Renewed Judaism*, has revisioned Lilith made of stars and describes her as "the shadowy side of our power, the power that has not yet been tamed and put to use in the service of our greatest personal gifts." She agrees that when repressed or dominated, the Lilith aspect of our feminine selves reacts negatively, neurotic or enraged. When engaged consciously and appreciated for her fire, her creative power is expressed. "Tracking our Lilith nature is the key to our spiritual awakening," Gottlieb writes.

Lilith's Dark Mirror

She looked into the obsidian mirror held before her. The shiny black surface flickered in the torch light. A dark shadowed face was reflected back to her, haloed by rings in the grain of the gemstone. She smiled and nodded in recognition of her deep secret self, honed from many years of inner reaching, searching, living, feeling. The dark face smiled in return and so did the mysterious woman in front of her holding the mirror.

Why does Lilith come now, at this time in your life? You wonder, you have called her; you are ready for deeper levels. Lilith is not to be trifled with. Wherever Lilith lives in your chart, whenever she comes by transit, take a moment of reflection. Like Perseus in front of Medusa: wait, watch and listen. The dark mirror holds your image, your fear, your desire.

Lilith can be felt as an ally when you look in the dark mirror that reflects your fears, those that get in the way of moving to the next level inside yourself and therefore are activated in outer experiences, especially compelling in relationships.

I am your trial and realizer
Real eyes: Her
You have not seen yourself
Until you meet me
In the root of your tree
And its fruit

Lilith speaks in her own secret tongue. Interpreting Lilith is a highly personal, subjective and individual endeavor. She works specifically with intimate details of our lives, delving into our soul's desires. In our mundane lives, we tend to exile or demonize Lilith, as in her myths, and fail to invite her in. Generally, she's not someone you would want at a posh party. Like the thirteenth fairy, she places a curse on those who would deny her presence and her validity. This curse is lifted only when we take up the quest to be who we really are. Lilith placements involve a level of biological necessity. As we consider Lilith in the signs, we can ask, "What would be the impact of the 'uninvited' in each zodiac placement?" This leads us to consider the difficult, challenging, darker territory of each sign, the shadow side. As these dimensions are worked through, the creative promise comes alive.

Lilith is present in all the filters that channel spirit into matter. As creation is inherently sexual, Lilith touches directly into our sexuality. All Lilith placements reflect our primal, passionate sexual expression, our freedom or inhibitions in relation to our sexual instincts. Parental attitudes impressed at the time of our conception, throughout pregnancy and in our childhood relationships with mother and father all effect our sexuality at such a deep, primal level, we can hardly recognize them. The impact of social genderization and religious mores continues the job of defining our sexual judgments and choice of partners. Lilith work moves us into a deeper, truer (dare I say "purer"?) relationship to our sexuality, undifferentiated from our spirituality.

Rumi, the great 11th century Sufi mystic, honored the greatness of the human being, but spoke of "veils and obfuscations" that prevent us from recognizing the knowledge within ourselves. He generally identified these as "various preoccupations, worldly stratagems, and desires" (as translated by Thackston, Jr. in *Signs of the Unseen.*) We can add a whole laundry list of resistances, avoidances and blind spots. When we become aware of this inner wisdom, a wealth of creative discovery ensues.

Lilith in her multiple facets both weaves and unravels the sheaths that make up our various bodies, demonstrating in a remarkably intimate way the many layers that make us human. She holds to the truth that physical being is inherently spiritual, yet denser. She stands for the light in the darkness, dark though that light may be in the shadows of our beings and in the Universe. Dark matter is dark mother, ultimate ground of universal being, moving in the aethers. In Hindu philosophy, aether is the fifth element out of which the other four emerge to create the geo-cosmos.

Lilith was present in the original Garden, at the beginning of creation. Like a spark in the dark, innocent as the wisdom of primordial being, effervescent, the cosmic unfolds from her dark aetheric body. "I am the first and I am the last," declares the Feminine Divine in the Gnostic Gospels.

We have already seen, through some examples, how the various Liliths show up in life, and how they can be interwoven in a chart for a particularly strong Lilith signature. The various Lilith points operate on different levels but, like the same musical note in different octaves, they have the same vibration and reflect each other. Let's review the four Liliths and their octaves of experience. As you read, keep in mind your four Lilith placements and you will make connections to how she shows up in your life.

Approaching Lilith

The first three Liliths are intriguing as a mirror of the triple goddess; the star resolves the trinity into a further dimension. Demetra George suggests that the Asteroid, Dark Moon and Black Moon represent different phases of Lilith's mythology. In *Mysteries of the Dark Moon*, she offers a rich discussion of a Lilithian process of rejection, shadow work and reintegration. This is a useful approach that gives a revealing angle to your Liliths. Essentially tantric, Lilith in her several forms transforms subjective to spiritual. Her impersonal energy opens transparent areas of the mind, not clouded by the weight of collective judgment or limitations of ego identity. The four aspects vibrate at different frequencies, in chords and octaves, opening channels to clear and spiritualize the emotional body.

As we seek our Lilith storyline, we can remember the mythic history of Lilith as seductress, child killer, sexual initiator, primordial mother and lover, magical woman, dakini dancer. Lilith resonates with other dark goddesses or witches of mystery and power. Clearly associated with magic, she ultimately regenerates us through direct experiences of sacrifice, surrender, sexuality and mysticism. Consider her themes of autonomy, exile, extremism, and denial, the clouds of regret and betrayal. Black Moon and Dark Moon transits, in particular, can provoke subconscious dynamics accompanied by troubling ripple effects in our daily lives. She can be an ally on the soul's journey, but she can also be intransigent. Lilith in the chart reveals, often in a blunt, unkind way, issues that are the most pressing from a soul point of view. Watch for her visits in transits and follow the threads of destiny.

Asteroid Lilith

The "hard rock" **Asteroid Lilith** is most likely to beat its drum out there in the world, shouting that "the emperor has no clothes!" This personal Lilith is often projected outward, as the most obviously anti-social or anti-societal placement of the four Liliths. By natal house placement, it shows where we reject what is given; we confront, push against an issue or exile ourselves, most specifically in relation to genderized behavior, but also social norms. We are engaged or pointedly disengaged in the area of life represented by the house placement. The sign shows the style we use in social commentary, as we seek to integrate a compelling inner urge with outer circumstances. Planets in aspect reveal more specifics.

As a factor in personal relationships, Asteroid 1181 can reflect all the issues in the mythology of Lilith: rejection, betrayal, self-exile, ostracism, anger (repressed or overt), contention/consensus, seduction, issues of autonomy, manipulation and dominance. The Asteroid, as well as the other Liliths, has a tendency for relationship triangles or voyeurism, whether subtle or obvious.

The asteroid is not connected to the Moon as are the other two Liliths. It has an orbit of somewhat over four years and is the most embodied, a verified object with an official number. Asteroid Lilith is about repressed elements that seek, even demand, expression and integration, relating to issues of sexuality, anger, assertion and conflict resolution.

Dark and Black Moons

Dark and Black Moons, arguably the more mysterious and elusive Liliths, share moon connections and shadowy nuances. There have been persistent doubts about the existence of the Dark Moon and confusion about how to monitor the movement of the Black Moon. These two positions can carry heritage from ancestral and/or spiritual lineages, by tradition and by blood. One of my thoughts about the difference between these two is that the Dark Moon is the Lilith of altered states of consciousness and visionary substances to move us beyond mundane reality, while the Black Moon requires us to come to her as we essentially are. The Dark Moon is astral, the Black Moon aetheric.

The **Dark Moon** has the quickest orbital cycle, ten days through a sign, like a cloud passing across the Sun. Veiled in shadow, Dark Moon seems to indicate dusky astral shrouds that dull the inherent light of the soul.

Alex Gordon, author of *Nine Deadly Venoms*, writes of his encounters with warrior-priestess Lilith, who tells him of nine "venoms" that must be mastered: karma, parental genetics, childhood conditioning, fear, language, gravity, time, tribal conditioning and human breath. Similarly, many spiritual teachings warn against five or seven deadly sins. In Hinduism they are greed, anger, lust, attachment and vanity. In all these areas, we work through Lilith's abhorrence of limited and limiting conditional states. Our Lilith placements point out where we contend with some of these issues and in what ways, pulling away the shadowed layers that obscure the light. Perhaps we can think of the Dark Moon as connected to the astral layers of psychic gobbledy-gook, residue of the unremembered, the unredeemed or the unborn, distorted configurations in the Earth's matrix. Karmic tendencies interface with this "stuff" and glob on to particular strains that feel darkly familiar.

Dark Moon Lilith slides in-between times. She comes in during twilight, both evening and morning gray light. She haunts your sleepless nights. She slips into those early morning dreams that come after you've been awake, but go back to sleep. The shadow lands of the Dark and Black Moons refer to aspects of the shadow in the Jungian sense, both as unperfected aspects of self and as untapped potentials, often linked. These shadow areas cast their distorted shapes through various moral disturbances, from raging jealousies, manipulative cruelties and depressive regrets, to gossip and unkind thoughts. These are the types of things we don't want to acknowledge in ourselves, the sides of ourselves we might even be afraid of and try to ignore. Yet that very ignorance holds us back. Lifting a spiritual candle into the dark, we explore these dusty psychological corners so we can offer up the hidden potential of that specific space inside ourselves.

The Dark Moon as a separate, though suspiciously tenuous entity, is renegade, not connected as intimately as the Black Moon to the Earth-Moon system. Perhaps it is the psychic memory of a dead moon, a once-upon-a-time moon that is no longer physical, or maybe never was. This suggests the links to the land of Faerie (especially when spelled that way) that wind through the Dark Moon-scape. The dusky astral remnants of this ancient or ghost moon constrict the Earth's energy, like an oil spill or air pollution. Life on Earth breathes a lot easier when this layer is cleaned up. The elementals, devas of flora and fauna, work on this level, but need the cooperation of human beings, who carry the potentially highest level of spiritual Self-consciousness on this plane. Described by such words as sinister, denial, and sacrifice, the Dark Moon insists that we rise beyond the subjective experience and egoistic cravings toward an impersonal delivery of the content of our Dark Moon for the betterment of Self and others.

Black Moon is the most-often used Lilith position, with an agenda similar to the Dark Moon. Black Moon is an energy vortex, a primordial pathway into incarnation with an energy like a diamond-sharp sword of truth. Its orbital cycle of eight years and ten months, coordinates with the Moon's Nodes, being half a nodal cycle. Like the Nodes, Black Moon is related to karmic imprints and our "calling" into this life. The nodes indicate eclipses, moments when the light is turned off and back on with an altered (or altared) manifestation. Similarly, the Black Moon shuts doors and opens only the One that is true. Black Moon brings us to the outer edges of the Earth system, as its position careens to the Moon's apogee, its outer orbital edge. Is it the Black Moon that is helping to pull the Moon infinitesimally further from Earth each year? Some day we won't experience eclipses. Surely the Black Moon has something to do with whatever that means to our evolution!

Black Moon has deep wisdom, will and desire power that can weave matter out of aether. Perhaps that's why she comes in dreams, when our bodies and rational minds are asleep. Our thoughts are then turned off and she can whisper her secrets in images and even, perhaps, transport us to other realms. She reasons not with the rational mind but communes at the soul level. Black Moon is the cosmic stripper, the Dancer of the Seven Veils, weaving kundalini power like a sinewy serpent around and through each chakra. Black Moon Lilith shines her invisible light to reveal esoteric dynamics and confront us with illusions that seem so real, as she indirectly guides us into and beyond the aetheric void to ultimate spiritual reality. Forgotten, dismissed or denied, she is the one that holds the light behind the darkness. Can we look into that darkness long enough to see the radiance in her dark visage? Otherwise we are distracted down a path of denial and self-destruction.

Black Moon will not allow lower frequencies and does not operate on such levels. If we go off Lilith's track, the situation becomes negative. Whatever it is that you want won't happen and can be very frustrating or, if it does happen, you might wish it didn't. Remember the caution, "Be careful what you ask for." Lilith works with the desire body. What is it that you are wanting? "I will show you what you really want," promises Lilith. She may reflect in her dark mirror exactly what you don't want, so then you'll know by contrast. You can turn it around, like reversing a photographic negative to develop the picture.

Black Moon experiences probably involve *sanskaras*. In the reincarnational philosophy of Hinduism, this word refers to impressions the soul carries over from life time to life time, unfinished business one could say, that orients the life path with a hidden agenda, fueled by unconscious desires. Perhaps the Black Moon and Dark Moon imprint similar suggestions by throwing dust and distractions in our spiritual third eye.

We all have quirky or disturbingly neurotic personality traits that confound us and interfere with relationships. It is in these areas that we are most desperately seeking reconnection to our wholeness. Lilith lives in these places. This perspective helps us to understand Lilith's deep impact on relationships when she is the key factor, as she seeks spiritual embrace within a worldly one. The emotional effects of despair and desperation lead away from spirit, to a falling/failing in love. In the "original" Fall, the judgment of good and evil created the perception of duality. One way or another, Lilith takes us beyond such judgments.

With two positions, the Black Moon is bivalent. In chemistry, bivalence refers to two or more atoms bound together as a single unit. A bivalent engine can use two different types of fuel. Black Moon is like that! It can be in two different signs. The two positions vary from each other, but work together. Some Lilith lovers swear by one or the other. In Shakespeare's play Juliet entreats Romeo, "Oh, swear not by the Moon, th' inconstant Moon that monthly changes in her circled orb, lest thy love prove likewise variable." True Black Moon is variable in its continual back-and-forth motion that reflects shifting gravitational effects in the Earth-Moon orbit. Mean Black Moon is a derivative constant, not an actual position. Lilith easily encompasses paradox; our rational minds struggle. In my experience, both positions work in life issues and by transit. I have tentatively found the mean Black Moon to be obvious in its effects, the true Lilith to be more subtle. But I don't hesitate to suggest that this impression could easily change with more back story or fresh experience. See what works for you.

Lilith weaves together the super-conscious and the personal, the aetheric and the physical, like the warp and woof of the loom. The true Black Moon retrogrades frequently, constantly picking up stitches from the past and weaving them into the present, constantly shuttling between the various subtle bodies and the physical. The mean Black Moon maintains a steady drum beat for its flamenco dancer other, the true Black Moon.

In its vibrationally shifting rhythms, the two Black Moon positions channel the soul's desire through the aethers surrounding Earth to directly influence the matrix of our experience in mundane "reality." An overlay of two sign placements indicates layered dimensions, as can happen with planets that retrograde across cusps. Playing with images that contain both signs can be a meaningful exercise, like I did earlier with the Sagittarius-Capricorn "Unicorn" cusp. Perhaps a broader Black Moon corridor between true and mean positions offers a wider time frame for manifestations to appear, a spatial spread, while a close coordination of the two positions may suggest instant feedback in experience, an intensified momentum in time.

Through her various means and truths, Lilith urges us to engage the interior process of self-realization that leads to God/dess realization. Her ultimate stillness silently (for we bring the noise) invites us to open a space for the flame to be lit, like the light often seen at the end of the tunnel in near-death experiences. In his book, *La Lune Noir*, Black Moon researcher Marc Beriault recalls Nietzsche's phrase, the necessity "to become what one is," as its essential soul motivation. In Dzogchen Buddhism, among other spiritual paths, we are told that we are already perfect in our spiritual essence, but we do not recognize (or live) this. Our task is to unwrap the dark veils that mask the light of the soul. This is Lilith's strategy, to uncover — to reveal the bare, naked Truth. How daunting and how threatening this prospect can seem. The very alchemical process Lilith beckons us into is indelibly transformational and can become the "hallmark" of our lives, as Beriault writes.

Algol

Algol, the Lilith star, is a collectively shared placement, a stellar doorway to the power of the Goddess, through which we leave behind the duality of darkness and light as well as judgments that lead to suppression and repression. Lilith factors are all linked to the opening of such a doorway and by sign qualify the questions asked by the dangerously seductive Sphinx as we approach her portal. This Star

Lilith most directly suggests the impact of history on the collective consciousness in relation to the cosmic feminine. Through innovative, multi-disciplinary research into pre-history we are becoming aware of the thousands of years of feminine repression and misogynistic misinformation from which we are emerging. This repression has taken many forms, such as slavery, racism, religious supremacy, colonialism and the many other ways in which judgments are made by one group against another.

In *A New Earth*, spiritual teacher Eckhart Tolle writes about the collective dimension of the female pain-body that carries the burden of thousands of years of repression by largely male ego supremacy. Certainly related to Algol, aspects of this pain-body ripple through all Lilith placements. Specifically feminine values of love, relationship, mutuality and harmony with Nature have been denigrated and deranged for millennia. Algol carries this history and the resulting hidden store of "demonic" rage and grief and the burden of slavery that continues to darken human existence. This undercurrent carries deeply buried attitudes toward the female half of the human family, as well as racial and cultural biases and ecologically unsound practices that dishonor the integrity of Nature. Our collective rage in front of this holocaust of suppression can be self-destructive when internalized, yet redemptive when channeled.

In *Lilith's Fire: Reclaiming our Sacred Lifeforce*, Deborah Grenn-Scott, High Priestess of the Lilith Institute, shares mythic lore as well as rituals to invite Lilith's transformational power into our lives. The book's foreword is written by Cosi Fabian, a modern courtesan studied in the history and techniques of sacred sexuality. Reclaiming Lilith is freeing and inherently experiential, states Fabian, teaching us to "fly free of our imposed 'sins': of being sexual, of not being silent, of being women. Lilith's divine rage is a transformative energy."

In the old Sumerian story, Inanna descends to the underworld to visit her sister, Ereshkigal, who is in mourning. Whether it be for her dead husband, for her banishment into the underworld, or for the suffering of the world, this sorrow is too much for her to bear. In the throes of her grief, Ereshkigal rages against bright Venusian Inanna and fixes her with her Eye of Death, the paralyzing Eye of Medusa.

Ereshkigal's world is upsetting and dangerous. Ego consciousness is stopped cold in its tracks, as is Inanna. Stripped naked, Inanna confronts and recognizes her underworld self in that demonic power. She faces the impersonality of nature and death with an immediacy that pierces through illusion and subjective thought forms to the underlying eternal void. Ereshkigal is raw instinctuality cut off from consciousness, pushed below and repressed into fear, resistance, chaos, aggression, sexual hunger. These can be Lilith effects, turned on oneself or others, when the soul's desire for transcendence is denied.

In the realm of Ereshkigal and Algol, primal forces confront us with our apparent inconsequence. A highly focused and introverted process is at work, like the kind that takes place in the frozen heart of interstellar clouds in outer space, impersonally cold yet burning with passion. Such a passionate fire seeks to be extinguished, wrote Marie Louise Von Franz in *Alchemy*, thus the "natural inordinate urge" for individuation "seeks impossible situations. It seeks conflict and defeat and suffering because it seeks its own transformation." Addictions provide a temporary substitute for suppressed passion, but as intense as they get, these never satisfy because the soul is not deeply engaged.

Emotional passion must consume itself. When in the grip of strong emotion, there is also a great potential for heightened awareness. We learn from what affects us most. Passion seeks to connect to something that matches its intensity, seeking yet resisting direction and control by a force than can contain it. In a state of surrender, passion is stilled and transformed to compassion and passionate, diamond-bright equanimity. This raging goddess demands complete submission, "a terrible empathy, one that surrenders, waits upon and groans with her," writes Sylvia Perera in *Descent to the Goddess*. Through all of her poisonous rages, destructive tantrums and repulsive ugliness, small creatures come to cry with her, to share the burden of her sorrow, like mourners at a funeral or responders to a tragedy. That very acknowledgment calms her, and she releases a transformed and empowered Inanna.

This is a process of Algol. At times, pent-up, often unconscious emotions, erupt like a volcano in a fit of rage. Volcanos are a glorious but dangerous phenomenon. The act of listening, being able to contain, to engage or to be a witness to such intense release can be deeply healing and loving. Such expression reveals the deeper truth of our experience; exposes self-denial, clears the air, inevitably changing the continuing course of events. This is a collective as well as personal process. Tapping such passionate depths also releases our capacity for sexual passion. In the collective context, we could say that Algol addresses the psycho-spiritual history of human sexuality. And love.

And wisdom. Yasmin Boland is a passionate Algol researcher, seeking to reclaim the goddess core of this star. Calling it the Saraswati star, she engages in an original discussion of the deep connections between Algol and the Hindu goddess Sarasvati, Goddess of Wisdom [see www.yasminboland.com/saraswatistar.htm].

A star generally maintains its placement in alignment with the precession of the zodiac. Algol stays in the same sign for around 2160 years, an entire astrological age. Every living person shares the same Lilith star degree for seven decades. Its house placement and planetary aspects will suggest individual factors that show how you participate in the liberation of the divine feminine. It marks out your piece of work on this collective project, how you reclaim the shakti, the feminine power and life force. If it is strongly aspected, you've got your job cut out for you, and not for yourself alone. We all contribute to the vision reflected in the Eye of Medusa.

One woman who was born when the Sun was in alignment with Algol feels that she brings out the worst in men, as if being herself evokes a response that confronts her partner with his own negativity. This is often an aspect of the shadow side in relationships. Algol may have exaggerated this process or her awareness of it. Another woman with Algol conjunct Sun/Mars/Ascendant reports similarly:

> *It explains an uneasy sort of power that I feel I have, one that makes me intense, feared, and attractive. My former partner re-acts to the "global rage" that he perceives I run, with a passing irritation. It frankly leads me to feel hopeless in finding a life partner that can look me in the eye and still love me.*
>
> [Personal communication]

Candice Covington, a Portland, Oregon-based aromatherapist with Algol in the 7th house, makes "potions" specifically and individually formulated to move clients through deep issues that interfere with their relationships. Especially for people with Algol plugged into a planet or potent point in their charts, there is also the relationship with Algol itself as a living energy system. Canadian astrologer Julie Simmons honored this connection one year when the New Moon was conjunct Algol — on her birthday. She wrote this "Letter to Algol," asking intimate questions that can guide the way for each of us in interpreting Algol in our charts:

> *Dear Algol,*
>
> *I'm writing this letter to you because I think you understand something about me that I have a hard time understanding about myself. I have so many questions for you but I know they are really about myself. If I could see myself through your eyes, so powerful they turn men to stone, perhaps I would see something of my truth. I do not think you turn women to stone because we are made of different stuff than men. I think you see us for who we really are.*
>
> *Are you lonely?*
> *What do you see when you look in the mirror?*
> *When you go to sleep at night are your eyes opened or closed?*
> *Do you cry in your sleep for your lost home and the impossibility of justice?*
> *Do you go over in your mind again and again the wounding of the children?*
> *Knowing the futility of justice do you take refuge in the possibility of revenge?*
> *Do tears form around the edges of your eyes and spill down your cheeks?*
> *Are they hot tears like the ones I might cry? Are your cheeks soft and human?*
> *When you are alone what happens to the snakes that slither on your gnarly head?*
> *Are they just curls? Girl curls or maybe priestess curls like the Minoan women wore back in the days before war and walls.*
> *Were you once a woman (like me),*
> *surprised by the knife in the back,*
> *the rapist at the door?*
> *Suspended in shock at*
> *pleasure destroyed,*
> *desire profaned?*

The Lilith Star, Algol, seemingly immortal in the ancient field of fixed stars, contains a collective, yet heightened stellar dimension of Lilith, that fixes her Eye on us dispassionately, winking mysteriously. If you find you have a strong connection with the Lilith star and like things hot, you might want to spice things up more by adding Asteroid

Medusa #149 into the mix. See where another Eye is staring at you. In the spirit of that famous Humphrey Bogart line, "Here's looking at you, kid."

Lilith Through the Signs

In ARIES

Lilith in Aries indicates a need to express oneself with clarity and integrity. In Aries, Lilith can press the point, and these people can be wildly and gloriously original and inventive, forging fresh paths into territory that appear foolhardy to others. With Lilith in Aries, it is best not to refer to other people's ideas beyond a certain point so as not to "contaminate" the clarity of perception.

Relationships are seldom smooth for Lilith in Aries. When pulled off-track by "others" through the Libra polarity, an Aries Lilith is undermined, frustrated and feisty. Confidence and courage are compromised, leading to poor results. The fire may die down or go out. At the same time seeing themselves reflected in others can help to show them how they really are in the world. Such insights help tame the shrew, without dulling her fiery spirit. Lilith is not constrainable, nor is she essentially reckless.

Yet patience is thin in fire signs. Sheer bravado, like high stakes bluffing in poker, often backfires. When challenged, they are likely to take an understated yet belligerent stand, becoming intransigent: "My way or the highway." They keep on keeping on, forwarding the progress and the process of soul making. When personal desires or agendas muddy the act, there is trouble. The soul fights for its integrity, for the necessity to experience life for its Self, in a pristine way.

At times Lilith in Aries can appear incredibly gullible and naive. When at their edge, perception and actions are sharply astute. Their charisma opens doors in collective consciousness, whether through great acts of courage or spiritually inspired flashes, and only when divested of all inner doubts and hesitations.

In TAURUS

Lilith in Taurus revels in the embodiment of Heaven on Earth. Mythically Lilith lives in the Tree of Life with roots that tap into the planetary core. Taurus, too, puts down deep roots to stabilize and be fruitful. Lilith typically chooses a rare type of fruit. Look at the effect of that first apple! People with this placement can find resources and produce results in places which look barren to everyone else.

As in Leo, there can be an identification with the divine right of kingship and queenship. Taurean Liliths tend to align with either the "haves" or those who "have not," experiencing the implications of both. The "stuff" of life can become a heavy burden to Lilith in Taurus, with its load of memory, responsibility, karma, desire and attachment that comes with it all. It can also be a pleasure when lightly but thoroughly enjoyed.

The earthiness of Taurus is deeply engaged by Lilith. The sensuality of this sign leads to basic, raw, ecstatic physicality and sexuality. Lilith in Taurus ultimately seeks beyond the tangible gloss of experience to the internal resonance. An inner sense of self-worth, not always reinforced by worldly definitions of success, is aligned with actualizing the spiritual quest. Natives here may buck tradition or plant their feet firmly in it. There is a relentless need to dig down to the fertile soil of their spiritual ground, the better to grow fruits that satisfy the soul and, perhaps, leave a meaningful legacy.

Taurean Lilith, wades through deeply-embedded thickets of financial, sexual and life style issues, seeking clarification of their values. The security-seeking aspect of Taurus is rocked to its core by the complexities of financial loss, sexual betrayal or illness, or any black hole of uncertainty. Lilith in Taurus can demonstrate extraordinary physical beauty and great physical endurance, when they let the light shine through.

Because Algol is now in Taurus, some people with this position will have a double Lilith-in-Taurus. The personal Lilith path merges with the collective call to free the creative power inherent in Mother Nature.

In GEMINI

Multifaceted Lilith in Gemini has a quicksilver mind that is endlessly curious and inventive. Gemini knows that the negative and positive poles together give the battery its charge, so a synthesis at a higher, intuitive level is required to resolve the paradox of duality. Gemini's inconsistencies and ambivalence will cease when the mind is calmed by the intelligence of the heart.

Lilith-in-Gemini people are often wired differently and misunderstood. Subtly reticent at times, they employ varied means of communication to convey their multivalent perceptions. Since most languages do not contain words with enough layers of meaning, they may find everyday language too stark or bare. With creative spontaneity they delight in impetuous responses. Chameleon-like, and able to pick up on signals at various wavelengths, they can instantly adapt to any environment and don't like to be pegged down. This Lilith position can move on astonishingly quickly, avoiding any hint of commitment unless both mind and heart are in synch.

The twinship theme of Gemini is likely to play out like a tennis match between the "good" twin and the "bad" twin, sometimes through relationships with siblings. Lilith does not engage in judgment, so the pair needs to unite like a yin-yang symbol. In astronomical fact, the two stars of the Gemini twins, Castor and Pollux, may look like twin stars, but are nothing alike. Castor, the mythic mortal twin, is a triple star system, and each of the three stars has a binary companion. Two of the binary stars are yellow stars like our Sun, and one is a pair of red dwarves. Pollux, the immortal twin and son of Zeus/Jupiter, is a huge star, still yellow but likely to evolve soon into a red supergiant star.

Gemini has a trickster tendency, so this Lilith position may be prone to witty white lies or darker deceits. There are many active sub-personalities with this placement. Like bees gathering pollen, their curiosity and thirst for knowledge leads them restlessly from one activity to another. Ceaseless internal conversations can yield the honey of wisdom in the most unlikely circumstances. They are capable of extracting every subtle nuance from both actions and words.

In CANCER

With Lilith in the sign of the Moon, layers of maternal impressions run deep. The early familial soup can be can feel thick and lumpy, with suffocating undercurrents of dependency. Emotional waters are easily rippled and disturbed, with the tendency of Cancer to reach out into the feelings of others. Retreating to her inner cavern, Lilith can purify the waters and even turn water to wine, distilling the best from the DNA.

This is a tricky placement of Lilith, similar to a conjunction of the Moon and Lilith which can also have a tougher time than other positions in detaching from early imprints that dull the original colors of the soul's light. One tends to set off in the wrong direction, burdened with false attachments to other people's needs. For some, it can be parental disaffection that sets one on Lilith's path, sometimes very young. Family bonds can be very complex, with dangerous eddies and undertows. The Cancer tendency to return to familiar patterns recreates difficulties until one detaches from these bonds and moves into a more independent life. A spacious internal clarity arises that feels like home and gives a sense of belonging to oneself.

The essence of Cancer is growth. Once a healthy emotional maturity and relational interdependency are established, this can be a wonderful placement, more intimately connected to the Lilith flow than any other. The work here is to resolve the contradiction between the subjective and highly personal mode of the Moon's watery sign with the ultimately impersonal and unconditional universality of Lilith. Lilith in Cancer can be like the mother bird who pushes the fledgling from the nest when it is ready to fly, but is always there, invisibly, to catch the fall. Her flowing cornucopia provides intimately, precisely and abundantly just what is needed for the soul's growth.

In LEO

Lilith in Leo evokes the heart of creativity in the midst of life's chaos. She courageously seeks the stage upon which she can best play her greatest role in the soul consciousness of humanity. Lilith in Leo creators may well find themselves center stage, but often enough behind the scenes. A piece of paper under a magnifying glass in the Sun will catch fire. Though it may look like spontaneous combustion, it is the result of focused intention and focused light. In esoteric astrology, Leo is ruled by the Sun on all levels: the personality, soul and spirit. Lilith navigates from one level to the other, testing the strength of the ego by putting it under that magnifying glass, requiring a purity of expression that allows the creative channels to be open to cosmic impulse.

Except at high noon, the Sun casts shadows. In full dramatic, sometimes operatic technicolor, the Sun spotlights any motivation hiding in the shadows, exposing personality games. Lilith is Leo "plays" better when sparked by creative impulses rather than overblown emotions. The driving force in Leo is to raise self expression to the spiritual level, in pure, shadowless light, thereby freeing the ego — a transcendent experience. When the heart isn't fully present in any activity or situation, it can be "broken" and the Sun's vitality dimmed. Personal fears are likely to stifle creative potential as in the past, certain behaviors may been dis-allowed, or even punished. Lilith cannot be tamed and does not behave "properly." As in the Fire sign Aries, Lilith in this sign can be willful, exaggerating the tendency of Leo to resist the imposition of others, though she may deign to bestow royal favors.

Sub-personalities can take turns dominating. Particular archetypal figures can walk onto the stage of one's life, taking over and demanding acknowledgement or some outlet for expression. How fun — playmates! Detachment from any particular aspect of self, no matter how fascinating, is key to opening to fuller expression of the true Self. The creative urge is large and heart-felt, not to be caged, but freed to roam and roar out its joy.

In VIRGO

The resonance to nature and natural rhythms can be felt most strongly with Lilith in Virgo. Intimately attuned to the pulse of the Earth, these people seem to be naturally in synch with the pulse of life rather than the artificial clock time that runs the daily business of the world.

With a common sense approach, Virgo analyzes subtle and detailed systems in any field of interest. This pragmatic sign tends to gather tools and techniques, honing and refining them to accomplish delicate tasks. Inevitably, in the midst of responding to the most pressing inner priority with instinctive wisdom, it transcends any single methodology. Lilith in Virgo people are highly skilled in unusual ways, and terribly frustrated when not able to develop or offer this skill. The high priest/ess side of Virgo is present in this position, as the soul seeks to offer a sublime service.

In this sign, singularly attuned to body systems and psycho-somatic awareness, Lilith natives may have health issues that require special attention and alternative therapies. Sometimes there are environmental sensitivities, or discomfort around electrical or radio wave technologies, such as cell phone towers, power lines, computer screens, etc. Some illnesses may be psycho-somatic or self-induced from hypochondriac tendencies. Often it is the body's response to unconsciousness self-criticism, which can be quite harsh, and idealistic perfectionism. Such mental-emotional tendencies can be deeply embedded, acquired even while in the womb.

The fix-it mentality of Virgo can tend to look for what is going wrong rather than what is going right. No one is perfect. Indeed our idiosyncratic "imperfections" are often the key to our path in life. When Lilith in Virgo people accept this, they thrive in accord with Nature, relishing its subtle beauties, seasonal cycles, elemental delights and the process of its evolution. Beauty is inherent in nature. This Lilith position can come to honor this most exquisitely.

In LIBRA

In Libra, Lilith is related to the Egyptian goddess Ma'at who maintains the harmony of the spheres and celestial law "on Earth as it is in heaven." She holds the Scales of Justice. On one side, she places the Feather of Truth; on the other side she places your heart or soul. If the heart and soul are as light as the Feather, the balance is even. Balance is the key, delicate as it may be. Especially here, Lilith does not want an easy compromise for the sake of a temporary peace.

Lilith in Libra weighs the give and take in each relationship, adjusting the subtle balance of karmic accounts known only at the soul level. There is an exchange going on in any encounter with another person — in the very air between you, in words spoken or not. Ideas can contrast or harmonize in heightened ways. The outcome will be based on the intent behind the words, whether it be a competitive or cooperative spirit and if there is a true desire to understand the other. When the desire to be in relationship outweighs self-integrity, frustrations and tensions develop.

As wide as the pendulum may swing, it will eventually come back to the center point. Libran Lilith is shrewd at finding the common ground and dancing lightly along the middle line. With Air sign objectivity, she holds to the higher, cosmic law, far beyond the jurisdiction of potentially politically-swayed judges.

Libran Lilith shows that the choices we make, even when we don't know we are making them, can drastically alter the course of our lives, and that of others. Lilith reveals inescapable truths in the paradox of our choices and life situations. Do the benefits and detractions balance each other? Choices don't need to be made before the crossroad is reached.

Liliths in Libra often have a special talent for meaningful connections and seeing relationships between ideas, philosophies and peoples of different cultures or time periods. The diplomatic side of Libra sets up dialogues between East and West, North and South, latitude and longitude, past and future. All polarities that are complementary eventually join in union and become one. Lilith in Libra agrees with Rumi: "Out beyond ideas of wrongdoing and rightdoing, there is a field. I will meet you there."

In SCORPIO

The passionate intensity of Scorpio is a natural stomping ground for Lilith. Think of the extreme tantric yogis who meditate in cremation ghats along the Ganges and even on disintegrating corpses, contemplating beyond the duality of life and death. With Lilith in Scorpio, no stone, thought or feeling is left unturned in the search for a direct line to Universal Source. "May the Force be with you." These people are capable of phoenix-like acts of regeneration, but may go to the very edge to tap such power, like thrill-seekers who would go over Niagara Falls in a barrel. Niagara Falls is one of Nature's finest demonstrations of the power of passionate water, generating enough electricity to light up our lives. No wonder it's a honeymoon destination.

In Scorpio, Lilith offers the power of influence. One can be stained or sustained by the use of it. Desire hones the will into a powerful tool. The best of Scorpionic Lilith is attained only by surrendering to the finest current of energy that empowers your very Being — love — while carefully analyzing the relationship between love and desire. Scorpionic suspicion is ignited by betrayal and distrust of deeply seated motivations and desires, their own as well as those of others. There are dark dealings in any interactions. We rarely discern all the reactive factors set off in daily encounters. We are rarely, if ever, free from personal agendas in the subconscious undercurrents between ourselves and others, and between ourselves and our surroundings. At times, we must just get on with it, let it go and flow.

Though fears darken her perception, Lilith in Scorpio will rise to the occasion, becoming a psychic martial artist, contending with "attacks" from within and without. The fixed frozen waters of Scorpio contain dangerous submerged icebergs of resistance that stop the flow of energy. Scorpio's water is too powerful to dam up for long, "for power unused, power neglected or refused, will find its own shape, its own destructive path in the world" (Patricia McKillip, *The Book of Atrix Wolf*). Lilith draws one into every resistance, suspicion, or shadow of a doubt that clouds the pure energetic stream of life force. She offers the agony and the ecstasy, seeing any situation through to the last drop, with a relentless resilience and capacity for regeneration.

The eroticism and intensity for fusion sought by Scorpio is never totally fulfilled by an "other," by a necessarily conditional love, but it can sometimes get close. Eventually all other desires dissolve in the power of love generated by the Source. Water wears down even hard stone over time. These resilient natives experience a relentlessness that seeks out the darkness in order to dispel it.

In SAGITTARIUS

Lilith shows her warrior nature in the sign of the Archer, with her Sword of Truth raised high and ready. These natives have a roaming heart, restless mind, and a tremendous thirst for adventure. Sagittarius is the sign of the truth-seeker, so the Ultimate Truth is part of the great Quest, the Holy Grail. What does it all mean? What is Real? This Lilith position indicates an urgency for "the Truth, the whole Truth and nothing but the Truth." Legal issues can be complex as Lilith in this sign seeks to align social law to cosmic law.

This quest is a never-ending story, as there is no ultimate Truth apart from the moment of Being. Liliths in Sagittarius can tell a good story. Their version of the truth can take on mythic proportions. They may impose it on others for the sake of a "cause," becoming the righteous dictator, inflated to a sense of personal godhood, being above one's own laws, stepping boldly across one's own professed ethical lines. Lilith eventually forces one to walk the talk.

When such high idealism takes the form of fundamentalism, it brings out the dark side of Lilith. She will eventually expose limited or corrupted belief systems. Lilith's Sagittarian arrow pierces through lies and deceptions, especially those in your own soul. She can instigate great discomfort and discontent with one's falsehoods, large and small. If we survive, we cannot fail to be impressed by the accuracy of her aim.

Like Eros with his love arrows, Lilith in Sagittarius is the Heavenly Huntress with an erotic mind that is transparent, with no attachments or limiting concepts. With the Milky Way's galactic center in the region of Sagittarius, Lilith in the sign of the Archer aims cleanly toward this centerpoint. Once there, we feel the inevitable tug of the Great Attractor, a power center that draws multiple galaxies into its heart. The dilemma can be how to encompass such expansive breadth and depth. How many angels dance on the head of an arrow tip? Lilith in Sagittarius imagines and re-imagines the answer.

In CAPRICORN

Control, capacity, contemplation — basic evolving agendas of Lilith in Capricorn. Capricorn continually tests levels of self-mastery and self-sufficiency. "No man is an island" is a much-needed lesson for the Capricorn loner. Lilith in Capricorn carries a burdened or Bodhisattva sense of responsibility for others. People with this position tend to take charge. After contending with the lesson of control over or by others, they emphasize self control.

Due to the opposition from Cancer, they may yield to pressure from others before they know it. They may find themselves caught in the weakness of their own needs or those of others that set up unconscious dependencies. Overt pressures are more easily defined, as one can push back at them. Authority figures may be encountered on a battle ground, as Lilith refuses to bend the knee to hierarchic convention. Covert pressures, often internal, wear away the rough surfaces to a marble-like polish. These natives stand for something, like a Rock of Gibraltar or a fine sculpture freed from its slab of stone.

An Earth sign, Capricorn can be most tangibly aware of the sacred geometries in nature and their reflection in social systems. Liliths in Capricorn raise the standing stones and pull the sword of power from the stone. Appreciating the use of ritual, they shape the life force into form and function, recognizing that function and form have mutual effect. Traditions, tried and tested through time often contain the potency sought by Liliths in Capricorn. Once they decide something is worth their attention, they will apply themselves and master it to the best of their ability. Often, they make a significant contribution along the way. Practical and contemporary, they are willing to alter or improve any tradition from the past, and must be careful to do so with integrity and honor. As in Native American philosophy, they may take on the alchemical responsibility for clearing the ancestral karma three generations back, and opening the way forward for three generations to come. The experience and test of their capability is what they relish, along with the magic that comes with the mastery.

Lilith in Capricorn skillfully employs the most appropriate modus operandi that will maintain simplicity, efficiency and quality of energy. Capricorn rules the skeletal system, which supports the body. Bones produce the marrow which is the basis of our lifeblood. In this sign Lilith gets down to the bare bones, constructing on the simple, basic platform of Nature. Contemplation on the basics brings Capricorn Lilith an enduring strength.

Capricorn Liliths are not always granted the recognition they deserve for their work. They must be satisfied with their own sense of accomplishment, and resist the tempting vipers of envy. After all, the real authority figure they seek to impress is within, their authentic Self. The essential task is the embodiment of a living legacy.

In AQUARIUS

As an electrically-charged conduit, Lilith in Aquarius is plugged in to the higher echelons of Earth's magnetosphere, where solar flare photons swirl like lightning, lightening and enlightening. With Lilith in Aquarius, the body's energy field can light up like an aurora borealis, affecting other people in ways that surprise all concerned into higher mind perspectives. The subtle systems of the body can be finely tuned, sometimes prone to short circuits. Disruptions in the energy system may at times create an uncomfortable ripple effect in the emotional body, very upsetting to this impersonal sign. Acupuncture works with meridian points to help reconnect the loose wires; cranio-sacral therapy, Shiatsu, Reiki and other therapies that align the subtle, aetheric energy fields with the physical vehicle can also help.

The Aquarian rationality can be rapidly informed, processing information quickly, with a heightened, broad and penetrating consciousness. Like Lilith in Gemini, Lilith in this Air sign is wired in an alternate, sometimes abnormal arrangement, with aberrant anomalies. This complex wiring allows for extraordinary sensitivity and attunement to subtle energies. In some cases, multidimensional connections can be channeled and these Liliths can be conversant with living archetypes. This can give rise to a self-conscious awareness of being different, odd; even alien.

Aquarian Lilith is often interested in broad social trends and wants to make a singular contribution that is not so much about the personality as about the work. She is often ahead of her time, with ideas not always readily accepted. These rainbow women and men are particular about their participation in group dynamics, preferring activities that accent consciousness change. In regular types of clubs or social situations, they may find themselves a scapegoat or the odd one out, feeling unwelcome in most mundane cliques. When working skillfully, this Lilith position allows one to connect in unusual ways and in rare situations; otherwise, it can create havoc in spite of trying to fit in.

Upon finding like-minded comrades, this Lilith can form strong associations while maintaining personal space; friendship and collegiality have special value for this sign, based on an open acceptance and appreciation of individuality.

In PISCES

What is the difference between illusions, dreams and reality? Not a simple question for Liliths in Pisces, prone to both waking and night-time dreams of great portent. They never lose their extraordinary psychic awareness. Not fully comfortable in the confines of the human form, a body can seem like a prison to these land-locked mermaids, used to flowing freely in fluid spiritual seas. For this reason, water can be healing, especially a salt bath or, even better, the salty sea. This helps cleanse the aura and wash away impressions that have gathered as dust on the soul or a stain in the DNA.

Feeling like fallen angels, it is painful for these souls to lose communion with higher realms as the impact of denser energy fields and distortions of human vibrations close in. Pisces soaks in vibrational streams and is open to the psychic states and disturbances of others. Liliths in Pisces can feel battered with a kaleidoscope of impressions, from heavenly to hellish. The world can feel brutal, so they seek to be transported beyond "normal" life and fear losing the way to do so. Dream states, altered states and alternate realities, fantasy, addictions or madness can seem like viable options. It takes subtle Lilith insight to distinguish where the energy comes from, also to clarify various levels of reality. Psychic distress arises when they try to seek sanctuary in some illusion of reality as their internal sense of purity won't allow it. They do well when surrounded by beauty, aromas and uplifting music that soothe the soul.

An unfulfilled yearning, a sacrifice, unfinished business or a compassionate gesture may bring one into this life, like a savior reluctant to leave anyone behind. Lilith in Pisces is a champion of the underdog, the disenfranchised or lost and must beware of being sucked down into those very waters. There is something in them that idealizes the glory of the martyr.

Like *The Little Sea-Maid* of Hans Christian Anderson, Lilith in Pisces yearns to see the world and falls in love at the sight of a prince. She makes painful sacrifices for him, and is desperately disappointed not to be recognized by her beloved. In the original, pre-Disney version, her deepest desire is for an immortal soul, which mermaids have not. Because she sacrifices her own life rather than betray the prince, she is lifted into the realm of the angels. As one of them, she can earn immortality by doing good deeds. Her longing for human love is not fulfilled, but her desire for an eternal soul, for which she has suffered and endured much pain, has returned her to the heaven from whence she came. This can be a true faerie tale for Lilith in Pisces.

LILITH and the Sabian Symbols

The meaning of image-loving Lilith can be amplified by the use of Sabian symbols. Fortified with the images for each of your Lilith placements, you'll have more clues for your Lilith story line. The literal way in which the Sabian symbols manifest leaves a trail which can be tracked in relation to Lilith's message. Let's look at our collectively shared image for Algol. Currently at 26 degrees 10 minutes Taurus, we round up and use *The Sabian Symbols as an Oracle* by Lynda Hill to find the image for 27 Taurus:

An Old Indian Woman Selling Beads and Trinkets

Native peoples are naturally attuned to Earth energy, the element of the sign of Taurus. A Cherokee woman once told me that her people worship through the Earth to Great Spirit. This symbol shows an elder carrying on a tradition, offering her wares — small items and beads, like little "earths." Simple, yet eternal, beads are made from many earth substances. They have been used as currency, reveal history, hold memories and carry a legacy. The worth of age and tradition are largely disregarded and undervalued by modern society.

This symbol well indicates the repressive themes of Algol in downgrading native peoples, women and elders, and the value of Earth-honoring traditions. Since entering this degree around the year 1966, there has been an increasing interest in the history, arts and spirituality of the First Peoples of the Americas, as well as in other cultures. In India the Dalit, or lowest-class "untouchables" of the long-held caste system, has been increasingly incorporated into society. Kumari Mayawati, a woman politician born to a lower class family, made history in 2007 when she became the leader of the large north India state of Uttar Pradesh. A controversial maverick, she has raised the self-esteem of low-caste people. (Her Venus-Pluto opposition squares Algol, and Asteroid Lilith is conjunct her Aquarius Moon/Ceres.)

Lynda Hill's analysis of this symbol cautions against underestimating yourself, your talents and skills, and also against looking down on those less fortunate or in menial jobs. Loss of culture and tradition undermines a sense of true values, of appreciation for the "simple things of life" and the basic "salt of the Earth" kind of people that keep the world going. In these times of Earth energy shift, it behooves us to keep the "simple" things is mind, to get back to the basics of life. What does this symbol say to you?

Keeping in mind Ptolemy's original projection of ecliptic degrees used by Bernadette Brady, let's briefly check out the Sabian symbol for the previous degree, 26 Taurus:

A Spaniard Serenading his Senorita

This romantic image suggests a Lilith-directed power of love that evokes compelling expression in music from the heart. Or is it a public show of affection without substance? The Eye of Medusa skewers any pretense.

Lilith and the Nakshatras

As a subtle, multivalent aspect of the cosmic feminine, an understanding of Lilith can be enhanced by reference to the Vedic Nakshatras, the twenty-seven Moon Mansions. Like a foundational, lunar-based zodiac, the Nakshatras are mini-constellations, each spanning 13 degrees 20 minutes and defined by the key stars that the Moon visits each night in its monthly weaving. The Man-in-the-Moon visits his various wives night by night, lighting and empowered by each in turn.

These star-lit faces/phases of the Moon are facets of the goddess and can inform the personal placement of Lilith in meaningful ways. You can locate the placement of each of your Lilith positions in a Nakshatra for interesting insights. The Nakshatras are sparkling doorways that lead deeper into goddess power. India has an unbroken tradition of goddess worship that goes back many millennia, with an especially rich and deep honoring of the dark faces of the goddess, her spiritual treasures and sacred wisdom.

Because they follow the sidereal zodiac, the Nakshatras change slowly over time. Below are given the tropical degree equivalents for around 1950. If your Lilith is very close to the cusp of a Nakshatra, you may need help from a practitioner to get a precise positioning. Each Nakshatra has a thematic name, a deity, animal, sacred syllables and various attributes, including specific shaktis, or powers, as well as certain wishes and desires. The deeper meaning of your Lilith unfolds through the help of such imagery and connections.

In *Mansions of the Moon*, Kenneth Johnson gives thematic names to each Moon mansion (given below), which help to convey its essence. His book and Dennis Harness's *The Nakshatras* are both fine introductions with basic interpretations that get one started on a rewarding journey into this lunar zodiac of the Vedic system. Dr. David Frawley offers articles on this material and more on the goddess in Hindu tradition that can be found on the website of the American Institute of Vedic Astrology (www.vedanet.com).

The Lilith Star Nakshatra

Again using Algol, the collective Lilith star, its location at 26-27 degrees Taurus places it in Krittika, the Nakshatra marked by the Pleiades, the Seven Sisters, known as Subaru in Japan. Perseus, who holds the head of Medusa with that Eye, seems to be standing on the Pleiades. This asterism is ruled by the Fire God, Agni, a very ancient god, who particularly prepares ritual sacred fires. The shakti of Krittika is the power to burn. It burns up negativity, purifies and cooks food for nourishment. We can imagine that this star that marks the Eye of Medusa is purifying negativity on the collective level, burning away repressive control of feminine power and policies damaging to Nature.

The Nakshatras (given in tropical degrees for 1950)

1 ASHWINI, The Horse Goddess
23 Aries 10 – 6 Taurus 30

2 BHARANI, The River of Souls
6 Taurus 30 – 19 Taurus 50

3 KRITTIKA, The Pleiades, Star of Fire
19 Taurus 50 – 3 Gemini 10

4 ROHINI, The Red Goddess, Star of Ascent
3 Gemini 10 – 16 Gemini 30

5 MRIGASHIRA, Orion, the Hunter, Star of Searching
16 Gemini 30 – 29 Gemini 50

6 ARDRA, The Teardrop
29 Gemini 50 – 13 Cancer 10

7 PUNARVASU, The Light Bringer, Star of Renewal
13 Cancer 10 – 26 Cancer 30

8 PUSHYA, The Lotus
26 Cancer 30 – 9 Leo 50

9 ASHLESHA, The Serpent
9 Leo 50 – 23 Leo 10

10 MAGHA, Regulus, the Royal Star
23 Leo 10 – 6 Virgo 30

11 PURVA PHALGUNI, The World Tree Goddess
6 Virgo 30 – 19 Virgo 50

12 UTTARA PHALGUNI, The Marriage Goddess
19 Virgo 50 – 3 Libra 10

13 HASTA, The Hand
3 Libra 10 – 16 Libra 30

14 CHITRA, Spica, the Jewel
16 Libra 30 – 29 Libra 50

15 SWATI, Arcturus, Star of Wind
29 Libra 50 – 13 Scorpio 10

16 VISHAKHA, The Moon of Power, Star of Purpose
13 Scorpio 10 – 26 Scorpio 30

17 ANURADHA, The Moon of Friendship
26 Scorpio 30 – 9 Sagittarius 50

18 JYESHTA, Antares, The Wisdom Crone
9 Sagittarius 50 – 23 Sagittarius 10

19 MULA, Foundation, the Root of All Things
23 Sagittarius 10 – 6 Capricorn 30

20 PURVASHADHA, Moon of Early Victory, the Invincible Star
6 Capricorn 30 – 19 Capricorn 50

21 UTTARASHADHA, Moon of Later Victory, The Universal Star
19 Capricorn 50 – 3 Aquarius 10

22 SHRAVANA, Moon of Listening, Star of Learning
3 Aquarius 10 – 16 Aquarius 30

23 DHANISHTA, The Drummer
16 Aquarius 30 – 29 Aquarius 50

24 SHATABHISHAK, The Divine Healer
29 Aquarius 50 – 13 Pisces 10

25 PURVA BHADRA, The Fire Dragon
13 Pisces 10 – 26 Pisces 30

26 UTTARA BHADRA, The Dragon of the Deep
26 Pisces 30 – 9 Aries 50

27 REVATI, Moon of Splendor
9 Aries 50 – 23 Aries 10

7

Living Lilith

The Call of Lilith

It's a big dose of Lilith to include all positions in your chart at once. It can take some time to unwind the meanings. Over my years of study, I have been delighted, dismayed and distressed, surprised, shocked and exasperated by the way Lilith works with me. She came at me from odd angles over the course of years — first, the George MacDonald book, as I remember it, though memory is variably suspect. I became vaguely aware of the asteroid first, I think, because of the publication of *Asteroid Goddesses* in 1986. Back then, I was giving my attention to the "more important" largest four asteroids.

When I walked into my first Black Moon lecture by Marc Beriault in 1987, true Black Moon was transitting my natal Moon. I was certainly interested in such a dark goddess, but she just gave me a knowing wink at that point. I did not get pulled in yet. Perhaps it was the confusion about having two sign placements. I do still have my lecture notes, with key phrases of "independence, laser-like penetration, enforced lucidity, perception of non-physical reality through the senses, the yang that comes out of the yin."

I zeroed in on Delphine Jay's books at a monthly meeting of the American Society of Dowsers at its headquarters in Vermont. I had been invited to speak to the group about Astrology and was able to participate in an experiential lesson in using dowsing rods to locate an invisible door that had been "placed" on the grounds. I was having a bit of trouble, so an old timer took my hand and charged me with dowsing ability, as he said. It worked; an effective transmission. Even then Dark Moon Lilith was inviting me deeper into subtle energy fields. The experiential context of Lilith is the real essence of her revelation. That's why you can't really THINK about her, too much. In my new copy of Jay's *Interpreting Lilith* I jotted down this quote from William Blake without thinking why; the book was handy

> *How do you know but ev'ry Bird*
> *That cuts the airy way*
> *Is an immense world of delight,*
> *Clos'd by your senses five?*

This is Lilith's kind instinctive thinking and a way in which she speaks. The Lilith star took a couple of times to penetrate into my awareness (thank goodness, thank goddess). I had to read Richard Hinckley Allen's book, *Star Names, Their Lore and Meaning*, more than once to have the Lilith connection sink in. Even when I underlined the Lilith reference, I didn't remember it by the time I looked at the book the next time. It wasn't until after the passing of Hyakutake and Hale-Bopp, the two comets that criss-crossed at Algol. I was starting to do regular star gazing, and became interested the Andromeda story. Then I truly looked and saw that star. I do recognize earlier influences through mythic weavings and drama. The work with Dragon Dance Theater, giving a dramatic voice to Lilith, was particularly profound and brought Lilith much more into my consciousness. *Brady's Book of Fixed Stars* offered a confirming nudge.

When was it that I found myself looking around at all four Liliths? I can't really say. Silently and seductively sliding close, serpent-like, through dreams and drama, there she was, not suddenly, smiling in the center. If Lilith "lets you," you can start simple, with sign and house placements, with aspects. See what planets Lilith connects to, what kind of cosmic conversations are suggested. Consider one factor at a time. It's best not to try to analyze too much right away. Lilith responds best to an indirect approach rather than abstract theory. We can't just sit down and figure her out. However, simple is not an option when you are plunged into a full-on Lilith journey.

Even after a couple of decades working with Lilith, I have had numerous revelations recently while writing this book — especially about the Dark Moon. I realized all over again that it is conjunct my Sun (a daring confession!). How could I have "forgotten" that? It's as if Lilith pulled a veil across. How is it that we become aware of our soul's path, the slippery slopes and the quicksands, as well as the blissful moments of spacious upliftment? How often do we pull back? What moves us, not so much forward, as deeper, fuller and freer? Like the tree, Lilith has deep roots and arching branches that reach to the sky.

You'll see Lilith out of the corner of your eye, in your life's subtle intricacies and nuances. You'll find Lilith in your hesitancies, when you stop mid-sentence and lose your mind, when thoughts are lost in little black holes. (I do believe our higher minds are opening up, so we are losing our lower minds more often.) Lilith speaks in body language, in bird feathers, a puff of wind, or a crack in the sidewalk that trips you up. She speaks through some weird statement that comes out of your partner's mouth — or yours. You may hear something different than was said. You may actually have said something other than you were thinking.

Lilith takes us beyond our personal reactions to a deeper core of truth, daring us to the far edges of our safety zone toward spiritual freedom. Activating desires at the soul level, Lilith also points to where personal desires may get in the way of what the universe wants or how it wants to live through us. Lilith lives in those places in our lives that we cannot make happen, but where the path is magic when we open her door. We walk her labyrinth, back and forth, round and around, leading to the center where we dissolve. All light is submerged in the black hole at the center of the galaxy, so goes the latest story from astro-physics. Perhaps that is where Lilith takes us. That is where she took my friend Jan.

Lilith Up Close

I'd like to introduce you to a few people, for personal stories that give a closer sense of Lilith's weavings. We can hear Lilith in their words, as well as through their experiences. This may stimulate some recognition of the presence of Lilith in your chart as well.

JAN

Jan is an Aries woman with a strong Lilith signature. Mean and true Black Moon (only one minute apart) conjunct her close Moon/ Neptune in Libra in the 10th house. She was born on the Full Moon, with Chiron squaring it. So she has a strong Lilith-infused T-Square.

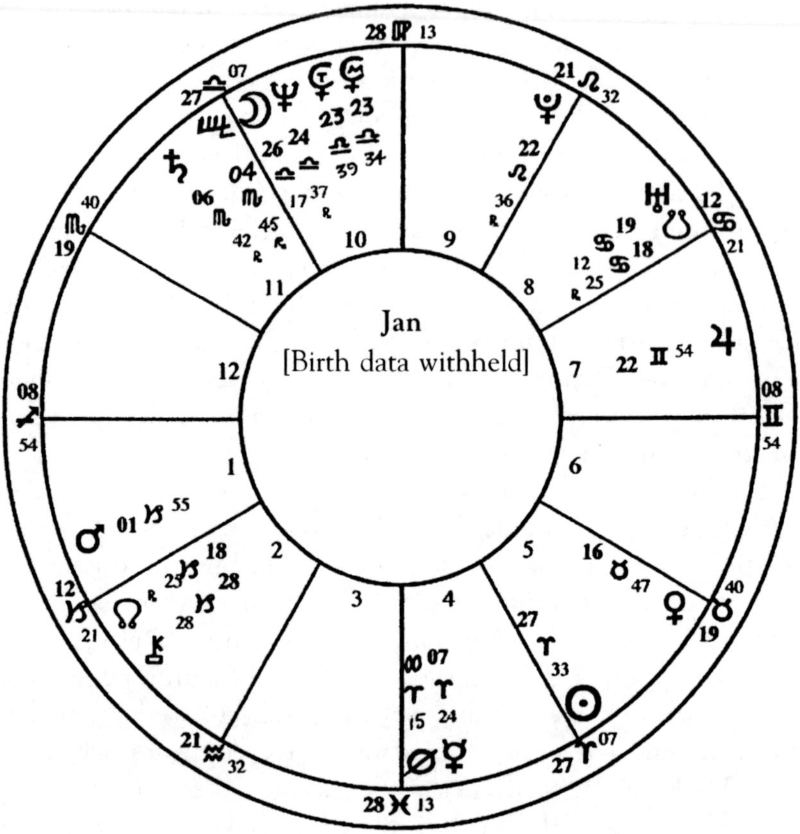

Jan is a bodywork and shamanic healer, working with sound and Authentic Movement. She is a pastel artist, writes poetry and has a very lively and alive dream world. The tree is one of her strongest experiential symbols, in art, movement and dream, as is the Black Hole. With the heightened sensitivity of Neptune deepened by the Black Moon, she feels subtle energies always at play. In her younger years this terrified her. She felt like she was never alone and that this energy put her in danger, as if it could strike at any moment, she was never safe. "It was quite tormenting because it started to make me feel like I was crazy." Then, at age 27 or 28 (at her progressed Moon return), it suddenly left.

> *This energy that had been inside of me, suddenly came out and was released into the room… Something was unleashed and it was loose in*

the room. I was so terrified I couldn't move for hours and hours... It was like terror itself was alive in the room. Then it left. It took days. My whole aura got blown apart. But whatever that was, left. Like somebody is gone now. Now I can feel these shadowy energies around but they don't scare me any more.

Her Dark Moon at 1 Aries in the 4th house squares Mars in Capricorn, giving a heavy sense of responsibility for absolute integrity.

I'm very aware of power and the use of power and the necessity when working with these energies, I have to be so clear that it's not for my own personal gain. If it is, then it's dangerous... it's just not right, I can't do it. Things fall apart, the energy stops if it's for my own... I feel I have to have the highest ethical standards. That I MUST, I HAVE TO, or it can't happen.

Another manifestation of Lilith happened for Jan at the death of her mother. Jan had been unable to conceive and was planning to adopt a child, which she and her husband later did. The night of her mother's death, without yet knowing that her mother was passing, she began to menstruate for the first time in many years. This biological separation from her birth mother released another level of her feminine experience, related to a level her Moon/Black Moon conjunction opposite her Sun on the cusp of the 5th house of creativity and children. Dark Moon in Mars's sign squared Mars adds another dimension to her work with movement and her experience of blood mysteries.

With Asteroid Lilith conjunct Saturn (retrograde) in Scorpio in the 11th house, Jan often feels that she channels the group unconscious in ways that are startling or out of context. Once she started to distinguish her own feelings, she recognized the process and now uses it when working with groups in transformative movement. This process started to become more conscious when Pluto moved to conjunct Saturn/Asteroid Lilith. She was feeling tremendous pressure, restriction and frustration about being in a body. The yearning for space and freedom and light was strong, but there seemed no way to get there, and the world of form and embodiment was antithetical to this desire. This opened deeper aspects of experience, involving the other Lilith placements and the Chiron healing journey. During this time she wrote:

> *I feel trapped by my own desires to know, to seek, to continue – further, deeper. There is no end... I see hungry mouths and pain but I can't stop it and the drops in the bucket are so small. There's not enough for me... It leaves too big a gap in my own life. My own hungry needs are left abandoned and they cry to me... I am sparked by so much, like a flint. Things strike up against me and I light, light, light little sparks. I need a fire: a long, slow smoldering fire that will sustain and grow...*
>
> *I feel it coming. Patience is needed and let go, let go... I should have been born a light, some kind of light that can flow in and out and expand and contract and take the shape of all things, get into the smallest places and flow out again. Because light cannot be trapped – only by the black holes in the sky. I will never visit a black hole when I turn into light. I will dance around the big black holes but stay far enough out of range.*
>
> *But what if I get caught? What if it sucked me right in and closed all around me, no way out, what could I do? I bet it could be nice in there. I bet it's another way in, another way to another universe.*
>
> *Black holes are just the door and don't really trap but always open up, open, open... to new and sparkling universes filled with color and light and space, space, so much space to fly and swirl and feel against the skin the air and movement of particles, cool and free...*
>
> *It's still in the swirl. Spin, spin, spin, but the center smiles, does not ever move. I am the center of the spin, of the twirl. The earth moves, and the universe spinning is me, and we don't stop. It brings love. Love is this. So full.*

This extraordinary process writing describes a transformative journey of psycho-spiritual import, taking her beyond the rational search for knowledge and irrational fears of darkness. The journey through the Black Hole became an essential aspect of her healing work, both with individuals and on a collective level that involves the whole Full Moon/Black Moon dynamic with Chiron — and Mars that energized the Dark Moon at the Aries point.

> *The Black Hole is a very alive for me, not a concept. I have a working relationship with that energy. There is the black hole in outer space. There's the Black Hole in my psyche. There's Black Hole when I'm working with people. I go into the Black Hole and through it ... It comes into me, like a two-way experience. I can put my hands on somebody's body and through feeling what is there, first physically and then ener-*

getically, I can go through actual tissue and any kind of memory or whatever that tissue holds. Then there is this place of limbo. If I keep going through that place, it takes me out into spirit, this very vast oneness, like pulling in light through that hole. When I go into the Black Hole and through it I connect with what is much larger, but you have to go all the way through. If you stop at the place which is the hole, you are stuck, in no-land. You have to keep all the way through it... Sometimes I feel like I am going down into these Black Holes in the Earth that are full of grief. I pull it up through my body, feel it, emote it, and something clears. It can be very intense.

In the way of Lilith, Jan has had numerous experiences with spirit trees, spiraling up through them into ecstatic states. Once coming out of such a hole, weighted down with grief, she made a great effort to stand up. She found herself in a circle of spirit trees, "a place where angels are born." Other people in the room heard the sound of a harp.

When she was a child, there was a willow tree outside the home that was a special friend and close companion. She felt that she actually lived inside of that tree, that it was her real home. Soon after her mother died she dreamt that the tree growing next to her childhood home was shattered by lightning. "It was a shock, like electricity going through me when the lightning struck that tree." In a later piece of movement work that largely involved her brother (Dark Moon in 3rd house), she lived in a tree and cut off her long braid so that he could not climb the tree.

The braid is a personal talisman, woven hair that records life experience. (Remember Lilith's theme of embodiment, and her magical hair). Jan was given her grandmother's braid and also that of a dear friend who ritually cut off her braided hair before beginning a course of chemotherapy. Jan assisted the process of this friend's eventual death. A big dream followed that death, again involving the tree, as if it were a black hole. In the dream she became aware that she was dreaming and began to dance and spin. She was led to a giant tree, a spirit tree, so old she knew she was looking back in time.

I started to spin like a dervish. I was hearing high pitched sounds like Peruvian whistles. My body was levitating higher and higher. I go into ecstatic states, which increased until I am way high above the earth in complete bliss. So high above the earth everything stops, no sound, no nothing, just bliss. Then eventually I come back. A crowd has gathered and are worried about me. My task is to tell them there is nothing to fear.

From terror to fearlessness is this woman's Lilith's journey.

LILLI

Lilli, with her Lilith name, has a double Lilith, with Asteroid 1181 conjunct Algol on her South Node in the 10th house, opposite her Sun in Scorpio. This is a very active Lilith signature, supported by Dark Moon conjunct Mars in Pisces in the 8th trine the Sun. Venus in Libra is quincunx Asteroid and Dark Moon Liliths. She has a wide Black Moon corridor, with the true Black Moon in mid-Capricorn in the 5th and mean Black Moon at 10 Aquarius conjunct Chiron in the 6th. How does this work in her life?

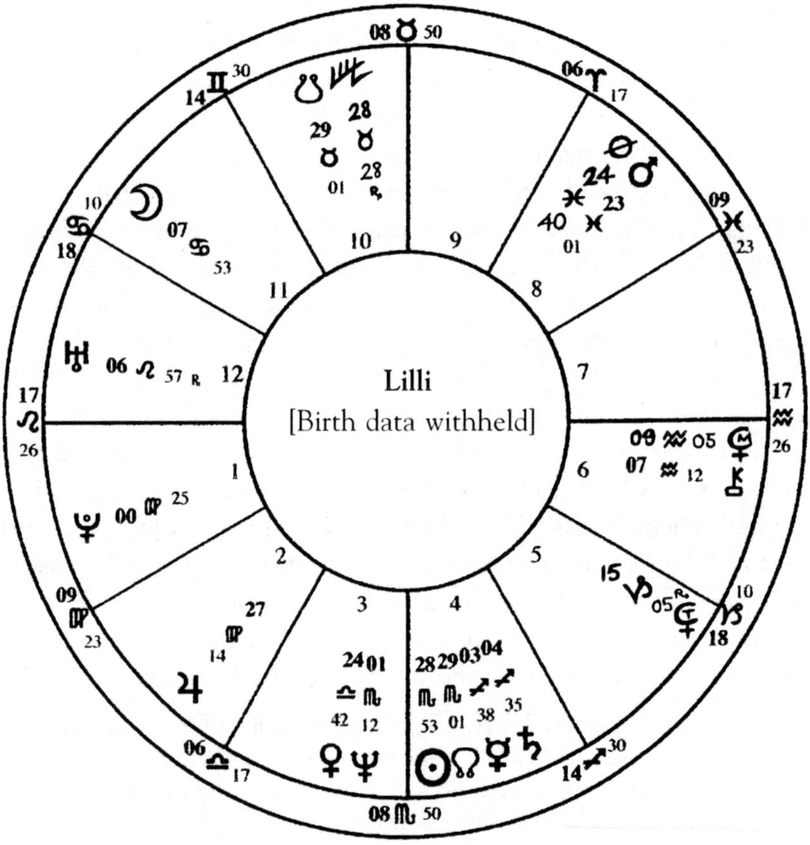

A strikingly lovely person, with long blond hair and large blue eyes, Lilli says, she was "demonized" even from the age of five. Girls used to bully her. "I'm just different. It's more acceptable now than it was in the 50s or 60s." She has studied women's history and sexuality and feels that, although social views of sexuality are changing, opening up and becoming more real, women's sense of worthiness still needs to be healed.

> *The issue of living up to expectations is a very Lilith-y trait, I think, like you are a representative in a way, not just of yourself. It's a signature or a paradigm that you step into. It's an archetypal thing. I've always been judged by the way that I look. Then, if people get over that, I am viewed as being able to handle everything. If you develop the persona of being so together, then you've made yourself invulnerable. If you have moments of failure or falling apart, you're not allowed to have them. Other people are depending on you. It's something you do to yourself. You create those expectations and rise to their expectations. If you don't hold that space all the time, people get disappointed.*

In these words we hear a mix of the social expectations of Asteroid Lilith brought to an archetypal level via Algol, and the burden of capability of true Black Moon in Capricorn. An ex-husband admits that he married her in order to control her. "I've never really felt I've been with someone who was really my equal or that I've been cherished. I imagine it would be divine," she says. "I don't really care if I'm with anybody or not, not if it's too hard to make it work. I really enjoy being alone."

The Capricorn fairy and elemental connection is strong as well. Four-leaf clovers are commonplace for Lilli. In half an afternoon, without even trying, she once found a baker's dozen five-leaf clovers and even a few six-leafs in a field in Italy. I never knew such things existed, did you?

Thinking about Algol as the Eye of Medusa, Lilli recognizes her ability to focus very intensely and has had to temper her power. "When I was streaming a lot of energy, unconsciously, into a given situation to get the job done, people sometimes got fried in the process." She views Lilith as a protector energy, like the demons that guard the sacred temple. "The overwhelming feeling I have when I think of myself as Lilith is that I would do whatever I need to do to achieve the goal and in many cases that energy comes about by protecting someone or something." What protects her?

Lilli met her first snake while modeling a wedding gown at an artsy fashion show. She was lowered down onto the stage in a coffin, from which she rose carrying a ten-foot python, and walked down a set of stairs in heels and the very tight dress to do the runway walk. This was the beginning of a life-long relationship with large snakes. "I would have been falling all over myself, nervous and self-conscious, but I was dealing with her and she was responding to the music and everything. She really hooked up with me and it was almost like a third energy came in — the both of us." The directors gave her the snake, soon named Daath Kundalini by her boyfriend who was a priest of the Golden Dawn (Mars conjunct Dark Moon).

> *Daath was an extraordinary animal. She was very protective of me. I once took her with me on a trip into the South. I was staying in a hotel. A bus boy brought me some ice. I turned away thinking he had gone out the door, but he closed the door and started coming back into the room. Oh shit, I thought. Then I saw a look come on his face and he turned and left. Daath had come out and risen behind me, so that she was standing like a cobra three and a half feet high. She scared the crap out of him, otherwise I might have been dealing with a rape situation.*

Currently she owns two albino pythons with golden diamonds on their backs. The older one, Seraphina, has been a guest teacher in several animal communication workshops. "Snakes are the clearest communicators with humans," says Lilli. "They can attain a level of inter-being link more easily and more readily than most other beings. They are clearer and stronger." The image of women and snakes has a long history, as old as Lilith, with more than a hint of kinky. Lilli confessed, "I used to let Daath sleep in the bed. She liked to curl up behind my knees. That takes ultimate kinkiness to another level." What about tongue kissing with her cockatoo? I asked, knowing of her pink companion. "It reassures him when he is feeling weird, she explains. "He used to bite. The kiss replaced the bite." Snakes and birds for Lilli and Lilith.

Lilli has strange, energetic health issues (mean Black Moon/ Chiron in 6th) that have led to extra-terrestrial communication and put her on Chiron's path of the wounded healer. She has facilitated healing in some critical cases. Her house is full of animals in rehab, mostly birds, but I've met a disabled squirrel there. She has trained horses and people on horses and most recently worked with orphaned baby elephants in Sri Lanka.

The true Black Moon in the 5th house is experienced through art and children. She is been the muse/manager for her art partner, who uses her as a model for mythic visionary art popular in Japan. A match for her Mars/Dark Moon conjunction, he was an award-winning artist for "creepy" and "eerie" art. Their recent series is centered around the aurora borealis and portrays her idealized image, hinting of the Japanese Sun goddess Amaterasu, surrounded by creatures and catching stars in her hands. She is currently developing her own work in photography (www.whispersinblue.com), necessary for her 5th house Black Moon, discovering a "new way of looking at nature that is full of beautiful surprises." Naturally, mysterious orbs show up in her work. Photographing at night, she was looking for a way to see through the dark and dispel fear of it.

> *The fear of the darkness and the unknown may be loosening up in this world, so we are allowed to see more light and other spiritual things. Hopefully the fear factor is starting to lose some power. That makes me wonder about this substance of negativity with the dark moon ...There is a price you have to pay for spiritual forces to help you.*

Lilli always knew she would never have her own children. With a Cancer Moon, she loves mothering things, but

> *If I had my own child, I wouldn't be as inclined to work with other people's children... As a child it is so special to be able to relate to an adult who is not your parent, especially an adult who sees who you are and can relate to it. It is such a privilege to be allowed to go into that place and share on that level with a child.*

A conversation with Lilli is often a time warp, tapping back into history and beyond. With South Node on Algol, she seeks a connection with something very ancient, before the duality of time and space. She feels the weight of dark matter and a primordial grief for being separated from the rest of the universe.

> *What I would love to bring to the world is a greater sense of connectedness — between people, between people and plants, people and animals, nature and the esoteric elements, so many layers. It's so nice when you feel a connection. That's what I feel I am called to work with.*

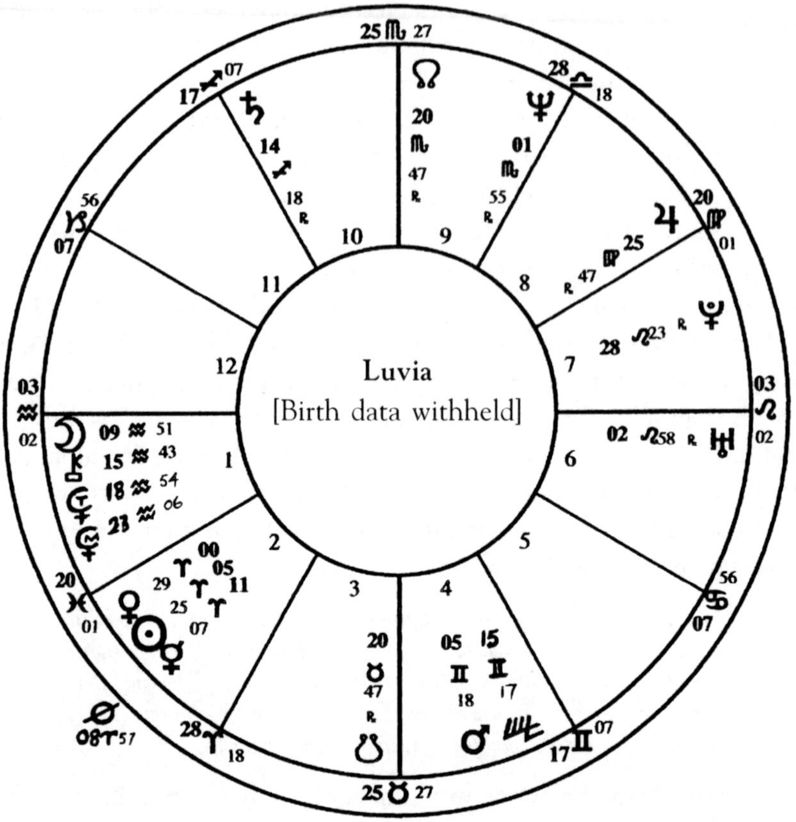

LUVIA

Luvia also has the Black Moon in Aquarius. She has a very strong Lilith signature. Black Moon conjuncts her Ascendant and Moon. The Dark Moon conjuncts her Aries Sun. The Dark Moon connection with the world of faerie is strong for her, as she "remembers" the destruction of Atlantis, at which time she withdrew from the human race into the faerie world. At the Dark Moon level, she is reintegrating into human being with a strong lingering communion with that other world over hill and vale, through the heart of the forest and beyond. She is often told she looks like a faerie, a dark-haired one with rippling Taino-type hair. She writes esoteric faerie tales for adults. On her property she dug a Chartres labyrinth, as a portal in which she planted herbs, flowers and crystals.

She embodies the high electrical charge of Aquarian Black Moon multi-dimensionality carried by her Ascendant and Moon. Her body is wired with surplus spinal nerves and an extra vertebra, requiring special attention and esoteric practice. She is an extraordinary healer working with subtle bodies fluids and energy fields.

Taken apart from the wider context of her chart, this Lilith slice offers an altered viewpoint, so Aquarian! We can only get hints about the true interweavings of Lilith in these briefings.

KAREN

I called Karen "out of the blue," when I found her chart and phone number in an old Lilith file from several years ago. Because of special interest in the Medusa connection with Lilith, we added in her Asteroid Medusa placement. Conjunct Chiron/South Node in Scorpio, it plays into the grand cross that includes her Sun/Black Moon in Aquarius, Saturn/Pluto in Leo, and Algol/North Node in Taurus. This deepens an already deep Lilith storyline.

The day before we spoke, Karen had had a soul retrieval session with a shamanic healer. The main issue that came up was the feeling that she had been "tamed" by authority figures in the course of her life, a feeling of being clamped down that undermined her sense of self. The image that spontaneously came up to represent the untaming of Karen was the flying horse. She had never heard of the story of Pegasus, the flying horse, who emerged from the severed neck of Medusa. Yet it spontaneously entered her inner journey and swept her up and free, up and free, strengthening her second chakra, containing sexuality, creativity and life force.

On that very day, the Sun was at 23 degrees Taurus, squaring her Sun and exactly opposite Asteroid Medusa/Chiron. It was the week of her second Saturn return, Saturn then opposite Neptune, both activating her Lilith-infused grand cross. Neptune was conjunct her Aquarian Sun/Black Moon, right after Black Moon had been conjunct her Neptune. Matching the moment, the Moon was exactly conjunct her Asteroid Lilith at 24 Aries.

Over the years Karen has had "to learn to express myself [Leo] in a larger way with groups and community [Aquarius]," but now is opening to the collective field at another level. "I feel the anxiety of

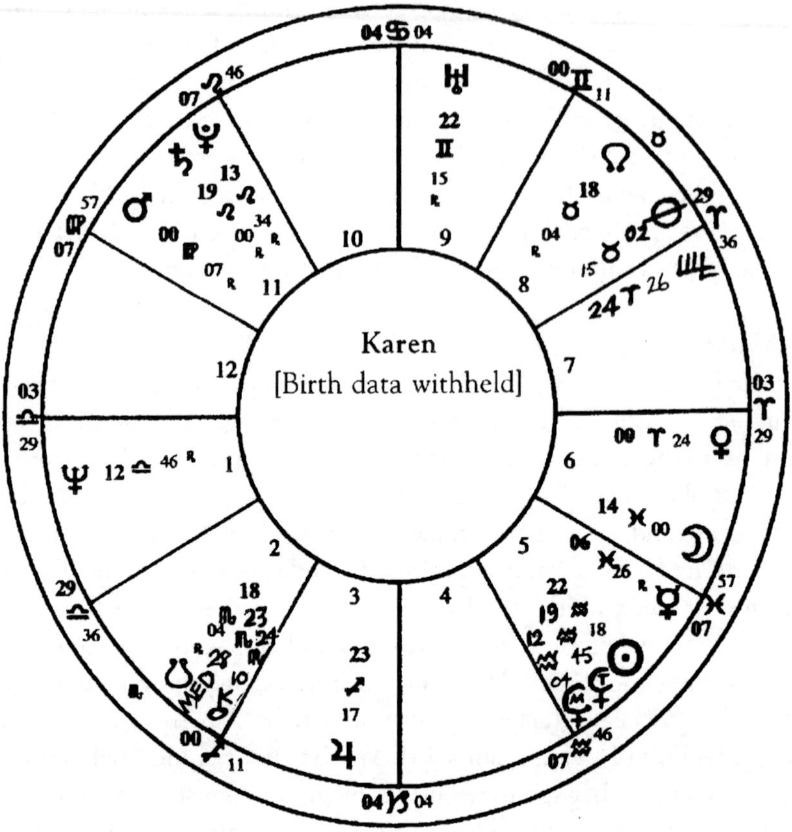

what is going on. I can physically feel it. Whenever another of our civil rights is taken away, I feel like I'm the one that is being taken away." She is tuned into the mental wavelengths of the collective consciousness and the anxiety that may hide the deep rage or grief of Algol. Black Moon in Aquarius may be insisting that she transcend the diffuse anxiety by de-personalizing it. By tuning her Aquarian antennae out to higher bands of the atmosphere, the broader bands that can receive cosmic download, this can clear the static she is reacting to in the lower bands. This can be a great service, as she contributes to the increasing upliftment of global consciousness. Now that she is astride the flying horse, she can go there into the unpolluted aetheric fields and send clear signals back.

In her 7th house, the Aries Asteroid Lilith describes something about her relationships. As a young woman, Karen was involved with a lot of "wild, crazy men," including a husband who was jailed and tried to cheat her out of her property. The nodal opposition involving Algol and Medusa/Chiron works in her 8th house/2nd house polarity activating the dynamic of joint vs. personal resources. With Asteroid Lilith trine Jupiter in Sagittarius, Karen learned about law and successfully defended her interests in court. She is now in her third marriage, to a man with strong feminine energy and a Scorpio stellium on her Medusa, thus involved with her Lilith signature. They appear to reverse the standard male-female roles. She is the one wielding tools and hammering away on the house, while he is a musician and artist. His Black Moon is on her Ascendant. "It's the most comfortable relationship," she says, describing a deep recognition one of the other. Lilith does not always promise comfort. One must be willing to completely let go. For such a Lilith woman, only a Lililth man will do.

BEN

Ben is very much a Lilith man, of the 1970s generation. Deeply involved in magic, mysticism and the arts, he feels an intimate relationship with Lilith. "Let me first say that I am dedicated to Lilith in her triple form as a witch and as her priest. I speak only of my personal experiences and relationship with her. I always think that Lilith was with me from my inception, even before." He experiences Lilith in his "absolute inability to submit to authority of any sort, unless it makes sense to me, my strong and dominant artistic intuitive and feminine side, and my honor of women in general."

Those words effectively summarize his four Liliths. Ben's Scorpio Sun/North Node is opposite Dark Moon/South Node, bringing Lilith directly into his karmic path in life — or he onto hers. Dark Moon is just a few degrees from the Algol degree. Ordinarily I prefer one-degree orbs with fixed stars, but this Dark Moon connection in Ben's chart is obviously active. Dark Moon casts a long shadow, so that 3 degrees is right in range. Dark Moon positioned in the 7th house astrologically reflects his strong feeling of relationship with Lilith; the South Node shows how ancient it is. Lilith also shows up in other relationships as well, including his magical partners in ritual. He speaks

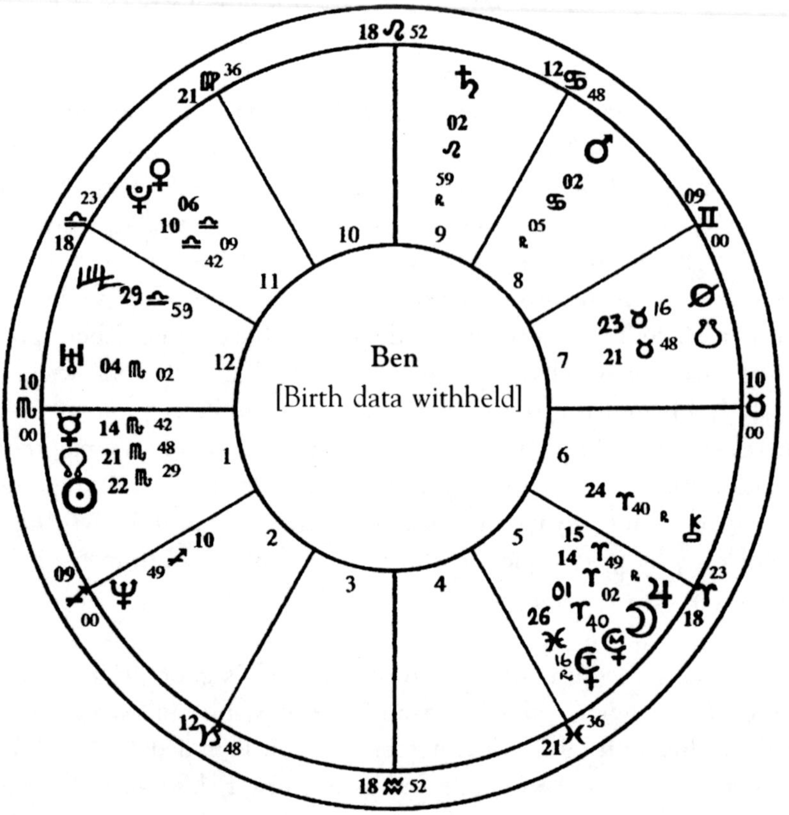

of his lineage to teachers and to ancestors, through tradition and blood ties. Dark Moon is always out of our sight, he says, a vibrational, mystical concept, a portal to the fey realms. With Dark Moon/South Node on Algol, Ben has been there.

The Black Moon spans two signs, with true Black Moon in late Pisces and mean Black Moon at 2 degrees Aries, both in the 5th house. The Lilith corridor spans only 5 degrees, but across the Pisces-Aries cusp, seeking to catch a flashing photon as it pops out of the cosmic sea. Musician, poet and screenplay writer, he is incessantly creative, but has yet to learn how to harness the energy into full manifestation. Mean Black Moon makes an emotionally-dynamic T-square in opposition to Venus/Pluto in Libra and square Mars retrograde in Cancer.

Raised in an "off the beaten path" reborn Christian missionary family (Moon conjunct Jupiter in Aries), Ben always sought his own truth. An experience of childhood sexual abuse brought feelings of shame and powerlessness. Shunned by the Christian church, deep questions stirred about male patriarchy, power, and sexuality. His father leaving home was the end of the old order. His two older brothers became his "parents" and abusers, mentally and emotionally. Asteroid Lilith is at the very cusp of Libra-Scorpio in Ben's chart opposite Chiron in Aries. He does not have a lot of compromise room when it comes to his integrity and following his path. We heard him speak above of his inability to submit to authority without a good reason.

> *My psychic and magickal abilities, that I had always been aware of, began to feel freakish to me. I began to run to the darker side of my psyche. All of these qualities Lilith wanted me to face; I understand this very clearly and my hands are radiating as I am writing this. Before I could become too dark, Lilith came to me full fledged at 9 years old. She came to me as a mantra that I could not get out of my head. I would see her face in the dark mid-west nights on the other side of mirrors and window reflections — the dark mother. She had come to spare me from going too dark or feeling too alone. When I would say her name I would become comforted or be physically protected. Then in my mystical and occult studies I came upon her story as the first wife of Adam. Her name which I had been chanting, and her face which I had been seeing, had all come to me in a realization. I knew her as my goddess and patron. The path had become clearer. The relationship has of course grown since.*

At age 9 when Lilith made her appearance, Ben's progressed Sun had moved into Sagittarius and was making a grand trine in Fire signs with his Black Moon at 2 Aries and Saturn at 3 Leo. He had completed a first Black Moon return with Lilith in Aries. A half-cycle of the Moon's Nodes brought the North Node right to his Dark Moon/South Node/Algol, a perfect moment for a Lilith encounter.

> *In the last few nights I went searching for owls. I drove to the ocean on the stretches of country road through deep hills and woods all the way to the ocean, looking for one of her most ancient symbols — a solitary night hunter, hunting with sound. Not one but four different owls came across my path early in the dark morning hours. With pure intention she always answers and in abundance for me. When I call and ask her to come and I allow her in, she manifests in amazing ways; peaceful*

> *ways. She wears the maiden form and guise of Queen Maeve, mother of all fairies. She is also Shiva's Shakti fully sexualized and fertile. She is the lust of all things, desires made whole and real, embracing themselves, being recognized, destroyed and being born anew, changed. If I resist her she comes as a darker image Kali-Ma. She will make her presence known in my life in all areas.*

Lilith is pure unbridled energy, Ben says, leading us along the intuitive path of hidden, even taboo forces, truly the unspeakable and unpronounceable. To harness her or to define her is to dishonour her. Lilith reaches into a consciousness of what cannot be known. She lives in a dimension of non-duality, from which she filters down elemental aspects of herself to us. Most of all Lilith changes all things by leaving them in their pure state. She is poetry as a goddess, the power of a mantra spoken over and over and the change – no, the process – of transmutation. Lilith's womb gives birth to magick, impregnated by Shiva's ecstatic dance.

> *Basically what I want to relay is that people who are drawn to her should reach deep within themselves and have a personal experience with her. That is what she requires and deserves. She is real, a real consciousness, not an archetype. The gods can be real. They can come up and shake your hand if they want to. I know from my own experience in the way she comes to me.*

Lilith in Relationship

Relationships can be powerful mirrors. Lilith likes to lurk and lark with lovers. Lilith evokes initiatory relationships, soul to soul meetings that open us to a deeper center of our experience and stretch us to edges of agony and ecstasy. A Lilith relationship is a spicy tango or a psychological duel, maybe both. Lilith can be the most powerful attractor in relationships, with compelling sexuality and other profound psychic dimensions, which may spur spiritual growth, but sometimes in a rather cruel way. Such relationships are not about having a family, a simple love affair, or going into business together, although these things may happen. Lilith does not care about the Moon concerns for comfort level or meeting subjective personality needs. Nor does she bow to Venusian emotional pleasure as the prime mover of the relationship, though she doesn't dismiss such sharing. The main agenda behind a Lilith connection is soul growth and spiritual liberation. It's as if the two people have an agreement for transcending ego levels; in other words, such relationships are ego-busters, requiring a willingness to let go of peripheral layers of self and relate from the center of one's truest essence. One of Lilith's significant strategies along the way can be to free up sexual inhibitions. Sometimes when emotional dependencies build up in a relationship, the raw passion and sexual fire may wane. At those times Lilith may show up as "the other woman" and the "femme fatale." When the emotional issues are worked through, deeper levels of intimacy can support a richer passion than ever.

Do I haunt you, haunt you, haunt you, haunt you
Hunt you, hurt you, cut you, desert you?
How can I be your one True Love
Oh mercy me, angels above
Why oh why this impossibly Other
Mother and Lover, Sister and Her
The whore, the star, the wonder, the liar,
Oh mystical She, so desired by me
My heart is yours.

JOHN

John lives with the powerful feminine energy of a strong Lilith signature, indicated in his chart by a Scorpio Moon exactly square Pluto/Jupiter in Leo and opposite a strong Venus in Taurus, conjunct Algol. Aquarius on the Ascendant completes a grand cross in fixed signs and indicates that this dynamic is to be directly lived through personal expression. It is clear that issues with the mother and family set up early dynamics of rejection and emotional abuse that re-surfaced in his marriage.

The true and mean Black Moons flank a Juno-Mars conjunction in Capricorn. Marriage and sexuality are areas in which experience is plumbed to the depths. With Mars in its exaltation and trine Venus, John was able to harness this energy, seeking to master the strength needed to channel the sensual earth energy of Venus/Algol in an effective way. Feelings about the emotional abuse in his marriage erupted in dream images of a fifteen-foot Scorpion emerging from his wife's vagina, helping him recognize a "murderous rage" pinpointing the activity of Algol conjunct Venus.

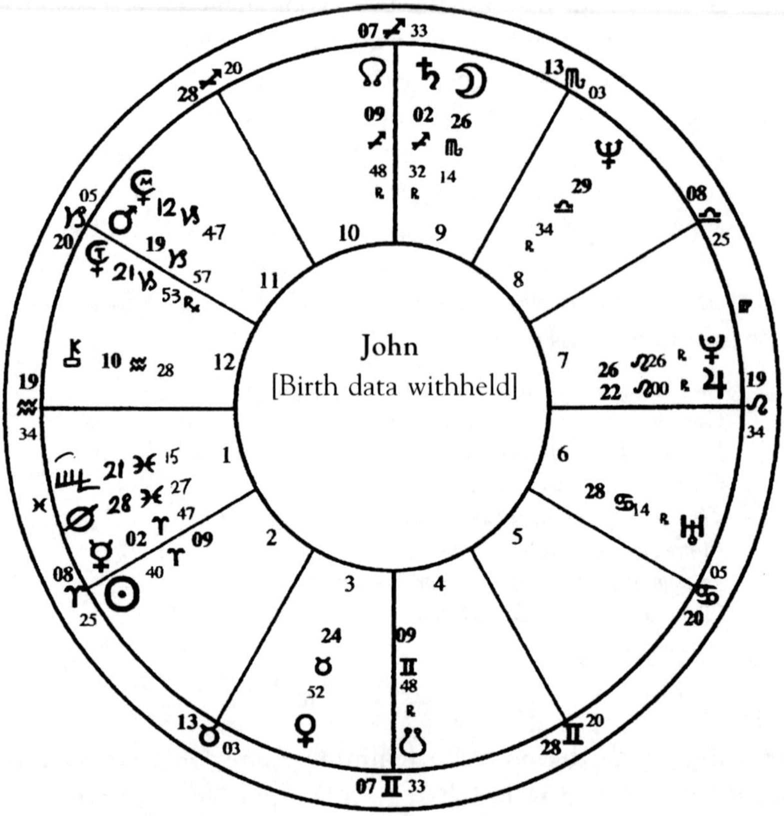

He began study and work with psycho-spiritual alchemy. As his Lilith work progressed, inner visions revealed the Divine Mother with many faces emerging from the Taj Mahal and giving birth to a huge star-like egg. This new, healing feminine energy transformed his emotional body, "enabling me to hold the whole," to delight in the "erotic, creative, juicy life force, beyond judgment."

> *The final notion revealed by the experience of the magnificent divine mother was a journey around the earth where she showed me the many, many forms of the mother in various countries — good, bad, indifferent, rich, poor, destitute. Humanity's needs are that vast. I realized that the divine mother is all these things including loving, and that each expression of her is a valid one that helped me because she is an expression of LIFE ITSELF.*

Asteroid and Dark Moon Liliths are conjunct in Pisces in the 1st house. When he left his marriage, he became a single father, still a non-typical social role. With such an extraordinary sensitivity to vibrational fields, John now applies the alchemical work through healing body and energy work. "A man's feminine can invigorate his masculinity to be as creative and strong as it wants to be."

SARAH

Sarah experienced psychic expansion through a new relationship with a strong Lilith connection. Her chart has a Lilith T-square, with the Asteroid in Virgo (7th house) opposite Black Moon/Moon in Pisces (1st house), both square Dark Moon/Saturn in Sagittarius (at the Midheaven). This is a strong Lilith signature. She dreams, draws and thinks a lot about snakes, she says. Ready to explore a deeper level of intimacy in her current relationship, she invited her lover to move in with her. For the two months that he stayed, they both experienced an unusual female presence in the house.

> *It moved things. It turned lights on and off. You could feel it. Its energy was here … I would know when she was here, because between my shoulder blades I would get gooseflesh – strong, strong, strong – and then usually something would manifest itself so we'd definitely know something was around.*

She found she could psychically communicate with this energy. Its aetheric dimension became more evident as it wove the energy fields into colors or images.

> *One time I saw a really interesting image of a snake in the air. It hung out there for a long time. It was beautiful colors. It was moving. It was looking at me. It was between me and my boyfriend. I saw it first. It was checking him out. It was staring at him and then me, him and then me. It was beautiful. Just before he moved out, there was a large cloud that he saw and it moved behind me.*

The presence left when her boyfriend did, as if it was evoked from what was going on between them. "The energy between him and me was very intense, very exploratory," she said. It sounds like Lilith to me.

Seeking the Sacred

On the other hand, Lilith interdynamics can lead to tragedy. Swiss astrologer Claude Weiss reports on a tragic manifestation of the Lilith connection in the charts of Roman Polanski and his wife, Sharon Tate. Well along in a pregnancy, she was one of those murdered by Charles Manson's Helter Skelter killers. Black Moon transits were active. I've always thought it mysteriously relevant that these murders occurred just a year after the release of Polanski's haunting film, *Rosemary's Baby*.

In Black Moon relationships, the two people are connected by a deep force that is the true source of what happens between them. In his book already mentioned, Peter Redgrove interviewed two neo-Gnostic initiates of a magical society, in which the central focus of contemplation is the Black Goddess seen as "the Virgin of the World, anima mundi, Star Maiden and the gateway to other worlds." An important part of their practice was sexual alchemy, enhanced by a conviction of the actuality of the goddess. "It was less that their goddess desired *worship* than that she rejoiced in being imagined."

One must be willing to completely let go when Lilith is present. Any of the Liliths show us where we are most likely to trip up on our life path, let ourselves be overpowered or underpowered in relationships. You may be overly determined (in Fire), grasping (Earth), rationalizing (Air) or elusive (Water). Do you see how the following underlying Lilithian tendencies could undermine a relationship?

Aries	stridently autonomous
Taurus	possessive
Gemini	ambivalent
Cancer	attached and dependent
Leo	selfish
Virgo	critical, looking for what is going wrong rather than right
Libra	overly accommodating
Scorpio	jealous
Sagittarius	overly independent
Capricorn	controlling

Aquarius	distant
Pisces	martyred

There are many other ways each sign can display its negative traits to undermine a relationship. Because life is inherently sexual, Lilith comes directly into play in this arena. She will show up in our sexual "politics," obsessions, fantasies, resistances, judgments, disappointments. Lilith will insist that you stay on your own soul path even, and especially, when in an intimate love relationship.

Related to what Jung called anima, the dark goddess mediates soul-making, as she opens a psychic awareness that links personal with consciousness. For women this is the soul aspect discovered through the shadow self, mirroring unrecognized potentials and self judgments, some of which have been accrued from ages of female repression. For men, it is the inner feminine that beckons to dimly lit corridors of the soul. The man's anima will attract relationships resonant to his capacity for emotional and spiritual depth. Feelings of vulnerability, rage, despair, rejection, regret and isolation are stirred up, echoed in Lilith's various mythologies. As if on an archaeological dig, layer after layer is uncovered and reclaimed as we sift through the dirt covering the soul and come home to ourselves. Committing to the spiritual may, at times, seem like a betrayal to others.

> *My dear man in the moon. Unknown to ourselves, we came together to explore the darkness. It was an initiation from temple days of long ago. We promised we would remind each other and make love once again and remember, from the dark to the black of the moon. The month was over and you left me abruptly. Your reasons were not entirely irrelevant. You were as honest as you could be. Now those reasons name the further work. Together we entered a deep space and now I am left alone in that space with the ghost of you, full with all that you have given me, yet empty with your sudden absence, desertion, betrayal. You asked, what did I want from you that I did not get? Time… My heart is turned in upon itself. Time….*

Taboos and morality are brought into question. Lilith will push you right over any moral edge you declare sacrosanct. Lilith challenges both men and women to connect with their instinctive passion for life. This natural force, if denied, unfulfilled, caged, or exiled, turns destructive. Lilith cannot exist in an atmosphere of betrayal, guilt, shame, criticism, judgment, self-doubt, or any such negative and subjective self-definitions or emotional projections that inhibit the freedom of love. When we identify with any negative emotion, Lilith is banished. She cannot exist in any limitation that shuts out the truth of our being. When that truth is honored, it shines in the relationship.

The Vesica Piscis is a lovely symbol in sacred geometry that conveys the essence of relationship, soul to soul. The symbol is made of two circles that touch each other's centers, creating an almond-shaped space, the *mandorla*, for mystical communion or "conjunctio" in the middle. This symbol is found on the cover of Chalice Well in Glastonbury, one of the oldest sacred springs in Britain. In a Lilith workshop once, we drew this symbol on large paper and used it as a double-circled mandala to create and color. We each learned more about Lilith in relationship.

Her Wild Dark Heart

To embrace Lilith requires courage, compassion, fascination, openness, love. Lilith taps into deep unconscious psycho-spiritual processes and a kind of erotic electromagnetism that connects with the life web. She engenders a subliminal spiritual crisis for being confined to an ego identity. She focuses on specific areas where small egoistic agendas interfere with soulful expression. Lilith taps a primordial space in ourselves which can't be summoned at will, but which responds to invitation.

This invitation can be a creative one. The deep soul territory of Lilith, the Black Madonna and other dark goddesses can be fruitfully explored by imagining from the heart, acknowledging intuitive sensations, feeling the vitality of living metaphors and dreams. Artistic expression is one way to dialogue with her essence. Perhaps that is why she plays a part in so many stories and songs, paintings and poems, fiction and drama. She catches the heart's eye in a nuance, in the color of a cloud, the hum of a bee, the close brush of a hummingbird, and in the little things she puts in your way — a serendipitous phone call, the right book at just the right time, the flash of fire in a future lover's eye — and especially in powerful feelings that leave one speechless.

Lilith seeks embodiment. Therefore, one way to discover her workings is through body therapies that address subtle energy fields. Lilith sneaks into stuck mental-emotional spaces. Various holistic modalities tune in to these unconscious areas and help release the vitality of Lilith trapped inside our bodies. Like the outer dakini that dances through the "winds" of our bodies, Lilith shows where the energy is not moving freely. She can influence systemic activities of the nervous system, the hormone-producing endocrine glands, neurotransmitter communication, chemical balance, chakra portals. Lilith choreographs the spiral dance of the electromagnetic currents.

In the most subjectively meaningful details and circumstances of our lives, she opens a psychic awareness that links the personal with the transpersonal, luring us through dimly lit passages of the magical, mystical and mysterious. Her revelation is our true nature and reason for being — no, not the reason for being, Lilith is not reason-able, she takes us beyond reason — rather she reveals our true nature and spaciousness of being. This is an a-logical approach, as the empirical mind cannot fathom this level of perception. Lilith calls for a surrender of logic into a deeper state of kinesthetic awareness and the transparent psyche. All that is worthwhile to yourself is held secret from the mind and permits life to function to its own great mystery. This is an essentially erotic experience, filled with pristine clarity and irrational dark delight. One shivers in the face of it, as in front of Medusa's Eye. Eros was the first god to emerge from chaos with Gaia, Earth. This god of desire evokes life. When we give the desire back to the Goddess, we are freed. With her Mona Lisa smile, she conveys a silent knowing that evokes ultimate stillness, a stillness that comes when you cease to fight the way it is "supposed" to be, and find out the way that it *truly* is with you.

Like a dakini, she is essentially tantric, transformer to higher octaves. She turns the cosmic mirror to face us with what we project. Beneath the soot of ages from candle smoke and incense, Madonnas in small chapels have been smudged dark, the colors of the Sistine Chapel have dimmed, the luminous windows of Chartres Cathedral have been dirtied. Thankfully these last two are being carefully cleaned, but many of us want our Madonnas to be black. Smoky mental and emotional chatter similarly smudges the luminescence of our spirit.

When unclouded by all the accumulated dross of personal and collective judgment, the mind opens into a vital attunement to the creative life force that expresses in extraordinary ways. The truer our perception becomes, the more fully we embody our wholeness and holiness. Lilith leads us to our True Desire, our innate passion for life. When we turn against it, Lilith turns demonic rather than daimonic.

With her several dark bodies, Lilith lures us into the Mystery. She severs our false sense of control and strongly suggests surrender to what is free and ecstatic beneath the shifting sands and myriad illusions of life. She opens a corridor into the heart through which we realize the yearnings of our souls. We can use our intuition to guide us, to imagine our way into the inner terrain. This is the inspiration and aspiration of the Divine Feminine.

Like cosmological dark energy, the invisible, pervasive, "aetheric" element underlying the universe, Lilith, as dark *mater*, dark mother, is the essential texture and subcurrent in our psyches. Lilith reflects our intimate connection to astral or aetheric levels that permeate individual and universe in a subtle stream of life force or consciousness. Through her many octaves of influence she taps into an urgent desire of the soul that seeks dramatization in life and will brook no denial. In her wild dark heart, Lilith dances in shiva-shakti ecstasy in the center of our inner galaxy, as she dances in the Galactic Center. In a time of renaissance such as ours, the Goddess, with her potent brilliancy and sweet spiritual impulse, illumines the inner pathway with the most heart for each seeker of Truth and Love.

Appendix
Locating Lilith

Astrology Programs

Some software programs offer options for one or two Liliths, most often Black Moon and Asteroid. I am not widely familiar with astrology programs.

Websites

The ASTRODIENST website is the only place I know that has tables for all four Liliths: http://www.astro.com. Basic membership is free.

1. On the home page click "Free Horoscopes."After entering chart data, click on name.
2. On page "Please select your horoscope here," choose "extended chart selection."
3. Toward bottom of page under "Additional Objects":

For the **mean Black Moon**, choose **LILITH** in the list of 'Additional objects.'

In the space for 'additional asteroids,' enter the following:

For **Asteroid Lilith,** insert **1181**
For **true** (oscillating) **Black Moon**, insert **h13**
For the **Waldemath Dark Moon** insert **h58**
For **Asteroid Medusa,** insert **149**

For **Lilith star, Algol**, check the option 'add some fixed stars' in the options on the right. On the chart you will see ALG in late Taurus.

Christian Borup's ASTROLOGY.DK site offers ephemerides for Asteroid Lilith, mean and true Black Moons from 1800-2090: www.astrology.dk/12hus/ephemeris.

Books

Starcrafts Publishing publishes an ephemeris with mean and true Black Moon, as well as Juno, Vesta, Pallas, Ceres, Eris and Chiron: www.starcraftspublishing.com

Demetra George's *Finding Our Way Through the Dark* has ephemerides for Asteroids Lilith and Medusa.

Other Resources

Recordings on the topic of Lilith from various astrology conferences are available byVerena Bachmann, Kelley Hunter, Antonia Langsdorf, Grazia Mirti, Claude Weiss.

Web Resources

A google search for Lilith resources yields immense results.

Lilith Bibliography

http://feminism.eserver.org/theory/papers/lilith/biblio.html

Lilith in Astrology

www.expreso.co.cr/centaurs/blackmoon/1181lilit.html
www.linda-goodman.com/ubb/Forum1/HTML
http://groups.yahoo.com/group/3Liliths/ founded by Sue Simmons

Lilith in Cultural Lore, Art and Literature

http://ccat.sas.upenn.edu/~humm/Topics/Lilith/
　Alan Humm of the University of Pennsylvania continues to gather resources on Lilith
www.lilithinstitute.com
www.lilithgallery.com
www.lilitu.com.au/Temple.htm
www.geocities.com/Wellesley/Garden/4240/apndx.html
　A Modern Development: Images of Lilith in Literature, Art and Artifacts
www.george-sterling.org/plays/Lilith:+A+Dramatic+Poem
www.youtube.com/watch?v=lW6hrYoT4hY&feature=related
　Video footage (rough) of the first showing of "The Huluppu Tree" portion of the Inanna myth at Bread and Puppet in Vermont in

1991, where Lilith was, more or less, "born". I was sent the link in March 2008, while writing this book.

www.myjewishlearning.com/ideas_belief/god/Overview_About_God/Angels/Demons/Lilith.htm

http://lilith.abroadplanet.com/Images.php

www.lilianbroca.com/ Artist with many Lilith images

Astronomy Sites

http://cfa-www.harvard.edu/iau/lists/NumberedMPs000001.html:
Discovery Circumstances: Numbered Minor Planets (1)-(5000)

http://ssd.jpl.nasa.gov/sbdb.cgi
NASA's Jet Propulsion Laboratory's Small-Body Data Base

http://virtualology.com/hallofwomen/MARTHAGRAHAM.NET

www.history.rochester.edu/class/sba/third.html 9/18/06

http://womenshistory.about.com/library/

www.nps.gov/archive/wori/ecs.htm

www.nps.gov/archive/wori/convent.htm

www.karinboye.se/verk/index-en.shtml

www.dalailama.com

www.bog.su.edu/col/senfalls1.htm

www.khandro.net/dakini_khandro.htm

www.spaceandmotion.com/Philosophy-Kundalini.htm

www.wyrdwords.vispa.com/heathenry/whatwyrd.html
An excellent discussion of "wyrd"

www.victorianweb.org/authors/gm/bio.html

www.sistersofmercy.org

Bibliography

Allen, Richard Hinckley. *(1963). Star Names: Their Lore and Meaning.* New York: Dover Publications.

Almaas, A.H. (1996). *The Void: Inner Spaciousness and Ego Structure.* Berkeley, CA: Diamond Books.

Anderson, Sherry Ruth, and Hopkins, Patricia. (1992). *The Feminine Face of God: The Unfolding of the Sacred in Women*, New York: Bantam Books.

Ankori, Gannit (2002). *Images of Her Selves: Frida Kahlo's Poetics of Identity and Fragmentation.* Westport, CT: Greenwood Press.

Arguelles, Miriam, and Arguelles, Jose. (1977). *The feminine: spacious as the sky.* Boulder, Co: Shamballa.

Bachmann, Verena. (1997). "Lilith: The Great Goddess in Everyday Life." tape from the Aquarian Revelation Conference.

Begg, Ean. (1985). *The Cult of the Black Virgin.* London, Penguin Books.

Bennerson, Vivian H. (1996). *Epheta, Universal Prayers and Thoughts.* Newport Beach, California: Brownell & Carroll, Inc.

Bento, William, Schiappacasse, Robert, and Tresemer, David. *(2000). Signs in the Heavens: A Message for Our Time.* Hygiene, CO: Sunshine.

Beriault, Marc. (2000). *La Lune Noire: Vers l'Autonomie de l'Etre.* Monaco: Editions du Rocher.

Bige, Luc. (2004). *La Lune Noire, un vertige d'Absolu.* Paris: Les Editions de Janus.

Birnbaum, Lucia. Chiavola. (2001). *dark mother: african origins and godmothers.* New York: Authors Choice.

Bloch, Doug and George, Demetra. (1990). *Asteroid Goddesses.* San Diego, CA, ACS Publications.

Borysenko, Joan. (1999). *A Woman's Journey to God: Finding the Feminine Path.* New York: Riverhead Books.

Brady, Bernadette. (1999). *Brady's Book of Fixed Stars.* York Beach, Maine: Samuel Weiser.

Briggs, John and Peat, F. David. (1989). *Turbulent Mirror.* New York: Harper & Ro.

Broca, Lilian and Kogawa, Joy. (2000). *A Song of Lilith.* Toronto: Polestar.

Brown, Robert G. (2006). *The Book of Lilith*. Lulu.com.

Calasso, Robert. (1990). *Ka: Stories of the Mind and Gods of India*. New York: Vintage.

Chamberlin, Ann. (1999). *Leaving Eden*. New York: Tom Doherty.

Clayton, Peter. (1990). *Great Figures of Mythology*. Greenwich, CT: Brompton Books.

Cleary, Thomas, trans., ed. (1996). *Immortal Sisters: Secret Teachings of Taoist Women*. Berkeley, CA: North Atlantic.

Cohen, Deborah Bodin. (2006). *Lilith's Ark: Teenage Tales of Biblical Women*. Jewish Publication Society.

Corelli, Marie. (1962). *Inspired Novels: The Soul of Lilith*. Mundelein, IL: Palmer.

Cott, Jonathan. (1994). *Isis and Osiris: Exploring the Goddess Myth*. New York: Doubleday.

Cunningham, Elizabeth. (1993). *The Wild Mother*. Barrytown, NY: Station Hill Press.

Danielou, Alain. (1991). *The Myths and Gods of India*. Rochester, VT: Inner Traditions.

David-Neel, Alexandra. and Yongden, Lama. (1967). *The Secret Oral Teachings in Tibetan Buddhist Sects*. San Francisco: City Lights.

De Gravelaine, Joelle. (1990). *Lilith, Der Schwarze Mond*. Zurich: Edition Astrodata.

Drabble, Margaret. (1979). *The Waterfall*. New York: Popular Library.

Eberhardt, Isabelle, translated by Paul Bowles. (1978). *The Oblivion Seekers*. San Francisco: City Lights.

Edinger, Edward. F. (1994). *The Eternal Drama: The Inner Meaning of Greek Mythology*. Boston: Shambhala.

Edwards, Meghan. (2004). "The Devouring Woman and Her Serpentine Hair in Late-Pre-Raphaelistism," *Pre-Raphaelites, Aesthetes, and Decadents*. Providence, RI: Brown University. http://www.victorianweb.org/painting/prb/edwards12.html

Eilberg-Schwartz, Howard and Donger, Wendy, edtiors. (1995). *Off with Her Head!: The Denial of Women's Identity in Myth, Religion, and Culture*. Berkeley: University of California Press.

Ellis, Normandi. (1995). *Dreams of Isis*. Wheaton, IL: Theosophical Publishing House.

Ernst, E. (1987). "Gorgon." *Middlebury College Magazine*, 61:4, 14-19.

Escobar, Thyrza. (1986). *The 144 Doors of the Zodiac*. Tempe, Arizona: American Federation of Astrologers.

Flinders, Carol. L. (1999). *The Root of This Longing. Reconciling a Spiritual Hunger and a Feminist Thirst*. HarperSanFrancisco,

Frawley, David. (2000). "The Shaktis of the Nakshatras." ACVA *Journal* 6:1, 3-7.

Frieden, Betty. (2001). *The Feminine Mystique*. New York: Norton and Co.

Froud, Brian. (2000). *The Faeries' Oracle*. Text by Jessica Macbeth. New York: Simon & Schuster.

Galland, China. (1990). *Longing for Darkness*. New York: Penguin.

George, Demetra. (1992). *Mysteries of the Dark Moon*. San Francisco: Harper.

Gerard, G. (1997). *Lumineuse Lilith: La Lumiere Cachee de l'Esprit*. Paris: Gandalf Editions.

Goldstein-Jacobson, Ivy M. *The Dark Moon Lilith in Astrology*. Self-published.

Gordon, Alex. (2004). *Nine Deadly Venoms*. England: Ebuilders.

Gottlieb, Lynn, (1995). *She Who Dwells Within: A Feminine Vision of a Renewed Judaism*. HarperSanFrancisco.

Grenn-Scott, Deborah J. (2000). *Lilith's Fire: Reclaiming Our Sacred Lifeforce*. Universal Publishers.

Griffin, Susan. (1987). *Unremembered Country*. Port Townsend, Washington: Copper Canyon Press.

Gustafson, Fred. (1990). *The Black Madonna*. Boston, Sigo Press.

____ editor. (2003). *The Moonlit Path: Reflections on the Dark Feminine*. Berwick, Maine: Nicolas Hays.

Harding, Elizabeth U. (1993). *Kali: The Black Goddess of Dakshineswar*. York Beach, Maine: Nicolas-Hays.

Harness, Dennis.(1999). *The Nakshatras: The Lunar Mansions of Vedic Astrology*. Twin Lakes, Wisconsin: Lotus.

Heath, Jennifer. ((1998). *On the Edge of a Dream: The Women of Celtic Myth and Legend*. New York: Plume-Penguin.

Hill, Lynda. (2002 edition). *The Sabian Symbols as an Oracle*. Australia: A White Horse Book.

Hillman, James, (1985). *Anima: An Anatomy of a Personified Notion*. Dallas: Spring.

____ (1997). "The Seduction of Black," Spring 61, 1-15.

Hixon, Lex. (1993). *Mother of the Buddhas: Meditation on the Prajnaparamita Sutra.* Wheaton, IL: Quest.

Hunter, M. Kelley. (1999). "The Dark Goddess Lilith." *The Mountain Astrologer* Issue 84, April/May 1999, 19-27.

____ (2000). *Black Moon Lilith.* San Diego, California: ACS.

____ (2009). *Black Moon Lilith.* Tempe, Arizona: American Federation of Astrologers.

Hurwitz, Siegmund. (1999). *Lilith, The First Eve.* Einsiedeln, Switzerland: Daimon-Verlag.

Jay, Delphine. (1981). *Interpreting Lilith,* Tempe, Arizona: American Federation of Astrologers.

____ 1983. *The Lilith Ephemeris,* 1900-2000 A.D, Tempe, Arizona: American Federation of Astrologers.

Johnsen, Linda. (1998). "The Legend of Lalita." *Yoga International,* No. 42.

Kahlo, Frida. (1995). *The Diary of Frida Kahlo: An Intimate Self Portrait.* New York: Harry N. Abrams, Inc.

Khanna, Madhu. (1979). *Yantra: The Tantric Symbol of Cosmic Unity.* London: Thames and Hudson.

Kinsley, David, (1997). *Tanric Visions of the Divine Feminine: The Ten Mahavidyas.* Berkeley, CA: University of California.

Koltuv, Barbara. (1986). *The Book of Lilith.* York Beach, Maine: Nicolas-Hays.

Kramer, Samuel N.(1983). *Gilgamesh and the Huluppu-tree: A Reconstructed Sumerian text.* Chicago, IL: University of Chicago.

Lang-Westcott, Martha. (1991). *Mechanics of the Future: Asteroids.* Conway, MA: Treehouse Mountain.

Lawrence, D.H., de Sola Pinto, Vivian and Roberts, Warren F. (1994). *Complete Poems.* New York: Penguin Classics.

Lehman, J. Lee and Morrison, Al. H. (1980). *Ephemeris of Lilith.* New York: CAO Times.

Lesur, Luis. (2005). *Las Claves Ocultas de la Virgen de Guadalupe. Barcelona:* Random House Mondadori.

Little, Stephen. (2000). *Taoism and the Arts of China.* Berkeley, CA: University of California Press.

Lorraine, Lilith. (1947). *Let the Patterns Break.* Rogers, Arkansas: Avalon Press.

MacDonald, George. (1964). *Phantastes and Lilith*, Grand Rapids, Michigan: Wm. B. Eerdsmans.

Mankiller, Wilma and Wallis, Michael. (1999.) *Mankiller: A Chief and Her People*. New York: St. Martin's Press.

Markale, Jean, (1986). *Women of the Celts*. Rochester, Vermont: Inner Traditions.

McKillip, Patricia. (1977). *Heir of Sea and Fire*. New York: Ballantine.

____ (2000). *The Book of Atrix Wolfe*. New York: Ace.

____ (2006). *Solstice Moon*. New York: Ace.

Midgette, Anne. (2001). "'Lilith' Is Made Flesh." *The New York Times*, November 9, 2001, p.E1.

Mirti, Grazia. (2000). "Encountering Lilith in the Individual and Collective Sphere through Transits." Presentation at ISAR conference in Anaheim, California.

Monaghan, Patricia. (1994). *O Mother Sun!: A New View of the Cosmic Feminine*. Freedom, California: The Crossing Press.

Mookerjee, Ajit. (1988). *Kali, The Feminine Force*. Rochester, Vermont: Destiny Books.

Neumann, Erich. (1974). *The Great Mother: An Analysis of the Archetype*. Princeton, New Jersey: Princeton University Press.

Needleman, Joseph. (1976). *A Sense of the Cosmos*. New York: E.P. Dutton and Co.

Noble, Vicki. (1991). *Shakti Woman*. HarperSanFrancisco.

O'Donnell, Kate. (2002). "The Lilith Archetype: A Feminist Mythology." *The Mountain Astrologer*, 15:4.

Pagels, Elaine. (1981). *The Gnostic Gospels*. New York, Random House.

Pereira, Filomena Maria. 1998. *Lilith: The Edge of Forever*. Las Colinas, Texas, Ide House.

Perera, Sylvia. (1981). *Descent to the Goddess*. Toronto, Inner City Books.

Phillips, Michael. (2005). George MacDonald: A Biography of *Scotland's Beloved Storyteller*. Minneapolis, MN: Bethany House.

Plaidy, Jean. (1967). *Lilith*, New York, Ballantine Books.

Pratt, Annis. (1994). *Dancing with Goddesses*. Bloomington, Indiana: Indiana University Press.

Purvis, Jane. (2002). *Emmeline Pankhurst: A Biography*. London: Routledge.

Rawson, Philip. (1968). *The Erotic Art of the East*. New York,:G.P. Putnam's Sons.

Redgrove, Peter. (1987). *The Black Goddess and the Unseen Real.* New York: Grove Press.

Reymond, Laya. (1974). *Shakti: A Spiritual Experience.* New York: Alfred A. Knopf.

Rilke, R. M., trans. Joanna Macy, Anita Barrow (2005). *Book of Hours.* New York: Riverhead Books,

Robson, Vivian B. (1969 edition). *The Fixed Stars and Constellations in Astrology.* New York: Samuel Weiser.

Rossen, Robert. (1964). *Lilith.* Centaur Films.

Salamanca, J.R. (1961). *Lilith.* New York: Simon and Schuster.

Sardello, Robert. (1992). *Facing the World with Soul.* Hudson, NY: Lindesfarne.

Schinn, Sharon. (1995). *The Shape-Changer's Wife.* New York: Ace Books.

Schwartz, Howard. (1998). *Lilith's Cave: Jewish Tales of the Supernatural.* New York: Oxford University Press.

Sepharial. (2005 edition). *The Science of Foreknowledge.* New York: Cosimo, Inc.

Shaw, George Bernard. (1927). *Back to Methuselah: A Metabiological Pentateuch.* London: Constable and Company.

Simmer-Brown, Judith. (2001). *Dakini's Warm Breath: The Feminine Principle in Tibetan Buddhism.* Boston: Shambhala.

Smulkis, Michael and Rubenfeld, Fred. (1992). *Starlight Elixirs and Cosmic Vibrational Healing.* Essex, England: The C.W. Daniel Company Limited.

Spielgelman, J. M., and Vasavada, A. U. (1987). *Hinduism and Jungian Psychology.* Phoenix, AZ: Falcon.

Sterling, George. (1926). *Lilith, A Dramatic Poem.* New York:The Macmillan Company.

Teilhard de Chardin, Pierre. (1978). *The Heart of Matter.* New York: Harcourt Brace Jovanovich.

Thackston, W.M., Jr., translator. (1999). Signs of the Unseen: The *Discourses of Jalauddin Rumi.* London: Shambhala.

Tolle, Eckhart. (2005). *A New Earth.* New York: Plume.

Von Franz, Marie-Louise. (1981). *Alchemy: An Introduction to the Symbolism and the Psychology.* Toronto: Inner City Books.

Waite, A. E. (1974). *Quest of the Golden Stairs.* Hollywood, CA: Newcastle.

Walker, Barbara G. (1983). *The Woman's Encyclopedia of Myths and Secrets.* New York: HerperCollins Publishers.

Weiss, Claude. (1999). "Black Moon Lilith through the Houses" (Parts one and two), *The Mountain Astrologer,* Aug./Sept. 1999, Oct./ Nov. 1999.

Welwood, J. (2000). "The Play of the Mind: Form, Emptiness, and Beyond," *The Quest.* 88:5, 190-195.

Williams, Grace Ellery. (2003). "Lilith, the Demon: Mythology and General Characteristics of Earth's 'Black Moon'". *Societas Rosicruciana in America.* www.sria.org/lilith_demon.htm 8/22/08.

Wilson-Ludlam, Mae R. (1997). *Lilith Insight: New Light on the Dark Moon.* Tempe, Arizona: American Federation of Astrologers.

Wolkstein, Diane and Kramer, Samuel. (1983). *Inanna, Queen of Heaven and Earth.* New York: Harper and Row.

Woodman, Marion. (1985). *The Pregnant Virgin: A Process of Psychological Transformation.* Toronto: Inner City.

Index

T

V

W

Y

Z

Other books by
The Wessex Astrologer

The Essentials of Vedic Astrology
Lunar Nodes - Crisis and Redemption
Personal Panchanga and the Five Sources of Light
Komilla Sutton

Astrolocality Astrology
From Here to There
Martin Davis

The Consultation Chart
Introduction to Medical Astrology
Wanda Sellar

The Betz Placidus Table of Houses
Martha Betz

Astrology and Meditation
Greg Bogart

Patterns of the Past
Karmic Connections
Good Vibrations
Soulmates and why to avoid them
Judy Hall

The Book of World Horoscopes
Nicholas Campion

The Moment of Astrology
Geoffrey Cornelius

Life After Grief - An Astrological Guide to Dealing with Loss
AstroGraphology
Darrelyn Gunzburg

The Houses: Temples of the Sky
Deborah Houlding

Temperament: Astrology's Forgotten Key
Dorian Geiseler Greenbaum

Astrology, A Place in Chaos
Star and Planet Combinations
Bernadette Brady

Astrology and the Causes of War
Jamie Macphail

Flirting with the Zodiac
Kim Farnell

The Gods of Change
Howard Sasportas

Astrological Roots: The Hellenistic Legacy
Joseph Crane

The Art of Forecasting using Solar Returns
Anthony Louis

Horary Astrology Re-Examined
Barbara Dunn

Living Lilith - Four Dimensions of the Cosmic Feminine
Kelley Hunter

You're not a Person - Just a Birthchart
Declination: The Steps of the Sun
Paul F. Newman